U.S. Copyright Documents

U.S. COPYRIGHT DOCUMENTS:

An Annotated Collection for Use by Educators and Librarians

By
Jerome K. Miller
Graduate School of Library Science
The University of Illinois

1981
Libraries Unlimited, Inc.
Littleton, Colorado

LIBRARIES UNLIMITED, INC.
P.O. Box 263
Littleton, Colorado 80160

Library of Congress Cataloging in Publication Data

Miller, Jerome K
U. S. copyright documents.

Bibliography: p. 281
Includes index.
1. Copyright--United States. I. Title.
KF2994.M54 346.7304'82 80-24768
ISBN 0-87287-239-4

To my brother,

DAVID D. MILLER

TABLE OF CONTENTS

Part II

THE COPYRIGHT REVISION ACT OF 1976 AND ITS SUPPORTING DOCUMENTS

ACKNOWLEDGMENTS

Although only one name appears on the title page of this book, a work of this size is, by necessity, a work of many hands. Suggestions by a colleague, D. W. Krummel, contributed to its design as a collection of documents accompanied by essays on some of the controversial or misunderstood points of the law. D. W. Krummel and W. C. Allen read portions of the manuscript and offered numerous comments for its improvement. Two excellent graduate assistants, Beth Stuckey Woodard and Margaret Ross, proved competent service as proofreaders, bibliographic sleuths, and friendly critics. Special thanks to Dean Charles H. Davis and Assistant Dean Lawrence W. S. Auld for their efforts to provide an environment which encourages the production of a work of this nature.

Finally, thanks are due to David D. Miller, who for many years has been very supportive of my work, both as a brother and as an attorney. This work is dedicated to him as a token of my appreciation.

An addendum to: Jerome K. Miller, *U.S. Copyright Documents: An Annotated Collection for Use by Educators and Librarians* (1981)

On December 12, 1980, President Carter signed Public Law 96-517, "The Patent and Trademark Amendment." Section 10 of the amendment includes a revision of sections 101 and 117 of the Copyright Law. The text of the Copyright Law amendment follows:

> Sec. 10. (a) Section 101 of title 17 of the United States Code is amended to add at the end thereof the following new language:
>
> "A 'computer program' is a set of statements or instructions to be used directly or indirectly in a computer in order to bring about a certain result."
>
> (b) Section 117 of title 17 of the United States Code is amended to read as follows:
>
> "§ 117. Limitations on exclusive rights:
> Computer programs
>
> "Notwithstanding the provisions of section 106, it is not an infringement for the owner of a copy of a computer program to make or authorize the making of another copy or adaptation of that computer program provided:
>
> "(1) that such a new copy or adaptation is created as an essential step in the utilization of the computer program in conjunction with a machine and that it is used in no other manner, or
>
> "(2) that such new copy or adaptation is for archival purposes only and that all archival copies are destroyed in the event that continued possession of the computer program should cease to be rightful.
>
> "Any exact copies prepared in accordance with the provisions of this section may be leased, sold, or otherwise transferred, along with the copy from which such copies were prepared, only as part of the lease, sale, or other transfer of all rights in the program. Adaptations so prepared may be transferred only with the authorization of the copyright owner."

Comment: Section 117 of the Copyright Revision Act of 1976 retained the existing law for the protection of computer programs to allow the National Commission on the New Technological Uses of Copyrighted Works (CONTU) time to study the problem and make recommendations for legislation. The CONTU recommendations were embodied in H.R. 6933 (96th Congress, 2nd Session) which were added to the Patent and Trademark Laws Amendment to facilitate passage in the closing days of the congressional session.

Source: PL 96-517 had not been printed at the time of writing. The above text appeared in the *Congressional Record* for November 21, 1980, p. H 11175.

INTRODUCTION

This volume is a collection of recent U.S. copyright documents useful to educators and librarians. The key document is the Copyright Revision Act of 1976, with its 1977 amendment, which appears in its entirety in Part II. It is supplemented by three important congressional reports (the Senate report, the House report, and the Conference Committee report).[1] These three reports, prepared by the congressional committees that wrote the Copyright Revision Act, offer an "official" explanation of the act.[2] Although the reports do not have the force of the law, the courts consult them to determine the "intent of the legislators" who drafted the act. Knowing the value the courts attach to these documents, attorneys consult the act and the reports in preparing briefs and in advising clients.

A few additional documents have been included to supplement the four major documents. These include: (1) passages in older congressional reports cited in the three key congressional reports, (2) selected Copyright Office regulations, and (3) copyright documents issued by the American Library Association and other recognized groups.

To keep the book as short and concise as possible, sections of the congressional reports that are of little interest to educators and librarians (e.g., the sections on background music and jukeboxes) were omitted to save space. These omissions are identified at the point of occurrence. Further space saving was achieved by editing the Senate report. The Senate passed its version of the copyright bill in 1975 and forwarded the bill and the report to the House of Representatives. Since the House and Senate were in general agreement on most parts of the bill, large sections of the Senate report were incorporated in the House report. For the sake of brevity and convenience, these redundant passages have been omitted and the text of the House report is supplied. Where the texts differ, the text of the House report and the conflicting passages of the Senate report are supplied. Although the House committee accepted almost all of the Senate report, it was edited to improve its accuracy and style. To avoid a proliferation of notes identifying minor changes in the texts, the following variations are not identified at the point of occurrence:

1. Variations in the dates on which the act would be implemented. The Senate committee anticipated an early passage of the act; when the dates in the Senate report could not be met, the House committee revised the dates for a later implementation. The dates in the House report are given.
2. Variations in dates used in examples of the application of the act. These changes reflect the changes in the implementation date noted above.
3. Incorrect references to certain subsections of the act. Revisions in the bill as it passed through the congressional committees prompted a renumbering or relettering of certain subsections.
4. Changes in the use of pronouns to reflect the role of women. The Senate report uses the traditional male forms which were changed in the House report.
5. Changes in the text to clarify the meaning. Numerous small changes of this nature were introduced in the House report. An example may be seen in Section 410:

   Senate: "...shifts the burden to him to do so."

   House: "...shifts the burden of doing so to the plaintiff."
6. Correction of typographical errors. The errors in the Senate report were corrected in the House report.[3] The errors in the House report were identified in the *Congressional Record* and corrected silently by the editor.[4]

Comments on these textual variations were omitted to accommodate the use of the book by its intended audience—educators and librarians who are neither interested in nor affected by these minor variations. Attorneys or scholars who discover this book would do well to examine the original documents so that they may identify each minor variation.

The unusual arrangement of the documents in this book should be noted. Most collections of documents are arranged chronologically or in the order of the documents' importance. This preserves the integrity of each document, but it does not accommodate a side-by-side comparison of the related passages, which is so important for an understanding of the difficult parts of the copyright law. The major documents have been disassembled on a section-by-section basis, and rearranged for convenient comparison. The overall outline follows the numerical arrangement of the act. A person consulting Section 108, on library photocopying, will find all of the relevant passages gathered in Section 108 of the book. These include Section 108 of the act, Section 108 of the three congressional reports, relevant passages from other government documents, and copyright documents issued by the American Library Association. Likewise, a person consulting Section 110, on the classroom use of copyrighted materials, will find the relevant passages of several documents gathered for convenient comparison.

To simplify the identification of the four major documents, the Copyright Revision Act is identified as "LAW," and the congressional reports are identified as: "HOUSE REPORT," "SENATE REPORT," and "CONFERENCE REPORT." Appropriate identifications are provided for the other documents. The editor's remarks appear as italicized comments interspersed among the documents and in a series of essays appearing in part I of the book. Readers should be aware that the editor is not an attorney and that in preparing this book he has not attempted to offer legal advice.

FOOTNOTES

[1]U.S. House of Representatives. *Report No. 94-1476: Copyright Law Revision* (Washington: Government Printing Office, 1976); U.S. Senate. *Report No. 94-473: Copyright Law Revision* (Washington: Government Printing Office, 1976); U.S. House of Representatives. *Report No. 94-1733: Copyright Law Revision* (Washington: Government Printing Office, 1976). They are hereinafter cited as: House report, Senate report, and Conference report.

[2]The House of Representatives Committee on the Judiciary, The Senate Committee on the Judiciary, and the House-Senate Conference Committee for P.L. 94-553.

[3]In unsigned correspondence dated October 12, 1978, the Copyright Office advised that an errata sheet had not been issued for the Senate report.

[4]*Congressional Record*, Vol. 122, No. 143 (daily edition of September 21, 1976), pp. H 10727-10728.

PART I

KEY POINTS IN THE LAW AFFECTING EDUCATORS AND LIBRARIANS

FAIR USE:
The Basis of User's Rights

Copyright is essentially a monopoly on creative works which permits the creator to profit from the work and to exercise some control over its use. Fair use contradicts this monopoly by granting certain rights to persons other than the copyright owner. These rights are defined in the new law as follows:

> Notwithstanding the provisions of section 106, the fair use of a copyrighted work including such use by reproduction in copies or phonorecords or by other means specified by that section for purposes such as criticism, news reporting, teaching (including multiple copies for classroom use), scholarship, or research, is not an infringement of copyright.[1]

The law identifies four criteria for applying the general principle of fair use to a given situation:

> In determining whether the use made of a work in any particular case is a fair use the factors to be considered shall include—
> (1) the purpose and character of the use, including whether such use is of a commercial nature or is for nonprofit educational purposes;
> (2) the nature of the copyrighted work;
> (3) the amount and substantiality of the portion used in relation to the copyrighted work as a whole; and
> (4) the effect of the use upon the potential market for or value of the copyrighted work.[2]

Because the courts use these criteria in deciding copyright infringement cases, it is imperative that educators and librarians apply them in resolving questions about the duplication of copyrighted materials. If a given situation falls within the bounds of all four criteria, one assumes that the action is a fair use. The four criteria are vague, but the congressional reports include numerous comments to assist in understanding and applying them. The Senate and House reports are especially useful, and from them one may identify several points which must be considered in applying each criterion. These items are listed in the Fair Use Checklist printed on page 16 and discussed in the following paragraphs.

I. PURPOSE AND CHARACTER OF THE USE

A. The Nonprofit Character of the Use
The Senate report suggests that although fair use is not limited to nonprofit institutions, they receive greater latitude in its application. There are two aspects in this regard which must be considered: will the copies be used in a nonprofit institution, and will there be a charge for the copies? The Senate report suggests that a teacher

---

Fair Use Checklist

This checklist is designed as a review of certain key points for applying the fair use criteria. It cannot substitute for a careful study of the law and the related congressional reports.

I. Purpose and Character of the Use
   A. The Nonprofit Character of the Use
   B. Spontaneity
   C. Collections and Anthologies
   D. Copying by Students

II. Nature of the Copyrighted Work
   A. Newspapers and News Magazines (but not newsletters or school news magazines)
   B. School Materials
   C. Consumable Materials
   D. Performance Materials

III. Amount and Substantiality of the Portion Used in Relation to the Work as a Whole
   A. Single Copies for Research, Study, or Teaching
   B. Multiple Copies for Class Distribution
      1. Amount that may be copied
      2. Frequency of the copying
      3. Distribution of the copies
      4. Disposition of the copies

IV. Effect of the Use on the Potential Market for or Value of the Work
   A. Direct Displacement
   B. Indirect Displacement

---

in a commercial school who charges students for the copies would have little basis for claiming that this was a fair use. On the other hand, a teacher in a nonprofit school who distributes the copies without charge has a much better claim that the action was a fair use.

B. Spontaneity

Single copies: The copying must be done at the volition of the person who will use the materials and not at the direction of a higher authority. This does not appear to prevent a teacher or a librarian from suggesting that a student or a patron copy an item for his or her personal use, as long as the decision to make the copy is freely made by the patron or student. Spontaneity is not a question of who pushes the button on the copying machine, but of who makes the decision to make the copy.

Multiple copies: In recent years a controversy has centered on the application of this point. To understand it, one must read both the general discussion of spontaneity in the Senate report and the narrowly based definition of spontaneity in the "Agreement on Guidelines for Classroom Copying in Not-for-Profit Educational Institutions" (hereafter cited as the "Agreement"), which appears in the House report. The Senate report states:

> *Spontaneity*–The fair use doctrine in the case of classroom copying would apply primarily to the situation of a teacher who, acting individually and at his own volition, makes one or more copies for temporary use by himself or his pupils in the classroom. A different result is indicated where the copying was done by the educational institution, school system, or larger unit or where copying was required or suggested by the school administration, either in special instances or as part of a general plan.[3]

The "Agreement" states:

> (i) The copying is at the instance and inspiration of the individual teacher, and
> (ii) The inspiration and decision to use the work and the moment of its use for maximum teaching effectiveness are so close in time that it would be unreasonable to expect a timely reply to a request for permission.[4]

There is no question that item (i) in the "Agreement" must apply to every application of fair use copying. The controversy centers on item (ii). Since both of the above statements are sustained in the conference report, there is room for controversy over their application.

Three interpretations have been offered to resolve the matter. A conservative interpretation advanced by many publishers suggests that the restrictive requirement for spontaneity in the "Agreement" supersedes the broader statement in the Senate report. The present writer has some difficulty accepting this interpretation since it appears to overlook an important statement in the introduction to the "Agreement": "The purpose of the following guidelines is to state the minimum and not the maximum standards of educational fair use . . . ."[5] The key word is "minimum." Quite clearly, a teacher who wants to pursue a cautious course should limit his or her copying to the narrow limit on spontaneity found in the "Agreement." However, the key word "minimum" does not preclude more liberal interpretations.

A second interpretation suggests that the "Agreement" is binding only upon those who signed it. This may have some merit since the "Agreement" was publicly repudiated by some professional associations, including the Association of American Law Schools and the American Association of University Professors.[6] This ingenious argument is not unique to educators, since some publishers employed the same argument to disassociate themselves from the "Gentlemen's Agreement of 1937," an early agreement between scholars and publishers to regulate the duplication of books and periodicals. Although this argument may have some value for professors who were not represented as signatories, the "Agreement" was ratified in the Conference Committee report and is a part of the legislative history of the law. It must be recognized as one of the several official explanations of the law.

A moderate interpretation suggests that both definitions of spontaneity can be employed on a nonexclusive basis to offer guidance in the matter. Since there is a general agreement that one should allow 30 days for a publisher or producer to respond to a request for permission to copy, this interpretation offers a convenient dividing line in resolving the question. If the use of the copies falls within 30 days of the inspiration to make the copies, it fits nicely within the narrow definition of spontaneity in the "Agreement." If the inspiration to copy and the use of the copies are separated by more than 30 days, then the person making the decision must proceed cautiously to be certain that the action falls within the bounds of fair use. In short, reproducing multiple copies of part of a work is not forbidden by the passage of more than 30 days between inspiration and use, but one must be particularly cautious in this application of the fair use criteria.

C. Collections and Anthologies

The House report comments:

> Spontaneous copying of an isolated extract . . . which may be a fair use under appropriate circumstances, could turn into an infringement if the copies were accumulated over a period of time with other parts of the same work, or were collected with other material from various workers so as to constitute an anthology.[7]

Most observers interpret this point liberally enough to permit a teacher or a scholar to maintain a personal file of photocopies of articles, essays, and the like for his or her research, study, or lesson planning. There is a general agreement, though, that this clause precludes the preparation of collections or anthologies for use by students.

D. Copying by Students

The Senate report suggests that a special exemption is provided for students:

> *Special uses*–There are certain classroom uses which, because of their special nature, would not be considered an infringement in the ordinary case. For example, copying of extracts by pupils as exercises in a shorthand or typing class or for foreign language study, or recordings of performances by music students for purposes of analysis and criticism, would normally be regarded as a fair use unless the copies or phonorecords were retained or duplicated.[8]

And further:

> The Committee has examined the use of excerpts from copyrighted works in the art work of calligraphers. . . . [A] single reproduction of excerpts from a copyrighted work by a student calligrapher or teacher in a learning situation would be a fair use of the copyrighted work.[9]

One may assume from these comments that copying by students as a learning exercise is a form of fair use, as long as some care is given to the disposition of the copies. Although the examples in the reports are limited to rather traditional learning exercises, it is a reasonable assumption that the principle can be applied to most student exercises, including the work of student printers, student video technicians, student photographers, and the like. Regardless of the copying format, it is important to control the disposition of the copies by recycling the paper, erasing the tapes, and so forth. Inasmuch as fair use is a sensible rule of reason, it seems acceptable to permit students to retain samples of their work for job application files or as mementoes of student days.

II. NATURE OF THE COPYRIGHTED WORK

A. Newspapers and News Magazines

The Senate report comments:

> With respect to material in newspapers and periodicals the doctrine of fair use should be liberally applied to allow copying of items of current interest to supplement and update the students' textbooks, but this would not extend to copying from periodicals published for student use.[10]

The first part of the Senate report comment is incorporated in the "Agreement":

> The limitation . . . [on the number of copies that can be produced each term] shall not apply to current news periodicals and newspapers and current news sections of other periodicals.[11]

The limited application of fair use to the duplication of newsletters also appears in the House report:

> [A] s a general principle, it seems clear that the scope of the fair use doctrine should be considerably narrower in the case of newsletters than in that of either mass-circulation periodicals or scientific journals.[12]

These statements can be summarized in two points. Considerable latitude applies to the duplication of articles in newspapers and news magazines for the use of teachers and students. The exception is limited, though, and has little application to the duplication of newsletters, such as the *Kiplinger Newsletter*, or to classroom news magazines, such as *My Weekly Reader*, since copying works of this nature could have an adverse effect on the sales of subscriptions. Although the comments in the congressional reports were addressed to the duplication of news publication in schools and commercial firms, the broad dispensation for copying news may be applied, within reasonable bounds, to the reproduction of news items by or for public library patrons. The suitability of such an action would depend on the use of the copies. It may be acceptable for a public library to make multiple copies of an article in *Time* for the Local Schools Committee of the League of Women Voters, but it might be an infringement to make multiple copies of the same material for an advertising firm.

B. School Materials

In speaking of the "character of the work," the Senate report comments:

> Textbooks and other material prepared primarily for the school markets would be less susceptible to reproduction for classroom use than material prepared for general public distribution.[13]

This statement was prompted by the ease with which copying school publications can reduce the market for a product. The question of the impact that copying has on the market for a work is treated at greater length on page 25.

C. Consumable Materials

Consumable materials are items designed for a single use, such as standard examinations, answer sheets, student workbooks, and student exercise sheets. The Senate report comments:

> Similarly, where the copyright [*sic*] work is intended to be 'consumable' in the course of classroom activities . . . the privilege of fair use by teachers or pupils would have little if any application.[14]

The "Agreement" states:

> There shall be no copying of or from works intended to be 'consumable' in the course of study or of teaching. These include workbooks, exercises, standardized tests and text booklets and answer sheets and like consumable material.[15]

Although consumable materials are copied frequently and in great quantities in some schools, the practice cannot be passed off as a fair use. Shortly after the law went into effect, one publisher began to sue educational agencies for copyright infringements in the duplication of its standard examinations.

D. Performance Materials

Performance materials include sheet music, plays, motion pictures, filmstrips, recordings of musical and dramatic performances, and other items designed for public performance. The Senate report comments on the duplication of these materials in its general discussion of "the character of the work":

> The character and purpose of the work will have a lot to do with whether its reproduction for classroom purposes is fair use or infringement. For example in determining whether a teacher could make one or more copies without permission, a news article from the daily press would be judged differently from a full orchestral score of a musical composition. In general terms it could be expected that the doctrine of fair use would be applied strictly to the classroom reproduction of entire works, such as musical compositions, dramas, and audiovisual works including motion pictures, which by their nature are intended for performance or public expression.[16]

In short, it is not an infringement to copy performance materials, as long as the other criteria are met and the copying is carefully limited to small amounts to avoid actions injurious to the proprietor. This is closely related to the fourth criterion, the effect of copying on the market for or value of the work.

III. AMOUNT AND SUBSTANTIALITY OF THE PORTION USED IN RELATION TO THE WORK AS A WHOLE

The amount of material that can be copied from a work is not always clear. A useful general statement appeared in the Register's 1961 report:

> Copyright does not preclude anyone from using the ideas or information disclosed in a copyrighted work. Beyond that, the work itself is subject to

> "fair use." That term eludes precise definition; broadly speaking, it means that a reasonable portion of a copyrighted work may be reproduced without permission when necessary for a legitimate purpose which is not competitive with the copyright owner's market for his work.

The 1961 report includes the following as an example of the kind of use that may be permitted under that concept:

> Reproduction by a teacher or student of a small part of a work to illustrate a lesson.[17]

A later and more detailed explanation appeared in the Senate report:

> In general, and assuming that the other necessary factors are present, the copying for classroom purposes of extracts or portions which are not self-contained and which are relatively 'not substantial in length' when compared to the larger, self-contained work from which they are taken, should be considered fair use. Depending on the circumstances, the same would also be true of very short self-contained works such as a brief poem, a map in a newspaper, a 'vocabulary builder' from a monthly magazine, and so forth.[18]

As the copyright revision bill progressed toward passage in the mid-1970s, most educators were willing to accept the Senate's general definition as a reasonable compromise. The picture changed with the publication of the "Agreement," which includes the following limitations on amount and substantiality:

> I. Single Copying for Teachers
>
> A single copy may be made of any of the following by or for a teacher at his or her individual request for his or her scholarly research or use in teaching or preparation to teach a class:
>
> A. A chapter from a book;
> B. An article from a periodical or newspaper;
> C. A short story, short essay or short poem, whether or not from a collective work;
> D. A chart, graph, diagram, drawing, cartoon or picture from a book, periodical, or newspaper.
>
> II. Multiple Copies for Classroom Use
>
> Multiple copies (not to exceed in any event more than one copy per pupil in a course) may be made by or for the teacher giving the course for classroom use of discussion; *provided that*:
>
> A. The copying meets the tests of brevity and spontaneity as defined below; *and*,
> B. Meets the cumulative effect test as defined below; *and*,
> C. Each copy includes a notice of copyright.

Definitions

Brevity

(i) Poetry: (a) A complete poem if less than 250 words and if printed on no more than two pages or, (b) from a longer poem, an excerpt of not more than 250 words.

(ii) Prose: (a) Either a complete article, story or essay of less than 2,500 words, or (b) an excerpt from any prose work of not more than 1,000 words or 10% of the work, whichever is less, but in any event a minimum of 500 words.

[Each of the numerical limits stated in 'i' and 'ii' above may be expanded to permit the completion of an unfinished line of a poem or of an unfinished prose paragraph.]

(iii) Illustration: One chart, graph, diagram, drawing, cartoon or picture per book or per periodical issue.

(iv) 'Special' works: Certain works in poetry, prose or in 'poetic prose' which often combine language with illustrations and which are intended sometimes for children and at other times for a more general audience fall short of 2,500 words in their entirety. Paragraph 'ii' above notwithstanding such 'special works' may not be reproduced in their entirety; however, an excerpt comprising not more than two of the published pages of such special work and containing not more than 10% of the words found in the text thereof, may be reproduced.

Spontaneity

[This section appears on page 17.]

Cumulative Effect

(i) The copying of the material is for only one course in the school in which the copies are made.

(ii) Not more than one short poem, article, story, essay or two excerpts may be copied from the same author, nor more than three from the same collective work or periodical volume during one class term.

(iii) There shall not be more than nine instances of such multiple copying for one course during one class term.

[The limitations stated in 'ii' and 'iii' above shall not apply to current news periodicals and newspapers and current news sections of other periodicals.] . . . .[19]

The limitations on amount and substantiality in the "Agreement" have not been well received in some quarters. It must be noted again that the terms of the "Agreement" represent the minimum rather than the maximum interpretation of fair use. The following points may be useful for sorting out some of the elements of amount and substantiality.

A. Single Copies for Research, Study or Teaching

There is a general agreement that teachers, scholars, librarians, library patrons, and others may make a single copy of an article, essay, poem, illustration, and the like for the purpose of private research, or study, or for lesson planning. The terms "research" and "study" are not limited to the work of professional scholars; they apply to everything from professional research to a search for a new garlic butter recipe.

B. Multiple Copies for Class Distribution

The problem here centers on (1) the amount of material that may be copied in each instance of copying, (2) the number of times multiple copies may be made for class distribution, (3) the distribution of copies outside of the classroom, and (4) the disposition of the copies when the students have finished using them.

1. Amount that may be copied: The amount of material that may be copied from a particular source for class distribution has usually been described as: a chapter from a book, an article from a periodical or newspaper, a short story or a poem from an anthology, or an illustration from a book or periodical. This has never been an entirely satisfactory explanation since copying under these broad terms may lead to the reproduction of a major part of a work. Copying a 20-line poem from an anthology seems acceptable but copying a long poem from a work containing only three poems is another matter. This is the basis for the insistence on both *amount* and *substantiality* as one criterion for fair use.

Substantiality is described in the Senate report as: "'not substantial in length' when compared to the larger, self-contained work from which they are taken. . . ."[20] Amount and substantiality were incorporated in the "Agreement" in the form of limits on the number of words which may be copied from a poem, article, or essay. Inevitably, limitations that work reasonably well for one situation do not fit another situation. The limit of 2,500 words from articles and stories may present no problems for a junior high school history teacher, but it creates an impossible situation for a university history professor. The journal articles that are the staple of upper-level university reading assignments commonly appear in multiples of 2,500 words. Wrenching a 2,500 word (or a 3,000 word) segment from a scholarly article may do violence to the author's presentation and is more likely to confuse students than to enlighten them.

The solution to this problem may rest in the opening statement of the "Agreement": "The purpose of the following guidelines is to state the minimum and not the maximum standards for educational fair use. . . ."[21] For teachers who feel they cannot observe the 2,500 word limit on articles or the 250 word limit on poems can probably exceed those limits if they observe the following rule of thumb in applying amount and substantiality:

Amount: An article from a periodical, or a chapter from a book, or a poem from an anthology or the equivalent amount from other works.

Substantiality: The amount taken must not exceed what the 1961 Register report calls "a small part of a work."[22] The "Agreement" suggests at two points that copying be limited to 10% of the work. Although copyright scholars abhor such arbitrary limits, as a rule of thumb 10% can probably be used as the outer limit for determining substantiality.[23] But, substantiality measures more than the quantity of material copied; it also applies to the significance of that portion in relation to the work as a whole. A key part of a work (e.g., a rare document or photograph which would be difficult to acquire without reproducing the original) may not be copied as freely as the text of illustrations pertaining to or describing the key part of the work.

If this two-part rule of thumb is applied *prudently*, and in conjunction with the other criteria, the action will probably fall within the bounds of fair use in most applications.

2. Frequency of copying: The Senate report speaks of "a reasonable number of copies," but it is unclear if this refers to the number of copies made or the frequency of making multiple copies.[24] The "Agreement" specifies a minimum limit of nine instances of copying per course, per term, not counting the duplication of news articles. This may be a reasonable limit for some courses, but it imposes a profound hardship in courses for which there are no textbooks or for which the textbooks are inadequate or out of date. If fair use is a sensible rule of reason, some teachers must substantially exceed the limit of nine instances per course, per term, plus news articles. However, they must consider an important comment in the Senate report:

> Fair use is essentially supplementary in nature, and classroom copying that exceeds the legitimate teaching aims such as filling in missing information or bringing a subject up to date would go beyond the proper bounds of fair use.[25]

3. Distribution of the copies: In reproducing multiple copies for class distribution, teachers frequently make a few extra copies for their files. The file copies are useful for planning lessons, or for individual assignments, or as gifts to needy colleagues. This common practice appears to violate the limitation on the distribution of multiple copies of a work. The Senate report indicates that one of the determining factors of fair use or infringement rests on the range of distribution:

> In the case of multiple copies, other factors would be whether the number reproduced was limited to the size of the class, and whether circulation beyond the classroom was permitted. . . .[26]

The "Agreement" does not comment on the distribution of copies outside the classroom, but it specifies that the number of copies shall not "exceed in any event more than one copy per pupil in a course. . . ."[27] This requirement is related to the concept of spontaneity. Reproducing copies for a single use in the classroom usually falls within the bounds of spontaneity, whereas reproducing copies for several uses is difficult to defend under any interpretation of spontaneity. Limiting the copies to a single distribution in a single class seems like a reasonable requirement that should be observed. If additional copies are needed for extra assignments or make-up assignments, it is a simple matter to obtain permission from the publisher or from the Copyright Clearance Center.

A closing comment must be addressed to the distribution of copies to several sections of the same class. If a teacher has several sections of a class and all of the students are receiving the same assignments, a reasonable interpretation suggests that enough copies may be reproduced for distribution to all of the students in the class, in as many sections as are required to accommodate the number of students.

4. Disposition of the copies: The Senate report suggests that the copies should be recalled or destroyed after a single use.[28] The "Agreement" is silent on this point, and most observers consider it unnecessary to recall and destroy the copies since most students will discard them anyway. The key point is not the destruction of copies but the careful observance of the spontaneous single-use concept. For this purpose, it is necessary only to avoid any reuse of the material without the permission of the publishers. The point is not seriously jeopardized by the occasional student who maintains a file of handouts for research or study.

IV. EFFECT OF THE USE ON THE POTENTIAL MARKET FOR OR VALUE OF THE WORK

Many commentators regard the effect of an action on the proprietor as the most important criterion in determining whether an action is an infringement or a fair use.

A. Direct Displacement: If copying a work deprives the publisher, producer, distributor, or agent of a sale, lease, or rental, it is not a fair use.

B. Indirect Displacement: Several instances of copying which in themselves appear to be a fair use can become an infringement if the cumulative effect of the copying deprives the publisher, producer, distributor, or agent of a sale, lease, or rental.

These are not always easy points to apply. Good judgement must be applied to arrive at an equitable rule of reason, especially when the copies are made from closely protected materials, such as sheet music, textbooks, and the like. It is very convenient to duplicate copyrighted materials for school or personal use, but if this action directly or indirectly deprives publishers or producers of a legitimate return on their investment, the supply of useful materials may be diminished. A spirit of fair play on the part of knowledgeable and fair-minded individuals may be the best way to apply this part of the fair use criteria.

CONCLUSION

Fair use has been an essential part of the Anglo-American copyright system for over a century, where it has been known as fair use, fair quotation, or fair dealing. It began through the court-developed common law and was later formalized through statutory law. This formalization process is quite apparent in the incorporation of the four court-developed fair use criteria in the new statute. Because of the vagueness of the four criteria and the difficulty in applying them in certain situations, the congressional reports provide suggestions for their application. Although the courts are not bound to observe the intent of the legislators, the reports will probably play an important role in shaping court decisions. If the reports are to be used by the courts in determining copyright infringement cases, it is essential that educators and librarians study the fair use section of the law and the related chapters in the reports in order to make informed decisions about the application of this difficult point of copyright law.

FOOTNOTES

1. *United States Code*, Title 17, "Copyrights," Sec. 107. Hereafter cited as Law.

2. Ibid.

3. U.S. Senate, *Report No. 94-473*, Sec. 107. Hereafter cited as Senate report.

4. "Agreement on Guidelines for Classroom Copying in Not-For-Profit Educational Institutions" in U.S. House of Representatives, *Report No. 94-1476*, Sec. 107. Hereafter cited as "Agreement."

5. Ibid.

6. U.S. House of Representatives, *Report No. 94-1476*, Sec. 107. Hereafter cited as House report.

7. Ibid.

8. Senate report, Sec. 107.

9. Ibid.

10. Ibid.

11. "Agreement," II.

12. House report, Sec. 107.

13. Senate report, Sec. 107.

14. Ibid.

15. "Agreement," III(B).

16. Senate report, Sec. 107.

17. U.S. Register of Copyrights, *Copyright Law Revision: Report of the Register of Copyrights on General Revision of U.S. Copyright Law* (Washington: Government Printing Office, 1961), p. 24.

18. Senate report, Sec. 107.

19. "Agreement," I and II.

20. Senate report, Sec. 107.

21. "Agreement," [Introduction].

22. U.S. Register of Copyrights, *Copyright Law Revision*, p. 24.

23. *Meeropol* v. *Nizer* (560 F.2d. 1061, 1068) states: "The line which must be drawn between fair use and copyright infringement depends on an examination of the facts in each case. It cannot be determined by resort to any arbitrary rules or fixed criteria."

24. Senate report, Sec. 107.

25. Ibid.

26. Ibid.

27. "Agreement," II.

28. Senate report, Sec. 107.

DUPLICATION OF JOURNAL ARTICLES FOR RESERVE READING COLLECTIONS*

Until recently, it was a common practice for academic libraries to place individual issues or bound volumes of journals in a reserve reading collection to accommodate class reading assignments. This arrangement was not entirely satisfactory because of the wear, mutilation, and theft of copies and because it failed to meet the students' demands for quick access to heavily used titles.

The advent of quick and inexpensive photocopying machines provided a convenient solution to the problem; instructors could make multiple copies of the articles for class distribution or libraries could place photocopies of the articles in their reserve collections. Both applications protected the original copies from wear, mutilation, and theft, and the students were assured of access to the assigned articles. Although some publishers voiced objections to the potential copyright infringements, none are known to have filed suits to prevent these practices or to recover damages. They preferred, instead, to see the matter resolved through the long-awaited copyright act. The publishers lobbied energetically to legislate a limit on educational and library copying, while the library and educational associations lobbied vigorously to retain the existing practices. The congressional committees, sensitive to the conflicting needs of the several groups, endeavored to arrive at a reasonable compromise. This compromise appears in Sections 107 and 108 of the Copyright Revision Act.

Section 108 permits a library to reproduce journal articles in the following situations:

1. to replace a damaged, deteriorating, lost or stolen work,[1]
2. to meet a patron's request for a copy,[2]
3. to meet an interlibrary loan request for a copy,[3] and
4. to meet a patron's request for a copy of an out-of-print work, when an unused copy is not available at a fair price.[4]

A copy of the damaged, deteriorating, lost, or stolen work may be placed in the library's collection, but copies made under the other three provisions must become the property of the patron.[5] Furthermore, copying under each of the above conditions is limited to a single copy at each request.[6] These conditions appear to prohibit the

---

*Although this essay speaks of copying journal articles, it is applicable to copying general circulation magazines for a reserve reading collection. The terms described here also apply to copying essays and poems in published collections and chapters of books for a reserve reading collection, as long as the amount of material copied conforms to the "Agreement on Guidelines for Classroom Copying in Not-For-Profit Educational Institutions." However, the copying terms described here do not apply to the duplication of most newsletters or to magazines designed for class distribution; these materials are closely protected since even a small amount of copying from them tends to be injurious to their publishers.

practice of making single or multiple copies of journal articles and placing them in a reserve reading collection. However, this practice appears to be authorized, with certain safeguards, by Section 107—the fair use section. The library's authorization to apply the fair use section to the duplication of single or multiple copies of journal articles for a reserve collection begins with Section 108(f)(4): "Nothing in this section [section 108] in any way affects the right of fair use as provided by section 107 . . . ."[7]

Section 107 was designed, among other things, to facilitate the duplication of journal articles for class distribution.[8] It also appears to authorize a few library services that are not available through Section 108.[9] The fair use section is far from perfect; librarians who have become accustomed to the specific requirements and authorizations of the photocopying section may be discouraged by its vague and imprecise nature. However, its vagueness is, in one sense, one of its great advantages. Instead of authorizing one set of activities and forbidding another (which would require frequent revision), the fair use section is based on the four court-developed criteria, which must be applied in each case to determine whether the act is a fair use or an infringement.[10] (The four criteria are identified in the preceding essay on fair use.) These criteria have broad application to areas "such as criticism, comment, news reporting, teaching . . . , scholarship, or research."[11] One of these uses includes the duplication of copyrighted materials for class distribution. If the practice of placing single or multiple copies of a journal article in a reserve collection is seen as an economical alternative to reproducing multiple copies of the article for class distribution, then the four fair use criteria dictate the terms under which the copies are made and used.[12]

Because of the difficulty in applying the fair use criteria to the duplication of copyrighted materials for class use, Congress urged the authors, trade, and educational associations to prepare a detailed set of fair use guidelines. These were completed shortly before the Copyright Revision Act passed, and were ratified by two congressional committees as appropriate guidelines for the application of the law.[13]

AGREEMENT ON GUIDELINES FOR CLASSROOM COPYING IN NOT-FOR-PROFIT EDUCATIONAL INSTITUTIONS

with respect to books and periodicals

The purpose of the following guidelines is to state the minimum and not the maximum standards of educational fair use under Section 107 of H.R. 2223. The parties agree that the conditions determining the extent of permissible copying for educational purposes may change in the future; that certain types of copying permitted under these guidelines may not be permissible in the future; and conversely that in the future other types of copying not permitted under these guidelines may be permissible under revised guidelines.

Moreover, the following statement of guidelines is not intended to limit the types of copying permitted under the standards of fair use under judicial decision and which are stated in Section 107 of the Copyright Revision Bill. There may be instances in which copying which does not fall within the guidelines stated below may nonetheless be permitted under the criteria of fair use.

GUIDELINES

I. *Single Copying for Teachers*
[*See* page 21.]

II. *Multiple Copies for Classroom Use*

Multiple copies (not to exceed in any event more than one copy per pupil in a course) may be made by or for the teacher giving the course for classroom use or discussion; *provided that*:

A. The copying meets the tests of brevity and spontaneity as defined below; *and*,
B. Meets the cumulative effect test as defined below; *and*,
C. Each copy includes a notice of copyright.

Definitions

Brevity

(i) Poetry: (a) A complete poem if less than 250 words and if printed on not more than two pages or, (b) from a longer poem, an excerpt of not more than 250 words.

(ii) Prose: (a) Either a complete article, story or essay of less than 2,500 words, or (b) an excerpt from any prose work of not more than 1,000 words or 10% of the work, whichever is less, but in any event a minimum of 500 words.

[Each of the numerical limits stated in 'i' and 'ii' above may be expanded to permit the completion of an unfinished line of a poem or of an unfinished prose paragraph.]

(iii) Illustration: One chart, graph, diagram, drawing, cartoon or picture per book or per periodical issue.

(iv) 'Special' works: Certain works of poetry, prose or in 'poetic prose' which often combine language with illustrations and which are intended sometimes for children and at other times for a more general audience fall short of 2,500 words in their entirety. Paragraph 'ii' above notwithstanding such 'special works' may not be reproduced in their entirety; however, an excerpt comprising not more than two of the published pages of such special work and containing not more than 10% of the words found in the text thereof, may be reproduced.

Spontaneity

(i) The copying is at the instance and inspiration of the individual teacher, and

(ii) The inspiration and decision to use the work and the moment of its use for maximum teaching effectiveness are so close in time that it would be unreasonable to expect a timely reply to a request for permission.

Cumulative Effect

(i) The copying of the material is for only one course in the school in which the copies are made.

(ii) Not more than one short poem, article, story, essay or two excerpts may be copied from the same author, nor more than three from the same collective work or periodical volume during one class term.

(iii) There shall not be more than nine instances of such multiple copying for one course during one class term.

[The limitations stated in 'ii' and 'iii' above shall not apply to current news periodicals and newspapers and current news sections of other periodicals.]

III. *Prohibitions as to I and II Above*

Notwithstanding any of the above, the following shall be prohibited:

(A) Copying shall not be used to create or to replace or substitute for anthologies, compilations or collective works. Such replacement or substitution may occur whether copies of various works or excerpts therefrom are accumulated or reproduced and used separately.

(B) There shall be no copying of or from works intended to be consumable in the course of study or of teaching. These include workbooks, exercises, standardized tests and test booklets and answer sheets and like consumable material.

(C) Copying shall not:

(a) substitute for the purchase of books, publishers' reprints or periodicals;

(b) be directed by higher authority;

(c) be repeated with respect to the same item by the same teacher from term to term.

(D) No charge shall be made to the student beyond the actual cost of the photocopying.

Agreed March 19, 1976.

Ad Hoc Committee on Copyright Law Revision:

By Sheldon Elliott Steinbach.

Author-Publisher Group:

Authors League of America:

By Irwin Karp, *Counsel*

Association of American Publishers, Inc.:

By Alexander C. Hoffman,
Chairman, Copyright Committee.[14]

The application of the "Agreement" to copying articles for reserve reading collections is based on the assumption that placing copies on reserve can substitute for distributing multiple copies to the class. Placing two or three copies of an article in a reserve collection can frequently substitute for making one copy for each of the 25 students in the class. Placing a few copies of an article in the reserve collection is a convenience for the instructor and greatly reduces the expenditure of funds and natural resources required to make multiple copies of the articles for class distribution. The legitimacy of this procedure depends on an understanding with the instructor that the copies placed on reserve are a substitute for copies distributed in class, and that they are not designed to supplement the items reproduced for class distribution. Several variations seem viable: (1) the instructor distributes all of the copies in class and none are placed on reserve, (2) all of the copies are placed on reserve in lieu of class distribution, or (3) copies of some articles are distributed in class while others are copied and placed on reserve, but the total number of items reproduced should not exceed the limits outlined in Section II of the "Agreement."[15]

In applying the "Agreement," a library should observe the following points:

1. The instructor agrees that the copies placed on reserve substitute for the copies he or she is entitled to reproduce and distribute to the class; this can be formalized with a statement on the library's reserve reading request form. The following is an example of such a statement:

> I agree that the photocopies of the copyrighted materials identified above are to be placed in the (name) library's reserve reading collection in lieu of making multiple copies of them and distributing them to my class.

The library may want the instructor to indicate his or her consent by signing the form.

2. The library maintains accurate records of the items copied for the reserve collection to prevent:

   a. exceeding the limit on the number of items copied for a class,[16] and
   b. repeated use of an article for a course by the instructor.[17] However, if the instructor teaches several courses, he or she may make multiple copies of an article to distribute (or place on reserve) for each course, as long as the other requirements are met. Also, the reproduction of an article for one instructor does nor prevent other instructors from reproducing that article (or placing it on reserve) for their classes.

3. The copies placed on reserve meet the tests of brevity, spontaneity, and cumulative effect.[18] (Brevity, spontaneity, and cumulative effect are discussed at length on pages 17-18, 23-24.)

4. Each photocopy placed on reserve includes a copyright warning notice.[19]

5. The copies placed on reserve do not appear to substitute for an available anthology.[20]

6. Consumable materials are not copied, but the original copies may be placed on reserve.[21]

7. The copies placed on reserve are destroyed at the end of the semester, or other appropriate steps are taken to prevent the copies from being placed on reserve again without the publishers' permission.[22] Either the library or the instructor may seek permission to reuse the copies; if the library undertakes that responsibility, it should establish orderly procedures for obtaining permission to make additional copies or to reuse the copies made earlier.[23] These procedures can also be used to obtain permission to copy items that are not authorized under the guidelines; these include copies of long articles that do not meet the brevity requirement, or copying in excess of the authorized quantities.

The limits of brevity, spontaneity, cumulative effect, and the like have been eliminated, in part, by the decisions of some of the professional and scholarly associations to grant a blanket permission to instructors and librarians to copy the articles in their journals for classroom or library use. Information about this policy usually appears in the fine print below the journal's masthead. An exemplary statement appears in each issue of *Instructional Innovator* (formerly *Audiovisual Instruction*), published by the Association for Educational Communications and Technology:

> Nonprofit organizations or individuals may quote from or reproduce from material copyrighted by AECT for non-commercial purposes provided full credit acknowledgments are given.[24]

Articles published under these or similar conditions appear to fall outside the limits in the "Agreement" in terms of (1) the numerical limits on the number of items copied, (2) the length of the items copied, and (3) repeated copying over several semesters or years. Other professional and scholarly associations should be encouraged to adopt this procedure, since many of the articles placed on reserve in academic libraries are taken from journals published by these associations.[25]

Finally, it must be noted that copies for the reserve collection can be made by the instructor, or the instructor may ask the library to make the copies; the question of fair use copying does not hinge on the identity of the person who operates the copying machine, but on who decides to make the copies and the conditions under which that decision is made (e.g., at the instructor's own volition or at the direction of higher authority). The practice of requiring the instructor to make the copies and send them to the library may be a convenient device for reducing the first-week-of-the-semester workload in the reserve department, but it does not appear to be dictated by the copyright law.

FOOTNOTES

1. *United States Code*, Title 17, Sec. 108(c). Hereafter cited as Copyright law.

2. Ibid., Sec. 108(d).

3. Ibid., Sec. 108(g).

4. Ibid., Sec. 108(e).

5. Ibid., Sec. 108 (c), (d)(l), and (g).

6. Ibid.; some may quarrel with the writer's conservative interpretation of "the copy" and "a copy" in Sec. 108(c), (d), and (e) to mean that a library is limited to making single copies. The single copy limitation is more explicit in Sec. 108(g), which regulates copying in response to interlibrary loan requests.

7. Ibid., Sec. 108(f)(4).

8. Ibid., Sec. 107; especially the statement "(including multiple copies for classroom use) . . . ."

9. This is brought out in several of the essays in Part I of this book.

10. Copyright law, Sec. 107.

11. Ibid.

12. Jerome K. Miller, ed., *Copyright and the Teaching/Learning Process: Issues Analyzed at the Critical Issues Conference 4, Washington, D.C., March 21-23, 1977* (Pullman, WA: Information Futures, 1977), p. 69.

13. The "Agreement on Guidelines for Classroom Copying in Not-For-Profit Educational Institutions" (hereafter cited as "Agreement") appears without comment in the U.S. House of Representatives, *Report No. 94-1476*, Sec. 107. One may reasonably assume, however, that its inclusion in the committee's report supplies at least tacit approval by the House Committee on the Courts, Civil Liberties, and the Administration of Justice (the committee responsible for the study and preparation of the Copyright Revision Bill). The Senate-House Conference Committee report (U.S. House of Representatives, *Report No. 94-1733*, Sec. 107) contains an explicit approval of the "Agreement": "The conferees accept as part of their understanding of fair use the Guidelines for Classroom Copying. . . ."

14. "Agreement."

15. Ibid., Sec. II.

16. Ibid., Sec. II(iii).

17. Ibid., Sec. II(ii).

18. Ibid., Sec. II.

19. Ibid., Sec. II(C); for further information on this point see pages 57-60.

20. Ibid., Sec. III(A).

21. Ibid., Sec. III(B).

22. Ibid., Sec. III(C)(c).

23. For a detailed discussion of procedures to follow in obtaining permission to duplicate journal articles, see Jerome K. Miller, *Applying the New Copyright Law: A Guide for Educators and Librarians* (Chicago: American Library Association, 1979), pp. 88-103.

24. *Instructional Innovator* 25 (January 1980): 4.

25. A directory of those journals which grant blanket copyright permission to instructors and libraries, and the nature of the blanket permission, would be very useful to reserve collection supervisors; it is to be hoped that an individual or a committee will prepare such a directory (in looseleaf format) and update it regularly.

DUPLICATION OF MUSICAL, PICTORIAL, GRAPHIC AND AUDIOVISUAL WORKS BY LIBRARIES AND ARCHIVES

Section 108(h) of the Copyright Act states that, with few exceptions, the rights accorded to libraries and archives by Section 108 do not apply to the duplication of musical works; pictorial, graphic, or sculptural works; or to motion pictures or audiovisual works. The isolated reading of this section is probably responsible for a common misinterpretation—that libraries and archives may never copy these materials. The confusion stems from a failure to compare Sections 108(h) and 108(f)(4) of the act. The former prohibits almost all forms of copying musical, pictorial, graphic, and audiovisual works by libraries and archives, while the latter opens the way to a limited reproduction of them under the broad provisions of Section 107—the fair use section. To be responsive to patrons' requests to duplicate these materials and at the same time stay within the limits of the law, a librarian or archivist must be familiar with both sections of the act. For convenience sake, the prohibitions and exceptions of Section 108(h) are described first, followed by a discussion of the more liberal provisions available under Section 108(f)(4).

SECTION 108(h)

Section 108 was written to facilitate and regulate the duplication of textual materials, television news programs, and phonorecords by libraries and archives. To insure that this provision is applied as it was intended, Section 108(h) identifies a list of works which may not be copied under the provisions of Section 108:

> The rights of reproduction and distribution under this section do not apply to a musical work, a pictorial, graphic or sculptural work, or a motion picture or other audiovisual work other than an audiovisual work dealing with the news, except that no such limitation shall apply with respect to rights granted by subsections (b) and (c), or with respect to pictorial or graphic works published as illustrations, diagrams, or similar adjuncts to works of which copies are reproduced or distributed in accordance with subsections (d) and (e).[1]

The materials which cannot be copied under Section 108 fall into four well-known categories of copyrightable works: (1) musical works, (2) pictorial, graphic, and sculptural works, (3) motion pictures, and (4) audiovisual works. The last three categories are defined in the law. (See pages 64-65).

Musical Works

The omission of a definition for musical works in this section is explained by the comment that it was unnecessary to define the term since it has a "fairly settled" meaning.[2] Unfortunately, the term is not understood by some of those who must apply the requirements of Section 108. In practical terms, "musical works" include published and unpublished musical compositions (i.e., sheet music), with or without lyrics, as well as lyrics issued independently of their musical notation (e.g., song books containing only the lyrics of popular or religious tunes). However, musical works do not include words arranged in a form that makes them adaptable to music, but which have never been integrated with a musical notation (e.g., poetry which lends itself to a musical rendition or scurrilous texts which lend themselves to certain patriotic tunes). These works fall within the definition of "literary works" (defined on page 65), which may be copied under the general provisions of Section 108.[3]

Libraries and archives may copy unpublished musical works for purposes of preservation or institutional exchanges under the terms of Section 108(b). Published works which are out of print and unavailable at a "fair price" may be copied for replacement purposes if the library or archive's copy is "damaged, deteriorating, lost, or stolen. . . ."[4] Musical works are excluded from the provisions of Section 108(e), which permits a library or an archive to reproduce all or a substantial part of an out-of-print work at the request of a patron.[5] The congressional reports do not indicate if the exclusion was a deliberate decision or an error in the legislative drafting process. This does not create an insurmountable hurdle, though, since there are well-established procedures for obtaining permission to duplicate most out-of-print sheet music.[6]

Phonorecords

There has been some confusion about a library or archive's right to duplicate phonorecords. The uncertainty stems from the frequent references in Section 108 to "a copy or phonorecord." "Phonorecord" merely describes the "material objects in which sounds . . . are fixed and from which the sounds can be perceived, reproduced, or otherwise communicated. . . ."[7] In brief, it describes the physical format of the work, and not its content. There appear to be three types of sound recordings which cannot be copied under the terms of Section 108: (1) musical works, (2) the musical portions of dramatico-musical works, and (3) sound tracks of motion pictures and audiovisual work. The prohibition of copying musical recordings appears in the preceding section on musical works; the prohibition against copying sound tracks appears under "Motion Pictures and Audiovisual Works" (see page 38-39).

Spoken word recordings of speeches, dramatic performances, folk tales, poetry readings, and the like may be copied under the provisions that regulate the duplication of textual materials in books and periodicals. Under those conditions, it may be appropriate for a library or archive to make a sound recording of a single story from an album of short stories, at a patron's request, just as it would make a photocopy of a single story from a book of short stories, at a patron's request.[8] The provisions for the duplication of out-of-print works, unpublished works, and "damaged, deteriorating, lost, or stolen works" apply equally to the duplication of textual materials and spoken word recording.[9] Finally, the provisions for unsupervised copying machines seem to apply equally to self-service audio duplicating equipment and self-service photocopying machines.[10]

Pictorial, Graphic, and Sculptural Works

Section 108(h) prohibits the duplication of pictorial, graphic, and sculptural works (the phrase is defined on page 65) by libraries and archives under the provisions of Section 108. The only exception applies to the duplication of:

> pictorial or graphic works published as illustrations, diagrams, or similar adjuncts to works of which copies are reproduced or distributed in accordance with subsections (d) and (e).[11]

Under this exemption, it is acceptable to reproduce the charts, diagrams, and illustrations accompanying a journal article or a chapter of a book, copied at a patron's request.[12] It is acceptable, also, to duplicate the illustrations accompanying the text of an out-of-print work which cannot be obtained at a fair price.[13] Although this exemption is generous in terms of duplicating the illustrations accompanying textual matter, some stretch of the imagination is required to use it to justify copying only the illustrations in a book or article (i.e., without copying the accompanying textual matter). A limited amount of copying of this nature can be justified under the terms of Section 107, the fair use section, but not under the terms of Section 108.

Motion Pictures and Audiovisual Works

Section 108(h) specifically prohibits the duplication of motion pictures and audiovisual works (defined on pages 64-65). This prohibition against duplicating sound tracks creates some special problems in handling "sound track" phonograph albums and tape recordings based on popular movies. These recordings frequently differ from the original sound track through the addition of new materials, editing, enchancing, and the like. Under these circumstances, the producer may choose to treat the work as a new edition of the original sound track or as a "phonorecord," depending on the firm's copyright procedures or its marketing plans for the work. If it is treated as a new edition of a sound track, the traditional Section 401 copyright notice (i.e., employing the word "copyright" or one of its derivatives) will be displayed on the work. Under these circumstances, the recording is a sound track of a motion picture and may not be copied under the terms of Section 108. On the other hand, if the producer regards it as a "phonorecord," it should display the Section 402 phonogram copyright notice (i.e., one employing the international phonogram Ⓟ symbol); this suggests that the recording falls within the provisions for copying phonorecords (discussed earlier in this chapter).

The situation is not always that simple. Peter F. Nolan, an attorney for Walt Disney Productions and a noted copyright authority, recommends that both types of copyright notices be displayed on the record, "if for no other reason than to avoid misunderstandings and to advise the public of the broader copyright protection afforded the sound track."[14] By displaying both copyright notices, the producer provides the maximum protection available to the original sound track while protecting the new material contained in the recording. A librarian or archivist who observes the dual notice on a sound track recording is thereby alerted that the recording may not be copied under the terms of Section 108, except in the unlikely event that he or she is able to identify and copy a nonmusical portion of the recording that did not appear in the original sound track.

The only major exception to the ban on duplicating audiovisual works in Section 108(h) appears in the Baker Amendment to the act (also known as the Vanderbilt Amendment):

> Nothing in this section–shall be construed to limit the reproduction and distribution by lending of a limited number of copies and excerpts by a library or archives of an audiovisual news program, subject to clauses (1), (2), and (3) of subsection (a).[15]

The Conference Committee report elaborates on this point:

> The conference committee is aware that an issue has arisen as to the meaning of the phrase "audiovisual news program" in section 108(f)(3). The conferees believe that, under the provision as adopted in the conference substitute, a library or archives qualifying under section 108(a) would be free, without regard to the archival activities of the Library of Congress or any other organization, to reproduce, on videotape or any other medium of fixation or reproduction, local, regional, or network newscasts, interviews concerning current news events, and on-the-spot coverage of news events, and to distribute a limited number of reproductions of such a program on a loan basis.[16]

Two important points in the House report restrict the application of this provision:

> It does not apply to documentary (except documentary programs involving news reporting as that term is used in section 107) [this reference has not been identified], magazine-format or other public affairs broadcasts dealing with subjects of general interest to the viewing public.
>
> It is intended to permit libraries and archives . . . to make off-the-air videotape recordings of daily network newscasts for limited distribution to scholars and researchers for use in research purposes.[17]

The first paragraph excludes documentary, magazine-format, and public affairs programs from copying under the terms of Section 108. The second paragraph indicates that the distribution of the copies is limited to research purposes, thus excluding the distribution copies or the transmission of the programs to classrooms.

Summary

Although Section 108(h) appears to impose an absolute ban on the duplication of most musical, pictorial, graphic, and audiovisual works, Congress recognized reasonable exceptions to this rule. The House report comments:

> Although subsection (h) generally removes musical, graphic, and audiovisual works from the specific exemptions of section 108, it is important to recognize that the doctrine of fair use under section 107 remains fully applicable to the photocopying or other reproduction of such works. In the case of music, for example, it would be fair use for a scholar doing musicological research to have a library supply a copy of a portion of a score or to reproduce portions of a phonorecord of a work. Nothing in section 108 impairs the applicability of the fair use doctrine to a wide variety of situations involving photocopying or other reproduction by a library of copyrighted material in its collections, where the user requests the reproduction for legitimate scholarly or research purposes.[18]

This exception is embodied in Section 108(f)(4) of the law.

SECTION 108(f)(4)

Section 108(f)(4) states:

> Nothing in this section . . . in any way affects the right of fair use as provided by section 107. . . .[19]

This provision opens up new avenues for libraries and archives to duplicate musical, pictorial, graphic, and audiovisual works at the request of a patron, or for use by the staff of the library or archive. Although Sections 107 and 108 stem from the basic concept of fair use, the methods of applying the two sections are quite different. Section 108 contains detailed requirements for the duplication of copyrighted materials, while Section 107 is limited to a brief definition of fair use and a vague set of guidelines.[20] Although Section 107 was discussed at length in the essay on fair use, it may be useful to emphasize the specific provisions of the law and the reports that apply to the duplication of musical, pictorial, graphic, and audiovisual works. All four of the fair use criteria must be applied to each application of the fair use doctrine, but the second criterion is of particular importance:

> In determining whether the use made of a work in any particular case is a fair use the factors to be considered shall include . . .
>
> (2) the nature of the copyrighted work.[21]

The Senate report offers one brief comment on the application of the second criterion:

> In general terms it could be expected that the doctrine of fair use would be applied strictly [i.e., narrowly] to the classroom reproduction of entire works, such as musical compositions, dramas, and audiovisual works including motion pictures, which by their nature are intended for performance or public exhibition.[22]

The House report adds:

> A problem of particular urgency is that of preserving for posterity prints of motion pictures made before 1942. Aside from the deplorable fact that in a great many cases the only existing copy of a film has been deliberately destroyed, those that remain are in immediate danger of disintegration; they were printed on film stock with a nitrate base that will inevitably decompose in time. The efforts of the Library of Congress, the American Film Institute, and other organizations to rescue and preserve this irreplaceable contribution to our cultural life are to be applauded, and the making of duplicate copies for purposes of archival preservation certainly falls within the scope of "fair use."[23]

It is a reasonable assumption that this exemption also applies to the reproduction of other pictorial, graphic, and audiovisual works which by their nature are subject to rapid and irreversible deterioration. These would seem to include out-of-print color photographs, paper audio tapes, and video recordings produced in the early non-standard formats.[24]

The most detailed exemption appears in the House report's "Guidelines for Educational Uses of Music" (pages 95-96). Under the terms of these guidelines, an employee of a library or archive may make a single copy of an entire piece of sheet music to serve as a temporary emergency replacement for music which was lost or damaged shortly before a school performance. They also permit the reproduction of single or multiple copies of a small part of a selection for "academic purposes other than performance . . . ,"[25] and the duplication of out-of-print sheet music "for a teacher solely for the purpose of his or her scholarly research or in preparation to teach a class."[26] Sound recordings of musical works may be copied for the purpose of creating "aural exercises or examinations. . . ."[27] These guidelines contain very specific terms which must be met if an instance of copying is to fall within the bounds of fair use. Although the guidelines are reasonably generous, the prologue to the guidelines states: "The purpose of the following guidelines is to state the minimum and not the maximum standards of educational fair use under Section 107. . . ."[28] This offers a bit of latitude in applying some of the specific terms of the guidelines (e.g., the limit of not more than 10% of a work in article 2[a]), but it does not appear to excuse significant departures from the spirit or the letter of the guidelines.

The example of copying films on nitrate stock and the guidelines for copying music represent only a few of the many situations in which librarians and archivists are asked to duplicate musical, pictorial, graphic, and audiovisual works. The fact that the other forms of copying were not mentioned in the House and Senate reports does not preclude their use; it only means that they must meet the four fair use criteria described at length in the essay on fair use. The reader who is unfamiliar with these criteria may find it useful to see them applied through the following example.

Example: A teacher asks a library to make one slide copy of each of three illustrations in an art book containing over 100 illustrations of the works of the American cartoonist Herbert Block. The teacher wants to use the slides the following week to illustrate key points in a lecture to be given at a tax-supported school. The three slides will be the only illustrations used in the lecture.

Answer: The first criterion, "the purpose and character of the use, including whether such use is of a commercial nature or is for nonprofit educational purposes," includes several tests. (1) Are the copies to be used in a nonprofit educational institution? (2) Is the copying done at the teacher's request and at the teacher's volition? (It is not a question of who pushed the button on the copying machine, the teacher or the librarian, but who makes the decision to copy the material.) (3) Will the copies be incorporated in a collection or anthology? Since the first two questions can be answered in the affirmative and the last in the negative, the first criterion appears to have been met.

The second criterion, "the nature of the copyrighted work," identifies certain materials, such as school materials and consumable materials (defined on page 90), to which fair use copying must be applied sparingly. Illustrations in books are not included in this list, so this criterion appears to have been met.

The third criterion, "the amount and substantiality of the portion used in relation to the work as a whole," contains two major tests, amount and substantiality. (1) Does the amount of material to be copied represent a small amount of the overall work, and (2) is the amount to be copied insubstantial in terms of quantity or, more importantly, in terms of its significance to the overall work? Since both questions can be answered in the affirmative, the third criterion appears to have been met.

The fourth criterion, "the effect of the use on the potential market for or value of the work," is regarded by many as the most important element in the application of fair use. If a nonprofit agency, a commercial firm, or an individual is deprived of a sale of a copyrighted work through this act of copying (or several instances of copying from a single work), even in such a small thing as making three slides from a large book of illustrations, then the fourth criterion is not met, and the act is an infringement. To properly meet this criterion, the librarian must make a reasonable search through the commonly used bibliographic tools to see if the slides are available through the normal trade sources for photographic slides. If they are not available, this criterion has been met, and the action appears to be a fair use.

This example is a very brief and superficial overview of a complicated part of the copyright law. Librarians and archivists who want to apply Section 107 to the duplication of musical, pictorial, graphic, and audiovisual works should make a careful study of the law (page 86), the congressional reports (pages 87-103), and the related documents (pages 100-101). It may be useful, as well, to read the commentaries on fair use (page 104).

CONCLUSION

The fair use and photocopying sections of the law have their origins in the theory of fair use developed in the Anglo-American common law. This nebulous concept was employed by the courts for over a century before it received statutory force in the British and American copyright acts. Although we benefit from the incorporation of this judicial concept in the U.S. statutes, it is unfortunate that the titles of Section 107 and 108 and their respective language tend to create the impression that they are unrelated sections that are coincidentally located side by side in the act. They are, in fact, interrelated parts of the broad concept of fair use. The separation of the broad concept into two sections of the act stems from the problem the congressional committees and the Copyright Office had in developing an "equitable rule of reason" for meeting the diverse needs of numerous constituent groups. A close reading of Section 108(f)(4) and statements in the congressional reports indicates that Sections 107 and 108 are related and that librarians and archivists may employ the provisions of either section when they are asked to duplicate performance and display materials. Section 108 is more generous in permitting the duplication of television news programs, "damaged, deteriorating, lost, or stolen" works, and the like, while Section 107 is a bit more generous in permitting the duplication of performance and display materials for internal use within a library or archive or at the request of a patron for his or her personal use. In short, a knowledgeable and conscientious use of both sections can expand a library or archive's repertory of services.

FOOTNOTES

1. *United States Code*, Title 17, "Copyrights," Sec. 108(h). Hereafter cited as Copyright law.

2. U.S. House of Representatives, *Report No. 94-1476*, Sec. 101. Hereafter cited as House report.

3. Musical works also include musical creations which exist only in sound recordings. This situation is occasionally observed in the music of primitive peoples and in jazz compositions which do not exist in a written or notational form. These works are usually identified by a Section 401 copyright notice in place of or in addition to the traditional Section 402 copyright notice found on sound recordings.

4. Copyright law, Sec. 108(c).

5. Ibid., Sec. 108(h).

6. The best description of this process appears in *The United States Copyright Law: A Guide for Music Educators*, available from the National Music Publishers' Association, 100 East 59th St., New York, NY 10022, or from the Music Publishers' Association of the United States, Third Floor, 130 West 57th St., New York, NY 10019.

7. Copyright law, Sec. 101.

8. Ibid., Sec. 108(d).

9. Ibid., Sec. 108(e), (b), and (c).

10. Ibid., Sec. 108(f)(1); some may quarrel with this statement, since the language of the act, and the accompanying comments in the House report, speak of unsupervised copying machines only in terms of "making a copy or a phonorecord." Inasmuch as the exclusionary provisions in Section 108 are quite specific, the writer assumes that the omission was not designed to be exclusionary, but stemmed from the legislators' unfamiliarity with self-service audio duplicating equipment, which was not commonly found in libraries and archives when the act was passed.

11. Copyright law, Sec. 108(h).

12. Ibid., Sec. 109(d) and (h).

13. Ibid., Sec. 108(e) and (h).

14. Peter F. Nolan, "A Brighter Day for the Magic Lantern: Thoughts on the Impact of the New Copyright Act on Motion Pictures," *Loyola of Los Angeles Law Review* 11, no. 1 (December 1977): 17.

15. Copyright law, Sec. 108(f)(3).

16. U.S. House of Representatives, *Report No. 94-1733*, Sec. 108.

17. House report, Sec. 108.

18. Ibid.

19. Copyright law, Sec. 108(f)(4).

20. Ibid., Sec. 107; and House report, Sec. 107.

21. Copyright law, Sec. 108.

22. Senate report, Sec. 108.

23. House report, Sec. 107.

24. The short life of the older video recordings is due to the growing unavailability of pre-EIAJ-I educational and industrial video tape recorders that are still in working condition. Dubbing the programs onto standard format tapes appears to be the only reasonable way to preserve these old programs.

25. House report, Sec. 108.

26. Ibid.

27. Ibid.

28. Ibid.

INTERLIBRARY LOAN REGULATIONS

Library photocopying was a controversial topic during the lengthy debates leading to the passage of the Copyright Revision Act. Much of the debate centered on the use of photocopies of journal articles and parts of books to meet interlibrary loan requests. Congress remained true to form in resolving the problem; it held public hearings and private conferences on the matter and referred one particularly troublesome point to a committee of experts. After due deliberation, a compromise was reached that was reasonably acceptable to most of the interested parties. The compromise appears in Section 108(g)(2) of the act and in the "Guidelines for the Provision of Subsection 108(g)(2)" issued by the National Commission on the New Technological Uses of Copyrighted Works (CONTU). The text of the act is fairly brief and straightforward. Having met the basic requirements of Sections 108(a) and (d), and assuming that it does not participate in interlibrary loan arrangements on a scale that substitutes copying for purchases or subscriptions, a library or archive may ask another library or archive to reproduce a journal article or a part of a book to meet a patron's request. Congress asked CONTU to determine the amount of copying that substitutes for a purchase or subscription; the CONTU guidelines (pages 116-18) may be summarized as follows.

CONTU GUIDELINES

Photocopying from periodicals

1. The recordkeeping and copying limitations are based on a calendar year.

2. The guidelines are based on filled or completed interlibrary requests. Unfilled requests must be recorded, but they do not apply to the limitation on the number of copies made each year.

3. A statement must be printed, typed, or stamped on the interlibrary request form indicating that the request complies with Section 108(g)(2). The revised interlibrary loan form of June 29, 1977 includes a check-off box to indicate compliance with this requirement.

4. A library or archive may receive no more than five photocopies per year of articles published in the restricted issues of a periodical. (They may be five copies of the same article or single copies of five different articles.) The restriction applies only to issues published within the last five years. The duplication of older issues is limited only by the broad provision in Section 108(g)(2) that prohibits copying which by its nature would substitute for a subscription.

5. The library or archive initiating the requests must maintain records of all requests and the disposition of each request, which must be retained for three years after the close of the calendar year. Although the requesting library must maintain these records, they are not required by the copyright act to make them available

to the public. (For further information on this requirement, see the American Library Association "Record Maintenance and Retention Guidelines for Interlibrary Loan Departments" on pages 120-22.)

6. The library or archive supplying the copies must examine each incoming interlibrary loan request to see if it contains information relative to item 3, above. If the request does not contain the required statement, it must be rejected.

Photocopying from Books

The rules for photocopying parts of books for the purpose of completing interlibrary loan requests are identical to the rules for periodicals, except for item 4, which limits the number of copies that may be made from periodicals published within the last five years. In requesting photocopies of books through interlibrary loan, libraries and archives are limited to receiving no more than five photocopies per title, per calendar year, for as long as the copyright on the book is in force. Under the 1909 copyright law, a book with a valid U.S. copyright receives 28 years of protection. If the copyright was renewed in the twenty-eighth year and it was in force on January 1, 1978, the copyright endures for 75 years. Works created on or after January 1, 1978 are protected for the life of the author, plus 50 years, or for a fixed term of 75 years, depending on the form of authorship.

Exceptions

The guidelines contain two exceptions:

1. If a library or archive owns a copy of a work but is prevented from making photocopies from it, the five-copies-per-year requirement is waived.

2. If the library or archive places a subscription or an order for the title, the five-copies-per-year requirement is waived.

The law and the guidelines were designed to prevent libraries and archives from ordering photocopies through interlibrary loan to avoid purchasing needed items. If the library or archive has demonstrated good faith by owning or ordering the title, the limitation on the number of copies is removed. This has many obvious applications; library and archives are frequently unable to meet a patron's request for a photocopy because the item is misshelved, or stolen, or because the condition of the copy (e.g., missing pages or tight binding) prevents reproduction.

The second exemption indicates that placing an order for a work removes the limitation on copying. The application of this section to copying from books is quite obvious, but there is an interesting twist in its application to orders for periodicals. By placing an order for the current and future issues of a periodical, a library or archives is excused from the five-copies-per-year requirement on the back issues of the periodical. This does not permit wholesale copying of articles in back issues, since the law prohibits copying "in such aggregate quantities as to substitute for a subscription,"[1] but it offers some relief from the five-copies-per-year restriction in the CONTU guidelines.

Requesting Entity

A question has arisen over the meaning of the phrase "requesting entity," which appears nine times in the guidelines. It is not defined in the document or in any other reliable source. The question concerns its application to multi-library public, school, and academic library systems. Is each individual library a requesting entity or is the entire system a single requesting entity? The best answer probably appears in the first appearance of the phrase in the guidelines: "filled requests of a library or archives (a 'requesting entity') within any calendar year. . . ."[2] "Library" and "requesting entity" are both used in the singular form, suggesting that any agency that calls itself a library or an archive may safely consider itself a requesting entity. This means that each departmental or branch library may apply the full quota of five copies per year to its own patrons. It also means that each departmental or branch library must meet the other requirements: "The requesting entity shall maintain records of all requests. . . ."[3] The writer takes the cautious view that the practice of claiming that each departmental or branch library is a requesting entity while operating a central interlibrary loan order department violates the spirit, if not the letter, of the guidelines. This should not preclude the use of central data processing systems for recordkeeping as long as the recordkeeping functions are controlled by the requesting entity.

CONCLUSION

The interlibrary loan provisions of the law were a source of controversy before the law was passed. Now that the law has taken effect and most librarians and archivists have become accustomed to its requirements (especially the recordkeeping requirements), interlibrary loan policies should cease to be a controversial matter. All in all, the law appears to present a fair balance of interests between copyright owners, patrons, and the librarians and archivists who must implement it. Section 108(i) of the law requires periodic reviews of Section 108 by the Register of Copyrights. The Register's first report, to be presented to Congress on January 1, 1983, is certain to concentrate on interlibrary loan practices and may include recommendations for the revision of Section 108. The writer suspects that any proposed revisions will consist of no more than a fine tuning of some parts of the section.

FOOTNOTES

1. *United States Code*, Title 17, "Copyrights," Sec. 108(g)(2).

2. "Guidelines for the Proviso of Subsection 108(g)(2)," Sec. 1(a) in U.S. House of Representatives, *Report No. 94-1476*, Sec. 108.

3. Ibid., Sec. 4.

REGISTRATION AND DEPOSIT

The requirements for registration and deposit of copyrighted works have been a source of confusion during most of the twentieth century. The first U.S. copyright act incorporated the British practice of requiring registration and the deposit of copies to secure copyright protection.[1] Under the Copyright Revision Act of 1867, the copyright proprietor was required to send a copy of the title page of a book, or a description of other works, to the Copyright Office prior to publication, and to deposit two copies of the new work within 10 days of publication. This was a burdensome responsibility, and there was a constant danger that the copyright in a valuable work would be lost through an error in complying with these requirements. Congress attempted to simplify the requirements in the Copyright Revision Act of 1909. The new act incorporated a simple, one-step deposit and registration system, which proved to be troublesome because of its ambiguity. The deposit requirement stated:

> [T]here shall be promptly deposited in the copyright office . . . two complete copies of the best edition thereof then published. . . .[2]

In 1939, the Supreme Court determined that the term "promptly" was too vague and that depositing copies at any time within the 28-year term of protection satisfied the requirement.[3] The registration requirements were equally imprecise:

> That such person may obtain registration of his claim to copyright by complying with the provisions of this Act, including the deposits of copies, and upon such compliance the register of copyright shall issue to him the certificate provided for in . . . the Act.[4]

The Copyright Office insisted, and continues to insist, that registration was required under the 1909 act. Many attorneys seized on the word "may" in the above quotation, suggesting that for most classes of works, registration was only required to renew the copyright for an additional term of protection or to institute an infringement suit. Since most works were not renewed and few were the subject of infringement suits, there was little compulsion to register most classes of works.

These deficiencies were remedied by the Copyright Revision Act of 1976. Under the new act, deposits are required, but registration is optional. Although it is optional, several benefits are offered to encourage prompt registration. First, registration is a prerequisite to an infringement suit. Second, registration within three months of publication is a prerequisite for receiving statutory damages or attorney's fees in the settlement of an infringement case. Third, registration within five years of publication constitutes *prima facie* evidence of the validity of the copyright. Finally, registration within five years of publication is one means of preserving the copyright in a work that was inadvertently published or distributed without a copyright notice. These benefits provide ample motivation for the registration of most works.

In spite of the relative simplicity and modest cost of registration and deposit, many educational institutions claim copyright protection for the bibliographies and instructional materials they produce (by inserting a copyright notice in all copies), yet do not complete the registration or deposit process. Representatives of these institutions contend that they cannot afford to bring a suit for an infringement, so they see little reason to devote the time and money to register the works and deposit the copies. This may justify not registering a work, but it does not excuse a failure to deposit copies. Neither fees nor forms are required to deposit copies, (the two copies are sent to: The Copyright Office, Library of Congress, Washington, DC 20559). A cover letter is not required, but may be included. Because of the cost of depositing certain types of materials (and the problem the Copyright Office has in storing copyrighted concrete birdbaths and other bulky objects), single copies are required for some items while others require only documentation in lieu of copies. For additional information see page 227.

The new copyright law gives the Copyright Office the right to force copyright proprietors to deposit copies. The Copyright Office deposit enforcement section has been expanded in an effort to identify proprietors who are not depositing copies. Proprietors who have not deposited copies may receive a letter from the Copyright Office "demanding" that the copies be deposited. An unresponsive proprietor will receive two more "demand" letters; if he or she does not comply with the third letter, the matter may be forwarded to the Justice Department for action. Upon receipt of such a case, the Justice Department sends the proprietor a letter advising of the omission and requesting that the matter be resolved. Failing that, the Justice Department may call the proprietor in an attempt to resolve the matter through persuasion instead of using the formal legal action available under the new copyright act.

During the 1979 fiscal year, 99% of the proprietors who received demand notices from the Copyright Office complied with the request. Fifteen non-compliance cases were forwarded to the Justice Department for action, but the Justice Department was able to resolve them through informal persuasion. During the first half of fiscal year 1980, 17 cases were forwarded to the Justice Department for action. One case, involving a publishing firm, could not be resolved through informal negotiation, and formal legal action was instituted. The case was resolved by a default judgement in favor of the plaintiff. The size of the fine and the right of the plaintiff to recover costs had not been determined at the time of this writing.[5]

FOOTNOTES

1. Under the act of 1890, the registration and deposit functions were handled by the clerks of the federal district courts.

2. *United States Code*, Title 17, "Copyrights" (1909 ed.), Sec. 12.

3. 306 U.S. 30, 59 S.Ct. 397.

4. *United States Code*, Title 17, "Copyrights" (1909 ed.), Sec. 10.

5. Information supplied during a visit to the Copyright Office on March 1, 1979 and through subsequent telephone conversations with Copyright Office officials.

REPRODUCTION OF UNPUBLISHED MATERIALS

Until recently, the American legal system offered a dual form of copyright protection. Under this system, common law copyright applied to works from the moment of their creation until they were published or disseminated in an uncontrolled distribution; upon publication or dissemination, they were eligible for a limited, renewable term of statutory copyright protection. The dual system began with the inauguration of statutory copyright in Great Britain in 1710.[1] The statute applied to the British colonies in North America, but most Americans ignored it. The American Revolution terminated statutory copyright protection in the breakaway colonies, but it was replaced in 1790 by a similar dual system of copyright protection. For all practical purposes, the dual system ended in the United States on January 1, 1978 with the implementation of the Copyright Revision Act of 1976.[2]

Common law copyright gave authors comprehensive and perpetual protection for their unpublished works. This was burdensome to those who studied or administered unpublished materials, particularly in cases where the ownership of literary rights to unpublished works of deceased authors was dispersed or unknown. Because of the ambiguity of the common law, it was unclear whether all or part of unpublished works could be duplicated to facilitate research or if they could be quoted in scholarly or popular publications. Equally serious doubts were raised about the right of libraries or archives to duplicate unpublished materials to preserve them or to share them with other libraries or archives.

Most of these problems were resolved by the Copyright Revision Act of 1976, which preempted common law copyrights in works "fixed in a tangible medium of expression" and subject to copyright protection when the law went into effect.[3] The preemption of existing common law copyrights has two significant benefits for the users and administrators of collections of unpublished materials. It fixes the duration of these copyrights, and removes uncertainty about the right to duplicate them for preservation or dissemination.

In the first matter, the law established the duration of copyright protection for all works, published or unpublished, as the life of the author, plus 50 years.[4] In implementing the new law, Congress faced the problem of the sudden expiration of copyrights in unpublished works which were near the end of their statutory term of protection. To compensate the copyright proprietors for the reduction in the term of protection, the duration for these works was extended to either December 31, 2002 or December 31, 2027:

> In no case, however, shall the term of copyright in such a work expire before December 31, 2002; and if the work is published on or before December 31, 2002, the term of copyright shall not expire before December 31, 2027.[5]

A specific termination date for copyrights in unpublished works resolves the problem of unclear or tangled ownership of the rights in many older works, which had prevented their fullest use by scholars and students. Although we must wait until 2002 or 2027 for these works to go into the public domain, the duration clause represents substantial progress in obtaining access to unpublished materials in or out of libraries and archives.[6]

The second significant benefit of the preemption of common law copyrights appears in Sections 107 and 108 of the new law. Section 108 contains the most significant provisions for the duplication of unpublished materials for the purpose of preservation or deposit in another institution. To qualify for these benefits, a library or archive must meet several conditions.

> Notwithstanding the provisions of section 106, it is not an infringement of copyright for a library or archives, or any of its employees acting within the scope of their employment, to reproduce no more than one copy or phonorecord of a work, or to distribute such copy or phonorecord, under the conditions specified by this section, if—
>
> (1) the reproduction or distribution is made without any purpose of direct or indirect commercial advantage;
>
> (2) the collections of the library or archives are (i) open to the public, or (ii) available not only to researchers affiliated with the library or archives or with the institution of which it is a part, but also to other persons doing research in a specialized field; and
>
> (3) the reproduction or distribution of the work includes a notice of copyright.[7]

The rights of reproduction and distribution under this section only apply if

> The library or archives displays prominently, at the place where orders [for copies] are accepted, and included on its order form, a warning of copyright in accordance with requirements that the Register of Copyrights shall prescribe by regulation.[8]

The House report indicates that the first requirement (the reproduction or distribution cannot be made for a direct or indirect commercial advantage) does not prevent libraries or archives from charging a modest fee for making copies. The report suggests that the clause was designed to prevent commercial firms from establishing a copying service under the terms of Section 108.[9]

Tax-supported or privately supported institutions that are open to the general public readily meet the second requirement. The problem arises with libraries and archives that restrict access to their collections. The congressional reports do not comment on this point, but it appears that a library or archive meets this requirement if its collections are open to authors, scholars, graduate students, and other researchers who meet certain reasonable requirements. This can be a problem for major libraries and archives that are heavily used by outside researchers. Some of these institutions attempt to reduce the pressure on their collections by requiring outside researchers to demonstrate their need or ability to use the collection or by requiring them to exhaust other available sources before being admitted to the collection. A library or archive that wants to benefit from the provisions of Section 108 must be careful that its admission requirements do not discriminate against certain classes of potential users.

The third requirement, that copies made under this provision display a notice of copyright, can be met by (1) reproducing the work's copyright notice on the copy, or (2) by including a copyright warning notice on all copies. The latter can be accomplished by stamping a warning notice on each copy or by having the warning notice printed on each copy by the copying machine. The law does not specify the text of the notice, so any reasonable notice should suffice. The American Library Association recommends the following: "Notice: This material may be protected by copyright law (Title 17 U.S. Code)."[10]

The last general requirement concerns the location and language of a notice which must appear at the place where orders for copies or interlibrary loans are accepted and on order forms for copies and interlibrary loans. The text of the required notice and the display requirements appear in the *U.S. Code of Federal Regulations, Title 37*, Sec. 201.14.[11] Unlike the advisories issued by the American Library Association, the specific requirements for this notice leave few opportunities for discretionary decisions by librarians and archivists. A discussion of this notice and the required text appear on page 57.

Having met the four basic requirements, a library or archive may duplicate unpublished materials in part or in their entirety for purposes of preservation and safety or for deposit in another library or archive. The act does not limit the number of copies that may be made, but imposes several requirements that tend to limit copying and the disposition of the copies:

1. The item that is copied must be "currently in the collections of the library or archives."[12] A conservative interpretation suggests that one may not borrow a document for a short time, make a microform master copy, and continue to reproduce it after the original is returned.

2. The copies must be made in "facsimile form."[13] Copies of manuscripts, films, photographs, sound recordings, and the like made by the electrostatic, photographic, or sound recording processes appear to meet this requirement, but copies made in machine-readable form do not meet the requirement.[14]

3. The copies must be made "for purposes of preservation and security or for deposit for research use in another library or archives."[15] The practice of making "convenience copies" of unpublished works for scholars does not appear to meet this requirement unless, of course, the copies are made with the permission of the copyright proprietor.

4. A library or archive receiving the depository copy must meet the requirement of Section 108(a)(2)–that the collections of the library or archive be open to the public and available to outside researchers.[16] This appears to prohibit making "deposit copies" of unpublished works for a scholar's personal library without the permission of the copyright proprietor.

These provisions appear to give libraries and archives enough latitude to copy unpublished materials for purposes of preservation or to deposit copies in another library or archive.

There are some limitations in this section that can be troublesome. The requirements in Section 108(a)(1) are designed to exclude commercial firms from the benefits of this section. The House report makes this point very clear:

> Under this provision, a purely commercial enterprise could not establish a collection of copyrighted works, call itself a library or archive, and engage in for-profit reproduction and distribution of photocopies. Similarly, it would not be possible for a non-profit institution, by means of contractual arrangements with a commercial copying enterprise, to authorize the enterprise to carry out copying and distribution functions that would be exempt if conducted by the non-profit institution itself.[17]

It appears that Congress wanted to prevent libraries and archives from turning their traditional photocopying services over to a commercial firm. In excluding this practice, the requirement also appears to prevent a library or archive from employing a commercial firm to make microform copies of all or part of its archival collection for purposes of preservation or to deposit the copies in another institution. The solution to this problem, through Section 107, appears below.

Another problem is presented by the restrictions in Section 108(b), which limit copying of unpublished works to making safety or deposit copies. This section appears to prevent libraries or archives from making convenience copies for scholars. The problem may be overcome, in part, if the library or archive loans its safety or deposit copies to researchers for temporary home use. This is not an entirely satisfactory solution, however, since safety or deposit copies do not exist for many unpublished materials and the libraries or archives that hold these copies may not allow them off the premises. A partial solution is found in Section 108(d), which permits a library or archive to copy an article from a periodical, a chapter from a book, or a small part of other works for a patron. This section was intended to facilitate the duplication of published materials at a patron's request, but nothing in the law or the reports suggests that a library or archive cannot employ this provision to copy a *small part* of an unpublished work for a patron at his or her request, as long as the copy is used for "private study, scholarship, or research."[18] Although this provision accommodates some patrons' needs, it does not satisfy all of them.

Solutions for some of these problems can be found in Section 107, which is based on the four historic criteria for fair use of a copyrighted work.[19] (The four criteria are discussed at length on pages 15-25.) The fair use criteria were designed to facilitate copying part of a work (or, in a few instances, a complete work) "for purposes such as criticism, comment, news reporting, teaching . . . scholarship, or research. . . ."[20]

The fair use section, which concerns both published and unpublished works, discusses three important applications to the duplication of unpublished works. Researchers benefit from the right to duplicate parts of unpublished materials on self-service copying machines. Although this does not appear to authorize copying in excess of the amounts indicated in Section 108(d), it enables researchers to copy selectively from the materials they are studying without seeking the assistance of a curator or clerk each time a copy is needed. (The library or archive's limited responsibility for self-service copying machines is treated on page 58.) More importantly, the fair use section permits researchers to incorporate brief passages from unpublished works in books and articles without the permission of the copyright proprietor, resolving much of the difficulty researchers sometimes face in attempting to include brief quotations from unpublished correspondence, diaries, taped interviews, and the like in scholarly books and articles. It also enables the film, video, and art critics to incorporate a small part of an unpublished visual work in their publications or productions. Although the fair use section was not designed to offer *carte blanche* permission to incorporate unpublished material in critical or scholarly works, a cautious application of the fair use criteria offers considerable relief from the burden of obtaining permission to duplicate *small parts* of unpublished works in scholarly or critical works.

Libraries and archives appear to benefit from another small point in the fair use section. Section 108(a)(1) appears to prohibit a library or archive from employing a commercial firm to duplicate all or part of a collection for preservation or deposit purposes; this limitation can probably be overcome through the fair use section. The clearest evidence is found in a statement in the Senate report:

> A problem of particular urgency is that of preserving for posterity prints of motion pictures made before 1942. Aside from the deplorable fact that in a great many cases the only existing copy of a film has been deliberately destroyed, those that remain are in immediate danger of disintegration; they were printed on film stock with a nitrate base that will inevitably decompose in time. The efforts of the Library of Congress, the American Film Institute, and other organizations to rescue and preserve this irreplaceable contribution to our cultural life are to be applauded, and the making of duplicate copies for purposes of archival preservation certainly falls within the scope of 'fair use.'[21]

Although these comments are addressed to the particular problem of preserving films printed on fragile nitrate stock, the point is clearly made in the last sentence: ". . . the making of duplicate copies for purposes of archival preservation certainly falls within the scope of 'fair use.'"[22] The fair use section, unlike the photocopying section, is based on a broad concept of fair use which accords only a limited consideration as to whether the duplicating service that makes the copies is operated on a for-profit or a non-profit basis. Under these circumstances, it may be acceptable for a library or archive to employ a commercial firm to conduct a major reproduction project designed to produce safety or deposit copies under the terms of the requirement in Section 108(b).[23]

CONCLUSION

The preemption of common law copyrights in the new copyright law and the inclusion of specific provisions for fair use and for library and archival copying mark a significant change in the administration and use of unpublished works. The problems which libraries and archives faced in obtaining permission to duplicate fragile materials or to share them with other libraries and archives are largely resolved. The availability of these safety or deposit copies improves access to these materials by researchers. The researcher's work is also enhanced by the right to duplicate a small part of a work to facilitate study and by the right to include brief excerpts in his or her publications. Both the researcher and the curator will benefit when the copyright protection on large bodies of unpublished works expires in 2002 or 2027. These changes were well designed to facilitate scholarly activities without inflicting serious injury on the copyright proprietor.

FOOTNOTES

1. 8 Anne, c 19 (1710).

2. *United States Code*, Title 17, "Copyrights." Hereafter cited as Copyright law. Common law copyright continues to protect works that are not fixed in a tangible form, such as speeches and sermons which exist only in the spoken form.

3. Ibid., Sec. 301.

4. Ibid., Sec. 302(a). Sec. 302(c) specifies that the duration for anonymous works, pseudonymous works, and works made for hire is 75 years from the date of publication or 100 years from the date of creation, whichever expires first.

5. Ibid., Sec. 303.

6. In spite of these progressive steps, some problems in access to unpublished materials remain. The limited duration of copyrights may prompt a few proprietors to restrict access to the materials as a means of controlling copying and dissemination, but that is a matter of collection management and not of copyrights.

7. Copyright law, Sec. 108(a).

8. Ibid., Sec. 108(e)(2).

9. U.S. House of Representatives, *Report No. 94-1476*, Sec. 108. Hereafter cited as House report.

10. "Warning Notices for Copies and Machines," *American Libraries* 8, no. 10 (November 1977): 530.

11. *U.S. Code of Federal Regulations, Title 37*, Sec. 201.14 (Washington: Government Printing Office, 1977). (The document appears on pages 119-20.)

12. Copyright law, Sec. 108(b).

13. Ibid.

14. House report, Sec. 108.

15. Copyright law, Sec. 108(b).

16. Ibid.

17. House report, Sec. 108.

18. Copyright law, Sec. 107.

19. Ibid.

20. Ibid.

21. U.S. Senate, *Report No. 94-473*, Sec. 107.

22. Ibid.

23. It should be noted that the highly regarded work of the Library of Congress to duplicate pre-1942 films involves the use of commercial film laboratories.

COPYRIGHT WARNING NOTICES FOR LIBRARIES, ARCHIVES, AND MEDIA CENTERS

Libraries, archives, and media centers are obliged to display a number of copyright notices. Although most librarians, archivists, and media specialists are familiar with the basic requirements, some confusion has arisen over the details of their application. The following are the approved and recommended notices and the locations in which they should appear:

1. Notices at the place where orders are accepted

This requirement in section 108(d)(2) and (e)(2):

> [T] he library or archives displays prominently at places where orders are accepted, and includes on its order form, a warning of copyright in accordance with the requirements that the Register of Copyrights shall prescribe by regulation.[1]

The required notice states:

NOTICE

Warning Concerning Copyright Restrictions

> The copyright law of the United States (Title 17, United States Code) governs the making of photocopies or other reproductions of copyrighted materials.
>
> Under certain conditions specified by law, libraries and archives are authorized to furnish a photocopy or other reproduction. One of these specified conditions is that the photocopy or reproduction is not to be 'used for any purpose other than private study, scholarship, or research.' If a user makes a request for, or later uses, a photocopy or reproduction for purposes in excess of 'fair use,' that user may be liable for copyright infringement.
>
> This institution reserves the right to refuse to accept a copying order, if in its judgment, fulfillment of the order would involve violation of copyright law.[2]

The notice must be printed on heavy paper or other durable material, in 18-point type, or larger, and it must be posted conspicuously at each place where orders are accepted for staff-operated copying services or for interlibrary loans.[3] The notice should also be posted in the audiovisual or microform areas of libraries and archives that offer staff-operated copying services. The requirements for the text, the size of type, and the placement of these notices are very specific, so it would be unwise to alter the language of the notice or to fail to meet any of the other requirements.

2. Notices at or on self-service copying machines

This notice is specified in Sec. 108(f)(1):

Nothing in this section–

> shall be construed to impose liability for copyright infringement upon a library or archives or its employees for the unsupervised use of reproducing equipment located on its premises: *Provided*, That such equipment displays a notice that the making of a copy may be subject to the copyright law.[4]

Unlike the previous requirement, the size and text of this notice are not prescribed. It is sufficient to have some sort of a copyright warning notice on or near each machine. This applies to all self-service "reproducing equipment" on "the premises" of the library or archive, both coin-operated and free-use machines which are likely to be used on the premises to reproduce copyrighted materials.[5] These would include photocopying machines, microform reader-printers, photographic copystands, animation stands, tape recorders, videotape recorders, and the like. Warning notices may be attached to duplicating equipment used off the premises, but they are not required.

The absence of a specified statement in the notice raises questions about the efficacy of some of the notices seen in libraries and archives. Since neither the law nor the Copyright Office specify the language of the notice, it appears that almost any understandable statement will meet the requirement. The American Library Association recommends that the following notice be used:

> Notice: The copyright law of the United States (Title 17 U.S. Code) governs the making of photocopies of other reproductions of copyrighted material. The person using this equipment is liable for any infringement.[6]

Several photocopying equipment manufacturers and distributors attach notices to the machines they place in libraries. The language of these notices varies considerably, but they all appear to satisfy the requirement.

3. Notices on copies

Section 108(a)(3) specifies that each copy made in a library or archive include "a notice of copyright."[7] The "Agreement on Guidelines for Classroom Copying in Not-For-Profit Educational Institutions" specifies that when multiple copies are reproduced for classroom use, "each copy includes a notice of copyright."[8] The "Guidelines for Educational Use of Music" prohibit the copying of sheet music "without inclusion of the copyright notice which appears on the printed copy."[9]

In the first two instances, the text of the notice is not specified, so any reasonable notice would seem to suffice. The American Library Association *recommends* that the following notice be used: "Notice: This material may be protected by copyright law (Title 17 U.S. Code)."[10] A notice can be applied by means of a rubber stamp or an adhesive label, and most photocopying machines can be adapted to print a warning notice on each copy. It is also possible to reproduce the copyright notice appearing in the work; this is the only procedure that meets the requirement in the "Guidelines for Educational Uses of Music." (See page 96.)

4. Notices on request forms

Sections 108(d)(2) and (e)(2) require that a warning notice appear on order forms for photocopying and interlibrary loans. One probably should appear on forms used to request the duplication of microforms or audiovisual materials as well. The notice, identical to the one appearing on signs at the places where orders are accepted (see page 57), must appear on a box "located prominently on the order form itself, either on the front side of the form or immediately adjacent to the space calling for the name or signature of the person using the form."[11] It must be printed in the type size used prominently in the form, but in no case is it to be in a type smaller than eight points.

Although the law specifically requires the use of this notice on order forms, it does not require a library, archive, or media center to initiate the use of request forms just to meet this requirement. The requirement applies only to institutions in which such forms are in use. Some confusion exists over the placement of this notice on interlibrary loan forms transmitted between institutions. It is generally agreed that the required notice need only appear on the forms used by patrons to request a copy of an interlibrary loan and that the notice is not needed on interlibrary loan forms exchanged between institutions. The coded notice in the lower left-hand corner of the Revised Interlibrary Loan Form of June 29, 1977 was not designed to comply with this requirement but to conform to Section 3 of the National Commission on the New Technological Uses of Copyrighted Works (CONTU) "Guidelines for the Provision of Subsection 108(g)(2)."[12] This notice states that the interlibrary request complies with the requirements of the CONTU guidelines or with other aspects of Sections 107 or 108 of the Copyright Act.

5. Warning notices required in independent media centers

Inasmuch as the requirements for copyright warning notices are almost all found in Section 108, media specialists wonder if they apply to media centers that are administratively independent of a library. Although the notices are only mentioned in Section 108 of the act, two references to them appear in Section 107 of the House report.[13] Both references apply to the notices on copies (see item 4, above). If the independent media center complies with that requirement, the need to comply with the three remaining requirements appears to depend on the type of services the center provides. If it employs some of the unique exemptions available in the photocopying section of the law (e.g., videotaping television news programs off-the-air, reproducing out-of-print works for a patron, etc.), then the center seems to be obliged to comply with the several requirements of Section 108, including the requirements for the use of warning notices.

FOOTNOTES

1. *United States Code*, Title 17, "Copyrights," Sec. 108(d)(2) and (e)(2). Hereafter cited as Copyright law.

2. *U.S. Code of Federal Regulations*, Title 37, Sec. 201.14 (Washington: Government Printing Office, 1977).

3. U.S. House of Representatives, *Report No. 94-1476*, Sec. 108. Hereafter cited as House report.

4. Copyright law, Sec. 108(f)(1).

5. Ibid.

6. "Three Words Added to Copyright Notice," *American Libraries* 9, no. 1 (January 1978): 22.

7. Copyright law, Sec. 108(a)(3).

8. House report, Sec. 107.

9. Ibid.

10. "Warning Notices for Copies and Machines," *American Libraries* 8, no. 10 (November 1977): 530.

11. Copyright law, Sec. 108(d)(2) and (e)(2).

12. House report, Sec. 108.

13. Ibid., Sec. 107.

PART II

THE COPYRIGHT REVISION ACT OF 1976 AND ITS SUPPORTING DOCUMENTS

The Congress shall have Power . . .
To promote the Progress of Science and useful Arts,
by securing for limited Times to Authors and Inventors
the exclusive Right to their respective Writings and Discoveries. . . .

Section 8, Article I
U.S. Constitution

LAW

Public Law 94-553 OCT. 19, 1976
94th Congress

An Act

For the general revision of the Copyright Law, title 17 of the United States Code, and for other purposes.

Be it enacted by the Senate and House of Representatives of the United States of America in Congress assembled,

TITLE I—GENERAL REVISION OF COPYRIGHT LAW

SEC. 101. Title 17 of the United States Code, entitled "Copyrights", is hereby amended in its entirety to read as follows:

TITLE 17—COPYRIGHTS

Chapter 1.—SUBJECT MATTER AND SCOPE OF COPYRIGHT

§ 101. Definitions

As used in this title, the following terms and their variant forms mean the following:

An "anonymous work" is a work on the copies or phonorecords of which no natural person is identified as author.

"Audiovisual works" are works that consist of a series of related images which are intrinsically intended to be shown by the use of machines or devices such as projectors, viewers, or electronic equipment, together with accompanying sounds, if any, regardless of the nature of the material objects, such as films or tapes, in which the works are embodied.

The "best edition" of a work is the edition, published in the United States at any time before the date of deposit, that the Library of Congress determines to be most suitable for its purposes.

A person's "children" are that person's immediate offspring, whether legitimate or not, and any children legally adopted by that person.

A "collective work" is a work, such as a periodical issue, anthology, or encyclopedia, in which a number of contributions, constituting separate and independent works in themselves, are assembled into a collective whole.

A "compilation" is a work formed by the collection and assembling of preexisting materials or of data that are selected, coordinated, or arranged in such a way that the resulting work as a whole constitutes an original work of authorship. The term "compilation" includes collective works.

"Copies" are material objects, other than phonorecords, in which a work is fixed by any method now known or later developed, and from which the work can be perceived, reproduced, or otherwise communicated, either directly or with the aid of a machine or device. The term "copies" includes the material object, other than a phonorecord, in which the work is first fixed.

"Copyright owner", with respect to any one of the exclusive rights comprised in a copyright, refers to the owner of that particular right.

A work is "created" when it is fixed in a copy or phonorecord for the first time; where a work is prepared over a period of time, the portion of it that has been fixed at any particular time constitutes the work as of that time, and where the work has been prepared in different versions, each version constitutes a separate work.

A "derivative work" is a work based upon one or more preexisting works, such as a translation, musical arrangement, dramatization, fictionalization, motion picture version, sound recording, art reproduction, abridgment, condensation, or any other form in which a work may be recast, transformed, or adapted. A work consisting of editorial revisions, annotations, elaborations, or other modifications which, as a whole, represent an original work of authorship, is a "derivative work".

A "device", "machine", or "process" is one now known or later developed.

To "display" a work means to show a copy of it, either directly or by means of a film, slide, television image, or any other device or process or, in the case of a motion picture or other audiovisual work, to show individual images nonsequentially.

A work is "fixed" in a tangible medium of expression when its embodiment in a copy or phonorecord, by or under the authority of the author, is sufficiently permanent or stable to permit it to be perceived, reproduced, or otherwise communicated for a period of more than transitory duration. A work consisting of sounds, images, or both, that are being transmitted, is "fixed" for purposes of this title if a fixation of the work is being made simultaneously with its transmission.

The terms "including" and "such as" are illustrative and not limitative.

A "joint work" is a work prepared by two or more authors with the intention that their contributions be merged into inseparable or interdependent parts of a unitary whole.

"Literary works" are works, other than audiovisual works, expressed in words, numbers, or other verbal or numerical symbols or indicia, regardless of the nature of the material objects, such as books, periodicals, manuscripts, phonorecords, film, tapes, disks, or cards, in which they are embodied.

"Motion pictures" are audiovisual works consisting of a series of related images which, when shown in succession, impart an impression of motion, together with accompanying sounds, if any.

To "perform" a work means to recite, render, play, dance, or act it, either directly or by means of any device or process or, in the case of a motion picture or other audiovisual work, to show its images in any sequence or to make the sounds accompanying it audible.

"Phonorecords" are material objects in which sounds, other than those accompanying a motion picture or other audiovisual work, are fixed by any method now known or later developed, and from which the sounds can be perceived, reproduced, or otherwise communicated, either directly or with the aid of a machine or device. The term "phonorecords" includes the material object in which the sounds are first fixed.

"Pictorial, graphic, and sculptural works" include two-dimensional and three-dimensional works of fine, graphic, and applied art, photographs, prints and art reproductions, maps, globes, charts, technical drawings, diagrams, and models. Such works shall include works of artistic craftsmanship insofar as their form but not their mechanical or utilitarian aspects are concerned; the design of a useful article, as defined in this section, shall be considered a pictorial, graphic, or sculptural work only if, and only to the extent that, such design incorporates pictorial, graphic, or sculptural features that can be identified separately from, and are capable of existing independently of, the utilitarian aspects of the article.

A "pseudonymous work" is a work on the copies or phonorecords of which the author is identified under a fictitious name.

"Publication" is the distribution of copies or phonorecords of a work to the public by sale or other transfer of ownership, or by rental, lease, or lending. The offering to distribute copies or phonorecords to a group of persons for purposes of further distribution, public performance, or public display, constitutes publication. A public performance or display of a work does not of itself constitute publication.

For further information about "publication," see Representative Kastenmeier's comments in the CONGRESSIONAL RECORD on page 67.

To perform or display a work "publicly" means—

(1) to perform or display it at a place open to the public or at any place where a substantial number of persons outside of a normal circle of a family and its social acquaintances is gathered; or

(2) to transmit or otherwise communicate a performance or display of the work to a place specified by clause (1) or to the public, by means of any device or processs, whether the members of the public capable of receiving the performance or display receive it in the same place or in separate places and at the same time or at different times.

"Sound recordings" are works that result from the fixation of a series of musical, spoken, or other sounds, but not including the sounds accompanying a motion picture or other audiovisual work, regardless of the nature of the material objects, such as disks, tapes, or other phonorecords, in which they are embodied.

"State" includes the District of Columbia and the Commonwealth of Puerto Rico, and any territories to which this title is made applicable by an Act of Congress.

A "transfer of copyright ownership" is an assignment, mortgage, exclusive license, or any other conveyance, alienation, or hypothecation of a copyright or of any of the exclusive rights comprised in a copyright, whether or not it is limited in time or place of effect, but not including a nonexclusive license.

A "transmission program" is a body of material that, as an aggregate, has been produced for the sole purpose of transmission to the public in sequence and as a unit.

To "transmit" a performance or display is to communicate it by any device or process whereby images or sounds are received beyond the place from which they are sent.

The "United States", when used in a geographical sense, comprises the several States, the District of Columbia and the Commonwealth of Puerto Rico, and the organized territories under the jurisdiction of the United States Government.

A "useful article" is an article having an intrinsic utilitarian function that is not merely to portray the appearance of the article or to convey information. An article that is normally a part of a useful article is considered a "useful article".

The author's "widow" or "widower" is the author's surviving spouse under the law of the author's domicile at the time of his or her death, whether or not the spouse has later remarried.

A "work of the United States Government" is a work prepared by an officer or employee of the United States Government as part of that person's official duties.

A "work made for hire" is—

(1) a work prepared by an employee within the scope of his or her employment; or

(2) a work specially ordered or commissioned for use as a contribution to a collective work, as a part of a motion picture or other audiovisual work, as a translation, as a supplementary work, as a compilation, as an instructional text, as a test, as answer material for a test, or as an atlas, if the parties expressly agree in a written instrument signed by them that the work shall be considered a work made for hire. For the purpose of the foregoing sentence, a "supplementary work" is a work prepared for publication as a secondary adjunct to a work by another author for the purpose of introducing, concluding, illustrating, explaining, revising,

commenting upon, or assisting in the use of the other work, such as forewords, afterwords, pictorial illustrations, maps, charts, tables, editorial notes, musical arrangements, answer material for tests, bibliographies, appendixes, and indexes, and an "instructional text" is a literary, pictorial, or graphic work prepared for publication and with the purpose of use in systematic instructional activities.

HOUSE REPORT

The significant definitions in this section will be mentioned or summarized in connection with the provisions to which they are most relevant.

These definitions can be located through the index.

CONGRESSIONAL RECORD

Representative Robert Kastenmeier offered the following explanation of the term "publication" during his remarks from the floor of the House of Representatives on September 22, 1976. The comment appears on page 10874 of the CONGRESSIONAL RECORD, daily edition, of September 22, 1976.

Mr. Chairman, before concluding my remarks I would like to discuss several questions which have been raised concerning the meaning of several provisions of S. 22 as reported by the House Judiciary Committee and of statements in the committee's report, No. 94-1476. One of these questions involves the meaning of the concept of "publication" in the case of a work of art, such as a painting or statue, that exists in only one copy. It is not the committee's intention that such a work would be regarded as "published" when the single existing copy is sold or offered for sale in the traditional way—for example, through an art dealer, gallery, or auction house. On the other hand, where the work has been made for reproduction in multiple copies—as in the case of fine prints such as lithographs—or where multiple reproductions of the prototype work are offered for purchase by the public—as in the case of castings from a statue or reproductions made from a photograph of a painting—publication would take place at the point when reproduced copies are publicly distributed or when, even if only one copy exists at that point, reproductions are offered for purchase by multiple members of the public.

LAW

§ 102. Subject matter of copyright: In general

(a) Copyright protection subsists, in accordance with this title, in original works of authorship fixed in any tangible medium of expression, now known or later developed, from which they can be perceived, reproduced, or otherwise communicated, either directly or with the aid of a machine or device. Works of authorship include the following categories:

(1) literary works;
(2) musical works, including any accompanying words;
(3) dramatic works, including any accompanying music;
(4) pantomimes and choreographic works;
(5) pictorial, graphic, and sculptural works;
(6) motion pictures and other audiovisual works; and
(7) sound recordings.

(b) In no case does copyright protection for an original work of authorship extend to any idea, procedure, process, system, method of operation, concept, principle, or discovery, regardless of the form in which it is described, explained, illustrated, or embodied in such work.

HOUSE REPORT

"Original works of authorship"

The two fundamental criteria of copyright protection—originality and fixation in tangible form—are restated in the first sentence of this cornerstone provision. The phrase "original works of authorship," which is purposely left undefined, is intended to incorporate without change the standard of originality established by the courts under the present copyright statute. This standard does not include requirements of novelty, ingenuity, or esthetic merit, and there is no intention to enlarge the standard of copyright protection to require them.

In using the phrase "original works of authorship," rather than "all the writings of an author" now in section 4 of the statute, the committee's purpose is to avoid exhausting the constitutional power of Congress to legislate in this field, and to eliminate the uncertainties arising from the latter phrase. Since the present statutory language is substantially the same as the empowering language of the Constitution, a recurring question has been whether the statutory and the constitutional provisions are coextensive. If so, the courts would be faced with the alternative of holding copyrightable something that Congress clearly did not intend to protect, or of holding constitutionally incapable of copyright something that Congress might one day want to protect. To avoid these equally undesirable results, the courts have indicated that "all the writings of an author" under the present statute is narrower in scope than the "writings" of "authors" referred to in the Constitution. The bill avoids this dilemma by using a different phrase—"original works of authorship"—in characterizing the general subject matter of statutory copyright protection.

The history of copyright law has been one of gradual expansion in the types of works accorded protection, and the subject matter affected by this expansion has fallen into two general categories. In the first, scientific discoveries and technological developments have made possible new forms of creative expression that never existed before. In some of these cases the new expressive forms—electronic music, filmstrips, and computer programs, for example—could be regarded as an extension of copyrightable subject matter Congress had already intended to protect, and were thus considered copyrightable from the outset without the need of new legislation. In other cases, such as photographs, sound recordings, and motion pictures, statutory enactment was deemed necessary to give them full recognition as copyrightable works.

Authors are continually finding new ways of expressing themselves, but it is impossible to foresee the forms that these new expressive methods will take. The bill does not intend either to freeze the scope of copyrightable subject matter at the present stage of communication technology or to allow unlimited expansion into areas completely outside the present congressional intent. Section 102 implies neither that that subject matter is unlimited nor that new forms of expression within that general area of subject matter would necessarily be unprotected.

The historic expansion of copyright has also applied to forms of expression which, although in existence for generations or centuries, have only gradually come to be recognized as creative and worthy of protection. The first copyright statute in this country, enacted in 1790, designated only "maps, charts, and books"; major forms of expression such as music, drama, and works of art achieved specific statutory recognition only in later enactments. Although the coverage of the present statute is very broad, and would be broadened further by the explicit recognition of all forms of choreography, there are unquestionably other areas of existing subject matter that this bill does not propose to protect but that future Congresses may want to.

Fixation in tangible form

As a basic condition of copyright protection, the bill perpetuates the existing requirement that a work be fixed in a "tangible medium of expression," and adds that this medium may be one "now known or later developed," and that the fixation is sufficient if the work "can be perceived, reproduced, or otherwise communicated, either directly or with the aid of a machine or device." This broad language is intended to avoid the artificial and largely unjustifiable distinctions, derived from cases such as *White-Smith Publishing Co.* v. *Apollo Co.*, 209 U.S. 1 (1908), under which statutory copyrightability in certain cases has been made to depend upon the form or medium in which the work is fixed. Under the bill it makes no difference what the form, manner, or medium of fixation may be—whether it is in words, numbers, notes, sounds, pictures, or any other graphic or symbolic indicia, whether embodied in a physical object in written, printed, photographic, sculptural, punched, magnetic, or any other stable form, and whether it is capable of perception directly or by means of any machine or device "now known or later developed."

Under the bill, the concept of fixation is important since it not only determines whether the provisions of the statute apply to a work, but it also represents the dividing line between common law and statutory protection. As will be noted in more detail in connection with section 301, an unfixed work of authorship, such as an improvisation or an unrecorded choreographic work, performance, or broadcast, would continue to be subject to protection under State common law or statute, but would not be eligible for Federal statutory protection under section 102.

The bill seeks to resolve, through the definition of "fixation" in section 101, the status of live broadcasts—sports, news coverage, live performances of music, etc.—that are reaching the public in unfixed form but that are simultaneously being recorded. When a football game is being covered by four television cameras, with a director guiding the activities of the four camermen and choosing which of their electronic images are sent out to the public and in what order, there is little doubt that what the cameramen and the director are doing constitutes "authorship." The further question to be considered is whether there has been a fixation. If the images and sounds to be broadcast are first recorded (on a video tape, film, etc.) and then transmitted, the recorded work would be considered a "motion picture" subject to statutory protection against unauthorized reproduction or retransmission of the broadcast. If the program content is transmitted live to the public while being recorded at the same time, the case would be treated the same; the copyright owner would not be forced to rely on common law rather than statutory rights in proceeding against an infringing user of the live broadcast.

Thus, assuming it is copyrightable—as a "motion picture" or "sound recording," for example—the content of a live transmission should be regarded as fixed and should be accorded statutory protection if it is being recorded simultaneously with its transmission. On the other hand, the definition of "fixation" would exclude from the concept purely evanescent or transient reproductions such as those projected briefly on a screen, shown electronically on a television or other cathode ray tube, or captured momentarily in the "memory" of a computer.

The two preceding paragraphs did not appear in the SENATE REPORT.

Under the first sentence of the definition of "fixed" in section 101, a work would be considered "fixed in a tangible medium of expression" if there has been an authorized embodiment in a copy or phonorecord and if that embodiment "is sufficiently permanent or stable" to permit the work "to be perceived, reproduced, or otherwise communicated for a period of more than transitory duration." The second sentence makes clear that, in the case of "a work consisting of sounds, images, or both, that are being transmitted," the work is regarded as "fixed" if a fixation is being made at the same time as the transmission.

Under this definition "copies" and "phonorecords" together will comprise all of the material objects in which copyrightable works are capable of being fixed. The definitions of these terms in section 101, together with their usage in section 102 and throughout the bill, reflect a fundamental distinction between the "original work" which is the product of "authorship" and the multitude of material objects in which it can be embodied. Thus, in the sense of the bill, a "book" is not a work of authorship, but is a particular kind of "copy." Instead, the author may write a "literary work," which in turn can be embodied in a wide range of "copies" and "phonorecords," including books, periodicals, computer punch cards, microfilm, tape recordings, and so forth. It is possible to have an "original work of authorship" without having a "copy" or "phonorecord" embodying it, and it is also possible to have a "copy" or "phonorecord" embodying something that does not qualify as an "original work of authorship." The two essential elements—original work and tangible object—must merge through fixation in order to produce subject matter copyrightable under the statute.

Categories of copyrightable works

The second sentence of section 102 lists seven broad categories which the concept of "works" of authorship" is said to "include." The use of the word "include," as defined in section 101, makes clear that the listing is "illustrative and not limitative," and that the seven categories do not necessarily exhaust the scope of "original works of authorship" that the bill is intended to protect. Rather, the list sets out the general area of copyrightable subject matter, but with sufficient flexibility to free the courts from rigid or outmoded concepts of the scope of particular caegories. The items are also overlapping in the sense that a work falling within one class may encompass works coming within some or all of the other categories. In the aggregate, the list covers all classes of works now specified in section 5 of title 17; in addition, it specifically enumerates "pantomimes and choreographic works".

Of the seven items listed, four are defined in section 101. The three undefined categories—"musical works," "dramatic works," and "pantomimes and choreographic works"—have fairly settled meanings. There is no need, for example, to specify the copyrightability of electronic or concrete music in the statute since the form of a work would no longer be of any importance, nor is it necessary to specify that "choreographic works" do not include social dance steps and simple routines.

The four items defined in section 101 are "literary works," "pictorial, graphic, and sculptural works," "motion pictures and audiovisual works", and "sound recordings." In each of these cases, definitions are needed not only because the meaning of the term itself is unsettled but also because the distinction between "work" and "material object" requires clarification.*The term "literary works" does not connote any criterion of literary merit or qualitative value: it includes catalogs, directories, and similar factual, reference, or instructional works and compilations of data. It also includes computer data bases, and computer programs to the extent that they incorporate authorship in the programmer's expression of original ideas, as distinguished from the ideas themselves.

In the preceding paragraph, the text following the asterisk did not appear in the SENATE REPORT.

Correspondingly, the definition of "pictorial, graphic, and sculptural works" carries with it no implied criterion of artistic taste, aesthetic value, or intrinsic quality. The term is intended to comprise not only "works of art" in the traditional sense but also works of graphic art and illustration, art reproductions, plans and drawings, photographs and reproductions of them, maps, charts, globes, and other cartographic works, works of these kinds intended for use in advertising and commerce, and works of "applied art." There is no intention whatever to narrow the scope of the subject matter now characterized in section 5(k) as "prints or labels used for articles of merchandise." However, since this terminology suggests the material object in which a work is embodied rather than the work itself, the bill does not mention this category separately.

In accordance with the Supreme Court's decision in *Mazer* v. *Stein*, 347 U.S. 201 (1954), works of "applied art" encompass all original pictorial, graphic, and sculptural works that are intended to be or have been embodied in useful articles, regardless of factors such as mass production, commercial exploitation, and the potential availability of design patent protection. The scope of exclusive rights in these works is given special treatment in section 113, to be discussed below.

The next five paragraphs did not appear in the SENATE REPORT.

The Committee has added language to the definition of "pictorial, graphic, and sculptural works" in an effort to make clearer the distinction between works of applied art protectable under the bill and industrial designs not subject to copyright protection. The declaration that "pictorial, graphic, and sculptural works" include "works of artistic craftsmanship insofar as their form but not their mechanical or utilitarian aspects are concerned" is classic language: it is drawn from Copyright Office regulations promulgated in the 1940's and expressly endorsed by the Supreme Court in the *Mazer* case.

The second part of the amendment states that "the design of a useful article . . . shall be considered a pictorial, graphic, or sculptural work only if, and only to the extent that, such design incorporates pictorial, graphic, or sculptural features that can be identified separately from, and are capable of existing independently of, the utilitarian aspects of the article." A "useful article" is defined as "an article having an intrinsic utilitarian function that is not merely to portray the appearance of the article or to convey information." This part of the amendment is an adaptation of language added to the Copyright Office Regulations in the mid-1950's in an effort to implement the Supreme Court's decision in the *Mazer* case.

In adopting this amendatory language, the Committee is seeking to draw as clear a line as possible between copyrightable works of applied art and uncopyrighted works of industrial design. A two-dimensional painting, drawing, or graphic work is still capable of being identified as such when it is printed on or applied to utilitarian articles such as textile fabrics, wallpaper, containers, and the like. The same is true when a statue or carving is used to embellish an industrial product or, as in the *Mazer* case, is incorporated into a product without losing its ability to exist independently as a work of art. On the other hand, although the shape of an industrial product may be aesthetically satisfying and valuable, the Committee's intention is not to offer it copyright protection under the bill. Unless the shape of an automobile, airplane, ladies' dress, food processor, television set, or any other industrial product contains some element that, physically or conceptually, can be identified as separable from the utilitarian aspects of that article, the design would not be copyrighted under the bill. The test of separability and independence from "the utilitarian aspects of the article" does not depend upon the nature of the design—that is, even if the appearance of an article is determined by esthetic (as opposed to functional) considerations, only elements, if any, which can be identified separately from the useful article as such are copyrightable. And, even if the three-dimensional design contains some such element (for example, a carving on the back of a chair or a floral relief design on silver flatware), copyright protection would extend only to that element, and would not cover the over-all configuration of the utilitarian article as such.

A special situation is presented by architectural works. An architect's plans and drawings would, of course, be protected by copyright, but the extent to which that protection would extend to the structure depicted would depend on the circumstances. Purely nonfunctional or monumental structures would be subject to full copyright protection under the bill, and the same would be true of artistic sculpture or decorative ornamentation or embellishment added to a structure. On the other hand, where the only elements of shape in an architectural design are conceptually inseparable from the utilitarian aspects of the structure, copyright protection for the design would not be available.

The Committee has considered, but chosen to defer, the possibility of protecting the design of typefaces. A "typeface" can be defined as a set of letters, numbers, or other symbolic characters, whose forms are related by repeating design elements consistently applied in a notational system and are intended to be embodied in articles whose intrinsic utilitarian function is for use in composing text or other cognizable combinations of characters. The Committee does not regard the design of typeface, as thus defined, to be a copyrightable "pictorial, graphic, or sculptural work" within the meaning of this bill and the application of the dividing line in section 101.

The five preceding paragraphs did not appear in the SENATE REPORT.

Enactment of Public Law 92–140 in 1971 marked the first recognition in American copyright law of sound recordings as copyrightable works. As defined in section 101, copyrightable "sound recordings" are original works of authorship comprising an aggregate of musical, spoken, or other sounds that have been fixed in tangible form. The copyrightable work comprises the aggregation of sounds and not the tangible medium of fixation. Thus, "sound recordings" as copyrightable subject matter are distinguished from "phonorecords," the latter being physical objects in which sounds are fixed. They are also distinguished from any copyrighted literary, dramatic, or musical works that may be reproduced on a "phonorecord."

As a class of subject matter, sound recordings are clearly within the scope of the "writings of an author" capable of protection under the Constitution, and the extension of limited statutory protection to them was too long delayed. Aside from cases in which sounds are fixed by some purely mechanical means without originality of any kind, the copyright protection that would prevent the reproduction and distribution of unauthorized phonorecords of sound recordings is clearly justified.

The copyrightable elements in a sound recording will usually, though not always, involve "authorship" both on the part of the performers whose performance is captured and on the part of the record producer responsible for setting up the recording session, capturing and electronically processing the sounds, and compiling and editing them to make the final sound recording. There may, however, be cases where the record producer's contribution is so minimal that the performance is the only copyrightable element in the work, and there may be cases (for example, recordings of birdcalls, sounds of racing cars, et cetera) where only the record producer's contribution is copyrightable.

Sound tracks of motion pictures, long a nebulous area in American copyright law, are specifically included in the definition of "motion pictures," and excluded in the definition of "sound recordings." To be a "motion picture," as defined, requires three elements: (1) a series of images, (2) the capability of showing the images in certain successive order, and (3) an impression of motion when the images are thus shown. Coupled with the basic requirements of original authorship and fixation in tangible form, this definition encompasses a wide range of cinematographic works embodied in films, tapes, video disks, and other media. However, it would not include: (1) unauthorized fixations of live performances or telecasts, (2) live telecasts that are not fixed simultaneously with their transmission, or (3) filmstrips and slide sets which, although consisting of a series of images intended to be shown in succession, are not capable of conveying an impression of motion.

On the other hand, the bill equates audiovisual materials such as filmstrips, slide sets, and sets of tranparencies with "motion pictures" rather than with "pictorial, graphic, and sculptural works." Their sequential showing is closer to a "performance" than to a "display," and the definition of "audiovisual works," which applies also to "motion pictures," embraces works consisting of a series of related images that are by their nature, intended for showing by means of projectors or other devices.

Nature of copyright

Copyright does not preclude others from using the ideas or information revealed by the author's work. It pertains to the literary musical, graphic, or artistic form in which the author expressed intellectual concepts. Section 102(b) makes clear that copyright protection does not extend to any idea, procedure, process, system, method of operation, concept, principle, or discovery, regardless of the form in which it is described, explained, illustrated, or embodied in such work.

SENATE REPORT

The following sentence appears in the SENATE REPORT but was omitted in the HOUSE REPORT:

The term "plan" in this context refers to a mental formulation for achieving something, as distinguished from a graphic presentation diagramming the mental concept.

HOUSE REPORT (Continued)

Some concern has been expressed lest copyright in computer programs should extend protection to the methodology or processes adopted by the programmer, rather than merely to the "writing" expressing his ideas. Section 102(b) is intended, among other things, to make clear that the expression adopted by the programmer is the copyrightable element in a computer program, and that the actual processes or methods embodied in the program are not within the scope of the copyright law.

Section 102(b) in no way enlarges or contracts the scope of copyright protection under the present law. Its purpose is to restate, in the context of the new single Federal system of copyright, that the basic dichotomy between expression and idea remains unchanged.

LAW

§ 103. Subject matter of copyright: Compilations and derivative works

(a) The subject matter of copyright as specified by section 102 includes compilations and derivative works, but protection for a work employing preexisting material in which copyright subsists does not extend to any part of the work in which such material has been used unlawfully.

(b) The copyright in a compilation or derivative work extends only to the material contributed by the author of such work, as distinguished from the preexisting material employed in the work, and does not imply any exclusive right in the preexisting material. The copyright in such work is independent of, and does not affect or enlarge the scope, duration, ownership, or subsistence of, any copyright protection in the preexisting material.

HOUSE REPORT

Section 103 complements section 102: A compilation or derivative work is copyrightable if it represents an "original work of authorship" and falls within one or more of the categories listed in section 102. Read together, the two sections make plain that the criteria of copyrightable subject matter stated in section 102 apply with full force to works that are entirely original and to those containing preexisting material. Section 103(b) is also intended to define, more sharply and clearly than does section 7 of the present law, the important interrelationship and correlation between protection of preexisting and of "new" material in a particular work. The most important point here is one that is commonly misunderstood today: copyright in a "new version" covers only the material added by the later author, and has no effect one way or the other on the copyright or public domain status of the preexisting material.

Between them the terms "compilations" and "derivative works" which are defined in section 101, comprehend every copyrightable work that employs preexisting material or data of any kind. There is necessarily some overlapping between the two, but they basically represent different concepts. A "compilation" results from a process of selecting, bringing together, organizing, and arranging previously existing material of all kinds, regardless of whether the individual items in the material have been or ever could have been subject to copyright. A "derivative work," on the other hand, requires a process of recasting, transforming, or adapting "one or more preexisting works"; the "preexisting work" must come within the general subject matter of copyright set forth in section 102, regardless of whether it is or was ever copyrighted.

The second part of the sentence that makes up section 103(a) deals with the status of a compilation or derivative work unlawfully employing preexisting copyrighted material. In providing that protection does not extend to "any part of the work in which such material has been used unlawfully," the bill prevents an infringer from benefiting, through copyright protection, from committing an unlawful act, but preserves protection for those parts of the work that do not employ the preexisting work. Thus, an unauthorized translation of a novel could not be copyrighted at all, but the owner of copyright in an anthology of poetry could sue someone who infringed the whole anthology, even though the infringer proves that publication of one of the poems was unauthorized. Under this provision, copyright could be obtained as long as the use of the preexisting work was not "unlawful," even though the consent of the copyright owner had not been obtained. For instance, the unauthorized reproduction of a work might be "lawful" under the doctrine of fair use or an applicable foreign law, and if so the work incorporating it could be copyrighted.

LAW

§ 104. Subject matter of copyright: National origin

(a) Unpublished Works.—The works specified by sections 102 and 103, while unpublished, are subject to protection under this title without regard to the nationality or domicile of the author.

(b) Published Works.—The works specified by sections 102 and 103, when published, are subject to protection under this title if—

(1) on the date of first publication, one or more of the authors is a national or domiciliary of the United States, or is a national, domiciliary, or sovereign authority of a foreign nation that is a party to a copyright treaty to which the United States is also a party, or is a stateless person, wherever that person may be domiciled; or

(2) the work is first published in the United States or in a foreign nation that, on the date of first publication, is a party to the Universal Copyright Convention; or

(3) the work is first published by the United Nations or any of its specialized agencies, or by the Organization of American States; or

(4) the work comes within the scope of a Presidential proclamation. Whenever the President finds that a particular foreign nation extends, to works by authors who are nationals or domiciliaries of the United States or to works that are first published in the United States, copyright protection on substantially the same basis as that on which the foreign nation extends protection to works of its own nationals and domiciliaries and works first published in that nation, the President may by proclamation extend protection under this title to works of which one or more of the authors is, on the date of first publication, a national, domiciliary, or sovereign authority of that nation, or which was first published in that nation. The President may revise, suspend, or revoke any such proclamation or impose any conditions or limitations on protection under a proclamation.

HOUSE REPORT

Section 104 of the bill, which sets forth the basic criteria under which works of foreign origin can be protected under the U.S. copyright law, divides all works coming within the scope of sections 102 and 103 into two categories: unpublished and published. Subsection (a) imposes no qualifications of nationality and domicile with respect to unpublished works. Subsection (b) would make published works subject to protection under any one of four conditions:

(1) The author is a national or domiciliary of the United States or of a country with which the United States has copyright relations under a treaty, or is a stateless person;

(2) The work is first published in the United States or in a country that is a party to the Universal Copyright Convention;

(3) The work is first published by the United Nations, by any of its specialized agencies, or by the Organization of American States; or

(4) The work is covered by a Presidential proclamation extending protection to works originating in a specified country which extends protection to U.S. works "on substantially the same basis" as to its own works.

The third of these conditions represents a treaty obligation of the United States. Under the Second Protocol of the Universal Copyright Convention, protection under U.S. Copyright law is expressly required for works published by the United Nations, by U.N. specialized agencies, and by the Organization of American States.

The last paragraph is not found in the SENATE REPORT.

The United States is a party to four international copyright conventions:

The Buenos Aires Convention of 1910
The Convention for the Protection of Producers of Phonograms, Geneva, 1971
The Universal Copyright Convention, Geneva, 1952
The Universal Copyright Convention, Paris, 1971

The texts of these agreements appear in Copyright Office Circular 38c; a list of the nations having copyright agreements with the United States appears in Copyright Office Circular R38a. These circulars are available without charge from the Copyright Office, Library of Congress, Washington, DC 20559.

LAW

§ 105. Subject matter of copyright: United States Government works

Copyright protection under this title is not available for any work of the United States Government, but the United States Government is not precluded from receiving and holding copyrights transferred to it by assignment, bequest, or otherwise.

HOUSE REPORT

Scope of the prohibition

The basic premise of section 105 of the bill is the same as that of section 8 of the present law—that works produced for the U.S. Government by its officers and employees should not be subject to copyright. The provision applies the principle equally to unpublished and published works.

The general prohibition against copyright in section 105 applies to "any work of the United States Government," which is defined in section 101 as "a work prepared by an officer or employee of the United States Government as part of that person's official duties." Under this definition a Government official or employee would not be prevented from securing copyright in a work written at that person's own volition and outside his or her duties, even though the subject matter involves the Government work or professional field of the official or employee. Although the wording of the definition of "work of the United States Government" differs somewhat from that of the definition of "work made for hire," the concepts are intended to be construed in the same way.

A more difficult and far-reaching problem is whether the definition should be broadened to prohibit copyright in works prepared under U.S. Government contract or grant. As the bill is written, the Government agency concerned could determine in each case whether to allow an independent contractor or grantee to secure copyright in works prepared in whole or in part with the use of Government funds. The argument that has been made against allowing copyright in this situation is that the public should not be required to pay a "double subsidy," and that it is inconsistent to prohibit copyright in works by Government employees while permitting private copyrights in a growing body of works created by persons who are paid with Government funds.

Those arguing in favor of potential copyright protection have stressed the importance of copyright as an incentive to creation and dissemination in this situation, and the basically different policy considerations applicable to works written by Government employees and those applicable to works prepared by private organizations with the use of Federal funds.

The last sentence in the above paragraph did not appear in the SENATE REPORT.

The bill deliberately avoids making any sort of outright, unqualified prohibition against copyright in works prepared under Government contract or grant. There may well be cases where it would be in the public interest to deny copyright in the writings generated by Government research contracts and the like; it can be assumed that, where a Government agency commissions a work for its own use merely as an alternative to having one of its own employees prepare the work, the right to secure a private copyright would be withheld. However, there are almost certainly many other cases where the denial of copyright protection would be unfair or would hamper the production and publication of important works. Where, under the particular circumstances, Congress or the agency involved finds that the need to have a work freely available outweighs the need of the private author to secure copyright, the problem can be dealt with by specific legislation, agency regulations, or contractual restrictions.

The prohibition on copyright protection for United States Government works is not intended to have any effect on protection of these works abroad. Works of the governments of most other countries are copyrighted. There are no valid policy reasons for denying such protection to United States Government works in foreign countries, or for precluding the Government from making licenses for the use of its works abroad.

The effect of section 105 is intended to place all works of the United States Government, published or unpublished, in the public domain. This means that the individual Government official or employee who wrote the work could not secure copyright in it or restrain its dissemination by the Government or anyone else, but it also means that, as far as the copyright law is concerned, the Government could not restrain the employee or official from disseminating the work if he or she chooses to do so. The use of the term "work of the United States Government" does not mean that a work falling within the definition of that term is the property of the U.S. Government.

The preceding paragraph did not appear in the SENATE REPORT; the following paragraph appeared in its place:

SENATE REPORT

Section 8 of the statute now in effect includes a saving clause intended to make clear that the copyright protection of a private work is not affected if the work is published by the Government. There is no need to restate this principle explicitly in the context of section 105; there is nothing in section 105 that would relieve the Government of its obligation to secure permission in order to publish a copyrighted work, and publication or other use by the Government of a private work could not affect its copyright protection in any way.

HOUSE REPORT (Continued)

The following five paragraphs did not appear in the SENATE REPORT.

LIMITED EXCEPTION FOR NATIONAL TECHNICAL INFORMATION SERVICE

At the House hearings in 1975 the U.S. Department of Commerce called attention to its National Technical Information Service (NTIS), which has a statutory mandate, under Chapter 23 of Title 15 of the U.S. Code, to operate a clearinghouse for the collection and dissemination of scientific, technical and engineering information. Under its statute, NTIS is required to be as self-sustaining as posisble, and not to force the general public to bear publishing costs that are for private benefit. The Department urged an amendment to section 105 that would allow it to secure copyright in NTIS publications both in the United States and abroad, noting that a precedent exists in the Standard Reference Data Act (15 USC § 290(e)).

In response to this request the Committee adopted a limited exception to the general prohibition in section 105, permitting the Secretary of Commerce to "secure copyright for a limited term not to exceed five years, on behalf of the United States as author or copyright owner" in any NTIS publication disseminated pursuant to 15 U.S.C. Chapter 23. In order to "secure copyright" in a work under this amendment the Secretary would be required to publish the work with a copyright notice, and the five-year term would begin upon the date of first publication.

Proposed saving clause

Section 8 of the statute now in effect includes a saving clause intended to make clear that the copyright protection of a private work is not affected if the work is published by the Government. This provision serves a real purpose in the present law because of the ambiguity of the undefined term "any publication of the United States Government." Section 105 of the bill, however, uses the operative term "work of the United States Government" and defines it in such a way that privately written works are clearly excluded from the prohibition; accordingly, a saving clause becomes superfluous.

Retention of a saving clause has been urged on the ground that the present statutory provision is frequently cited, and that having the provision expressly stated in the law would avoid questions and explanations. The committee here observes: (1) there is nothing in section 105 that would relieve the Government of its obligation to secure permission in order to publish a copyrighted work; and (2) publication or other use by the Government of a private work would not affect its copyright protection in any way. The question of use of copyrighted material in documents published by the Congress and its Committees is discussed below in connection with section 107.

Works of the United States Postal Service

The intent of section 105 is to restrict the prohibition against Government copyright to works written by employees of the United States Government within the scope of their official duties. In accordance with the objectives of the Postal Reorganization Act of 1970, this section does not apply to works created by employees of the United States Postal Service. In addition to enforcing the criminal statutes proscribing the forgery or counterfeiting of postage stamps, the

Postal Service could, if it chooses, use the copyright law to prevent the reproduction of postage stamp designs for private or commercial non-postal services (for example, in philatelic publications and catalogs, in general advertising, in art reproductions, in textile designs, and so forth). However, any copyright claimed by the Postal Service in its works, including postage stamp designs, would be subject to the same conditions, formalities, and time limits as other copyrightable works.

CONFERENCE REPORT

Copyrightable Subject Matter: Publications of the U.S. Government

Senate bill

Under section 105 of the Senate bill, both published and unpublished works of the United States Government were excluded from copyright protection.

House bill

The House bill retained the general prohibition against copyright in U.S. Government works, but made one specific exception in favor of any publication of the National Technical Information Service. The Secretary of Commerce was authorized to secure copyright in such works, on behalf of the United States as author or copyright owner, for a limited term not to exceed five years.

Conference substitute

The conference substitute conforms to the Senate bill. Because of the lack of Senate hearings on the issue, the conferees recommended that the NTIS request for limited copyright in order to control foreign copying be considered at hearings early in the next session. In the interim, consideration should also be given to compensatory appropriations to NTIS in lieu of revenues lost as a result of unauthorized foreign copying.

The Department of Commerce testified on May 8, 1975, before the House Subcommittee on Courts, Civil Liberties, and the Administration of Justice that the lack of copyright protection in publications of its National Technical Information Service (NTIS) posed special problems, since NTIS is required (15 USC 1151–7) to be self-sustaining to the fullest extent feasible. Widespread copying of NTIS publications is especially prevalent in foreign nations. In Japan it is reported that NTIS reproductions are sold having a value of $3,000,000 annually. A United Kingdom copier sells nearly twice as many copies of NTIS publications as NTIS does directly to the U.K. The USSR buys substantial volume of NTIS publications from European copiers for further copying in the USSR. The lack of copyright protection in NTIS publications also results in widespread foreign use of U.S. tax-funded research and development without any return to the U.S. U.S. organizations also sell NTIS publications to foreign buyers without recouping for the taxpayer, as represented by NTIS, monies adequately reflecting the value of the scientific, engineering, and technical information contained therein.

LAW

§ 106. Exclusive rights in copyrighted works

Subject to sections 107 through 118, the owner of copyright under this title has the exclusive rights to do and to authorize any of the following:

(1) to reproduce the copyrighted work in copies or phonorecords;

(2) to prepare derivative works based upon the copyrighted work;

(3) to distribute copies or phonorecords of the copyrighted work to the public by sale or other transfer of ownership, or by rental, lease, or lending;

(4) in the case of literary, musical, dramatic, and choreographic works, pantomimes, and motion pictures and other audiovisual works, to perform the copyrighted work publicly; and

(5) in the case of literary, musical, dramatic, and choreographic works, pantomimes, and pictorial, graphic, or sculptural works, including the individual images of a motion picture or other audiovisual work, to display the copyrighted work publicly.

HOUSE REPORT

General scope of copyright

The five fundamental rights that the bill gives to copyright owners—the exclusive rights of reproduction, adaptation, publication, performance, and display—are stated generally in section 106. These exclusive rights, which comprise the so-called "bundle of rights" that is a copyright, are cumulative and may overlap in some cases. Each of the five enumerated rights may be subdivided indefinitely and, as discussed below in connection with section 201, each subdivision of an exclusive right may be owned and enforced separately.

The approach of the bill is to set forth the copyright owner's exclusive rights in broad terms in section 106, and then to provide various limitations, qualifications, or exemptions in the 12 sections that follow. Thus, everything in section 106 is made "subject to sections 107 through 118," and must be read in conjunction with those provisions.

The exclusive rights accorded to a copyright owner under section 106 are "to do and to authorize" any of the activities specified in the five numbered clauses. Use of the phrase "to authorize" is intended to avoid any questions as to the liability of contributory infringers. For example, a person who lawfully acquires an authorized copy of a motion picture would be an infringer if he or she engages in the business of renting it to others for purposes of unauthorized public performance.

Rights of reproduction, adaptation, and publication

The first three clauses of section 106, which cover all rights under a copyright except those of performance and display, extend to every kind of copyrighted work. The exclusive rights encompassed by these clauses, though closely related, are independent; they can generally be characterized as rights of copying, recording, adaptation, and publishing. A single act of infringement may violate all of these rights at once, as where a publisher reproduces, adapts, and sells copies of a person's copyrighted work as part of a publishing venture. Infringement takes place when any one of the rights is violated: where, for example, a printer reproduces copies without selling them or a retailer sells copies without having anything to do with their reproduction. The references to "copies or phonorecords," although in the plural, are intended here and throughout the bill to include the singular (1 U.S.C. §1).

Reproduction.—Read together with the relevant definitions in section 101, the right "to reproduce the copyrighted work in copies or phonorecords" means the right to produce a material object in which the work is duplicated, transcribed, imitiated, or simulated in a fixed form from which it can be "perceived, reproduced, or otherwise communicated, either directly or with the aid of a machine or device." As under the present law, a copyrighted work would be infringed by reproducing it in whole or in any substantial part, and by duplicating it exactly or by imitation or simulation. Wide departures or variations from the copyrighted work would still be an infringement as long as the author's "expression" rather than merely the author's "ideas" are taken. An exception to this general principle, applicable to the reproduction of copyrighted sound recordings, is specified in section 114.

The last sentence did not appear in the SENATE REPORT.

"Reproduction" under clause (1) of section 106 is to be distinguished from "display" under clause (5). For a work to be "reproduced," its fixation in tangible form must be "sufficiently permanent or stable to permit it to be perceived, reproduced, or otherwise communicated for a period of more than transitory duration." Thus, the showing of images on a screen or tube would not be a violation of clause (1), although it might come within the scope of clause (5).

Preparation of derivative works.—The exclusive right to prepare derivative works, specified separately in clause (2) of section 106, overlaps the exclusive right of reproduction to some extent. It is broader than that right, however, in the sense that reproduction requires fixation in copies or phonorecords, whereas the preparation of a derivative work, such as a ballet, pantomime, or improvised performance, may be an infringement even though nothing is ever fixed in tangible form.

To be an infringement the "derivative work" must be "based upon the copyrighted work," and the definition in section 101 refers to "a translation, musical arrangement, dramatization, fictionalization, motion picture version, sound recording, art reproduction, abridgment, condensation, or any other form in which a work may be recast, transformed, or adapted." Thus, to constitute a violation of section 106(2), the infringing work must incorporate a portion of the copyrighted work in some form; for example, a detailed commentary on a work or a programmatic musical composition inspired by a novel would not normally constitute infringements under this clause.

Use in information storage and retrieval systems.—As section 117 declares explicitly, the bill is not intended to alter the present law with respect to the use of copyrighted works in computer systems.

Public distribution.—Clause (3) of section 106 establishes the exclusive right of publication: The right "to distribute copies or phonorecords of the copyrighted work to the public by sale or other transfer of ownership, or by rental, lease, or lending." Under this provision the copyright owner would have the right to control the first public distribution of an authorized copy or phonorecord of his work, whether by sale, gift, loan, or some rental or lease arrangement. Likewise, any unauthorized public distribution of copies or phonorecords that were unlawfully made would be an infringement. As section 109 makes clear, however, the copyright owner's rights under section 106(3) cease with respect to a particular copy or phonorecord once he has parted with ownership of it.

Rights of public performance and display

Performing rights and the "for profit" limitation.—The right of public performance under section 106(4) extends to "literary, musical, dramatic, and choreographic works, pantomimes, and motion pictures and other audiovisual works and sound recordings" and, unlike the equivalent provisions now in effect, is not limited by any "for profit" requirement. The approach of the bill, as in many foreign laws, is first to state the public performance right in broad terms, and then to provide specific exemptions for educational and other nonprofit uses.

This approach is more reasonable than the outright exemption of the 1909 statute. The line between commercial and "nonprofit" organizations is increasingly difficult to draw. Many "non-profit" organizations are highly subsidized and capable of paying royalties, and the widespread public exploitation of copyrighted works by public broadcasters and other noncommercial organizations is likely to grow. In addition to these trends, it is worth noting that performances and displays are continuing to supplant markets for printed copies and that in the future a broad "not for profit" exemption could not only hurt authors but could dry up their incentive to write.

The exclusive right of public performance is expanded to include not only motion pictures, including works recorded on film, video tape, and video disks, but also audiovisual works such as filmstrips and sets of slides. This provision of section 106(4), which is consistent with the assimilation of motion pictures to audiovisual works throughout the bill, is also related to amendments of the definitions of "display" and "perform" discussed below. The important issue of performing rights in sound recordings is discussed in connection with section 114.

Right of public display.—Clause (5) of section 106 represents the first explicit statutory recognition in American copyright law of an exclusive right to show a copyrighted work, or an image of it, to the public. The existence or extent of this right under the present statute is uncertain and subject to challenge. The bill would give the owners of copyright in "literary, musical, dramatic, and choreographic works, pantomimes, and pictorial, graphic, or sculptural works", including the individual images of a motion picture or other audiovisual work, the exclusive right "to display the copyrighted work publicly."

Definitions

Under the definitions of "perform," "display," "publicly," and "transmit" in section 101, the concepts of public performance and public display cover not only the initial rendition or showing, but also any further act by which that rendition or showing is transmitted or communicated to the public. Thus, for example: a singer is performing when he or she sings a song; a broadcasting network is performing when it transmits his or her performance (whether simultaneously or from records) ; a local broadcaster is performing when it transmits the network broadcast; a cable television system is performing when it retransmits the broadcast to its subscribers; and any individual is performing whenever he or she plays a phonorecord embodying the performance or communicates the performance by turning on a receiving set. Although any act by which the initial performance or display is transmitted, repeated, or made to recur would itself be a "performance" or "display" under the bill, it would not be actionable as an infringement unless it were done "publicly," as defined in section 101. Certain other performances and displays, in addition to those that are "private," are exempted or given qualified copyright control under sections 107 through 118.

To "perform" a work, under the definition in section 101, includes reading a literary work aloud, singing or playing music, dancing a ballet or other choreographic work, and acting out a dramatic work or pantomine. A performance may be accomplished "either directly or by means of any device or process," including all kinds of equipment for reproducing or amplifying sounds or visual images, any sort of transmitting apparatus, any type of electronic retrieval system, and any other techniques and systems not yet in use or even invented.

The definition of "perform" in relation to "a motion picture or other audio visual work" is "to show its images in any sequence or to make the sounds accompanying it audible." The showing of portions of a motion picture, filmstrip, or slide set must therefore be sequential to constitute a "performance" rather than a "display", but no particular order need be maintained. The purely aural performance of a motion picture sound track, or of the sound portions of an audiovisual work, would constitute a performance of the "motion picture or other audiovisual work"; but, where some of the sounds have been reproduced separately on phonorecords, a performance from the phonorecord would not constitute performance of the motion picture or audiovisual work.

The corresponding definition of "display" covers any showing of a "copy" of the work, "either directly or by means of a film, slide, television image, or any other device or process." Since "copies" are defined as including the material object "in which the work is first fixed," the right of public display applies to original works of art as well as to reproductions of them. With respect to motion pictures and other audiovisual works, it is a "display" (rather than a "performance") to show their "individual images nonsequentially." In addition to the direct showings of a copy of a work, "display" would include the projection of an image on a screen or other surface by any method, the transmission of an image by electronic or other means, and the showing of an image on a cathode ray tube, or similar viewing apparatus connected with any sort of information storage and retrieval system.

Under clause (1) of the definition of "publicly" in section 101, a performance or display is "public" if it takes place "at a place open to the public or at any place where a substantial number of persons outside of a normal circle of a family and its social acquaintances is gathered." One of the principal purposes of the definition was to make clear that, contrary to the decision in *Metro-Goldwyn-Mayer Distributing Corp.* v. *Wyatt*, 21 C.O. Bull. 203 (D. Md. 1932), performances in "semipublic" places such as clubs, lodges, factories, summer camps, and schools are "public performances" subject to copyright control. The term "a family" in this context would include an individual living alone, so that a gathering confined to the individual's social acquaintances would normally be regarded as private. Routine meetings of businesses and governmental personnel would be excluded because they do not represent the gathering of a "substantial number of persons."

Clause (2) of the definition of "publicly" in section 101 makes clear that the concepts of public performance and public display include not only performances and displays that occur initially in a public place, but also acts that transmit or otherwise communicate a performance or display of the work to the public by means of any device or process. The definition of "transmit"—to communicate a performance or display "by any device or process whereby images or sound are received beyond the place from which they are sent"—is broad enough to include all conceivable forms and combinations of wired or wireless communications media, including but by no means limited to radio and television broadcasting as we know them. Each and every method by which the images or sounds comprising a performance or display are picked up and conveyed is a "transmission," and if the transmission reaches the public in my form, the case comes within the scope of clauses (4) or (5) of section 106.

Under the bill, as under the present law, a performance made available by transmission to the public at large is "public" even though the recipients are not gathered in a single place, and even if there is no proof that any of the potential recipients was operating his receiving apparatus at the time of the transmission. The same principles apply whenever the potential recipients of the transmission represent a limited segment of the public, such as the occupants of hotel rooms or the subscribers of a cable television service. Clause (2) of the definition of "publicly" is applicable "whether the members of the public capable of receiving the performance or display receive it in the same place or in separate places and at the same time or at different times."

LAW

§ 107. Limitations on exclusive rights: Fair use

Notwithstanding the provisions of section 106, the fair use of a copyrighted work, including such use by reproduction in copies or phonorecords or by any other means specified by that section, for purposes such as criticism, comment, news reporting, teaching (including multiple copies for classroom use), scholarship, or research, is not an infringement of copyright. In determining whether the use made of a work in any particular case is a fair use the factors to be considered shall include—

(1) the purpose and character of the use, including whether such use is of a commercial nature or is for nonprofit educational purposes;

(2) the nature of the copyrighted work;

(3) the amount and substantiality of the portion used in relation to the copyrighted work as a whole; and

(4) the effect of the use upon the potential market for or value of the copyrighted work.

HOUSE REPORT

General background of the problem

The judicial doctrine of fair use, one of the most important and well-established limitations on the exclusive right of copyright owners, would be given express statutory recognition for the first time in section 107. The claim that a defendant's acts constituted a fair use rather than an infringement has been raised as a defense in innumerable copyright actions over the years, and there is ample case law recognizing the existence of the doctrine and applying it. The examples enumerated at page 24 of the Register's 1961 Report, while by no means exhaustive, give some idea of the sort of activities the courts might regard as fair use under the circumstances: "quotation of excerpts in a review or criticism for purposes of illustration or comment; quotation of short passages in a scholarly or technical work, for illustration or clarification of the author's observations; use in a parody of some of the content of the work parodied; summary of an address or article, with brief quotations, in a news report; reproduction by a library of a portion of a work to replace part of a damaged copy; reproduction by a teacher or student of a small part of a work to illustrate a lesson; reproduction of a work in legislative or judicial proceedings or reports; incidental and fortuitous reproduction, in a newsreel or broadcast, of a work located in the scene of an event being reported."

The significant passages of the Register's 1961 Report, cited in the preceding paragraph, appear on page 104, under the heading: COPYRIGHT OFFICE, 1961 REPORT.

Although the courts have considered and ruled upon the fair use doctrine over and over again, no real definition of the concept has ever emerged. Indeed, since the doctrine is an equitable rule of reason, no generally applicable definition is possible, and each case raising the question must be decided on its own facts. On the other hand, the courts have evolved a set of criteria which, though in no case definitive or determinative, provide some guage for balancing the equities. These criteria have been stated in various ways, but essentially they can all be reduced to the four standards which have been adopted in section 107: "(1) the purpose and character of the use, including whether such use is of a commercial nature or is for non-profit educational purposes; (2) the nature of the copyrighted work; (3) the amount and substantiality of the portion used in relation to the copyrighted work as a whole; and (4) the effect of the use upon the potential market for or value of the copyrighted work."

The following three paragraphs did not appear in the SENATE REPORT.

These criteria are relevant in determining whether the basic doctrine of fair use, as stated in the first sentence of section 107, applies in a particular case: "Notwithstanding the provisions of section 106, the fair use of a copyrighted work, including such use by reproduction in copies or phonorecords or by any other means specified by that section, for purposes such as criticism, comment, news reporting, teaching (including multiple copies for classroom use), scholarship, or research, is not an infringement of copyright."

The specific wording of section 107 as it now stands is the result of a process of accretion, resulting from the long controversy over the related problems of fair use and the reproduction (mostly by photocopying) of copyrighted material for educational and scholarly purposes. For example, the reference to fair use "by reproduction in copies or phonorecords or by any other means" is mainly intended to make clear that the doctrine has as much application to photocopying and taping as to older forms of use; it is not intended to give these kinds of reproduction any special status under the fair use provision or to sanction any reproduction beyond the normal and reasonable limits of fair use. Similarly, the newly-added reference to "multiple copies for classroom use" is a recognition that, under the proper circumstances of fairness, the doctrine can be applied to reproductions of multiple copies for the members of a class.

The Committee has amended the first of the criteria to be considered—"the purpose and character of the use"—to state explicitly that this factor includes a consideration of "whether such use is of a commercial nature or is for non-profit educational purposes." This amendment is not intended to be interpreted as any sort of not-for-profit limitation on educational uses of copyrighted works. It is an express recognition that, as under the present law, the commercial or non-profit character of an activity, while not conclusive with respect to fair use, can and should be weighed along with other factors in fair use decisions.

General intention behind the provision

The statement of the fair use doctrine in section 107 offers some guidance to users in determining when the principles of the doctrine apply. However, the endless variety of situations and combinations of circumstances that can rise in particular cases precludes the formulation of exact rules in the statute. The bill endorses the purpose and general scope of the judicial doctrine of fair use, but there is no disposition to freeze the doctrine in the statute, especially during a period of rapid technological change. Beyond a very broad statutory explanation of what fair use is and some of the criteria applicable to it, the courts must be free to adapt the doctrine to particular situations on a case-by-case basis. Section 107 is intended to restate the present judicial doctrine of fair use, not to change, narrow, or enlarge it in any way.

SENATE REPORT

The next two paragraphs did not appear in the HOUSE REPORT.

Section 107 is intended to restate the present judicial doctrine of fair use, not to change, narrow, or enlarge it in any way. However, since this section will represent the first statutory recognition of the doctrine in our copyright law, some explanation of the considerations behind the language used in the list of four criteria is advisable. This is particularly true as to cases of copying by teachers, and by public libraries, since in these areas there are few if any judicial guidelines.

The statements in this report with respect to each of the criteria of fair use are necessarily subject to qualifications, because they must be applied in combination with the circumstances pertaining to other criteria, and because new conditions arising in the future may alter the balance of equities. It is also important to emphasize that the singling out of some instances to discuss in the context of fair use is not intended to indicate that other activities would or would not be beyond fair use.

HOUSE REPORT (Continued)

Intention as to classroom reproduction

Although the works and uses to which the doctrine of fair use is applicable are as broad as the copyright law itself, most of the discussion of section 107 has centered around questions of classroom reproduction, particularly photocopying. The arguments on the question are summarized at pp. 30–31 of this Committee's 1967 report (H.R. Rep. No. 83, 90th Cong., 1st Sess.), and have not changed materially in the intervening years.

The passage in H.R. 90-83, cited above, appears on pages 101-103 under the heading: HOUSE REPORT 90-83.

The Committee also adheres to its earlier conclusion, that "a specific exemption freeing certain reproductions of copyrighted works for educational and scholarly purposes from copyright control is not justified." At the same time the Committee recognizes, as it did in 1967, that there is a "need for greater certainty and protection for teachers." In an effort to meet this need the Committee has not only adopted further amendments to section 107, but has also amended section 504(c) to provide innocent teachers and other non-profit users of copyrighted material with broad insulation against unwarranted liability for infringement. The latter amendments are discussed below in connection with Chapter 5 of the bill.

In 1967 the Committee also sought to approach this problem by including, in its report, a very thorough discussion of "the considerations lying behind the four criteria listed in the amended section 107, in the context of typical classroom situations arising today." This discussion appeared on pp. 32–35 of the 1967 report, and with some changes has been retained in the Senate report on S. 22 (S. Rep. No. 94-473, pp. 63-65. The Committee has reviewed this discussion, and considers that it still has value as an analysis of various aspects of the problem.

The above-mentioned passage from S.R. 94-473 follows.

SENATE REPORT

The next 12 paragraphs do not appear in the HOUSE REPORT; however, the HOUSE REPORT cites this section and comments that "it still has value as an analysis of the various aspects of the problem" of fair use.

The purpose and nature of the use

Copyright recognized.—Section 107 makes it clear that, assuming the applicable criteria are met, fair use can extend to the reproduction of copyrighted material for purposes of classroom teaching.

Nonprofit element.—Although it is possible to imagine situations in which use by a teacher in an educational organization operated for profit (day camps, language schools, business schools, dance studios, et cetera) would constitute a fair use, the nonprofit character of the school in which the teacher works should be one factor to consider in determining fair use. Another factor would be whether any charge is made for the copies distributed.

Spontaneity.—The fair use doctrine in the case of classroom copying would apply primarily to the situation of a teacher who, acting individually and at his own volition, makes one or more copies for temporary use by himself or his pupils in the classroom. A different result is indicated where the copying was done by the educational institution, school system, or larger unit or where copying was required or suggested by the school administration, either in special instances or as part of a general plan.

Single and multiple copying.—Depending upon the nature of the work and other criteria, the fair use doctrine should differentiate between the amount of work that can be reproduced by a teacher for his own classroom use (for example, for reading or projecting a copy or for playing a tape recording), and the amount that can be reproduced for distribution to pupils. In the case of multiple copies, other factors would be whether the number reproduced was limited to the size of the class, whether circulation beyond the classroom was permitted, and whether the copies were recalled or destroyed after temporary use.

Collection and anthologies.—Spontaneous copying of an isolated extract by a teacher, which may be a fair use under appropriate circumstances, could turn into an infringement if the copies were accumulated over a period of time with other parts of the same work, or were collected with other material from various works so as to constitute an anthology.

Special uses.—There are certain classroom uses which, because of their special nature, would not be considered an infringement in the ordinary case. For example, copying of extracts by pupils as exercises in a shorthand or typing class or for foreign language study, or recordings of performances by music students for purposes of analysis and criticism, would normally be regarded as a fair use unless the copies of phonorecords were retained or duplicated.

The nature of the copyrighted work

Character of the work.—The character and purpose of the work will have a lot to do with whether its reproduction for classroom purposes is fair use or infringement. For example, in determining whether a teacher could make one or more copies without permission, a news article from the daily press would be judged differently from a full orchestral score of a musical composition. In general terms it could be expected that the doctrine of fair use would be applied strictly to the classroom reproduction of entire works, such as musical compositions, dramas, and audiovisual works including motion pictures, which by their nature are intended for performance or public exhibition.

Similarly, where the copyright work is intended to be "consumable" in the course of classroom activities—workbooks, exercise, standardized tests, and answer sheets are examples—the privilege of fair use by teachers or pupils would have little if any application. Text books and other material prepared primarily for the school markets would be less susceptible to reproduction for classroom use than material prepared for general public distribution. With respect to material in newspapers and periodicals the doctrine of fair use should be liberally applied to allow copying of items of current interest to supplement and update the students' textbooks, but this would not extend to copying from periodicals published primarily for student use.

Availability of the work.—A key, though not necessarily determinative, factor in fair use is whether or not the work is available to the potential user. If the work is "out of print" and unavailable for purchase through normal channels, the user may have more justification for reproducing it than in the ordinary case, but the existence of organizations licensed to provide photocopies of out-of-print works at reasonable cost is a factor to be considered. The applicability of the fair use doctrine to unpublished works is narrowly limited since, although the work is unavailable, this is the result of a deliberate choice on the part of the copyright owner. Under ordinary circumstances the copyright owner's "right of first publication" would outweigh any needs of reproduction for classroom purposes.

The amount and substantiality of the material used

During the consideration of this legislation there has been considerable discussion of the difference between an "entire work" and an "excerpt". The educators have sought a limited right for a teacher to make a single copy of an "entire" work for classroom purposes, but it seems apparent that this was not generally intended to extend beyond a "separately cognizable" or "self-contained" portion (for example a single poem, story, or article) in a collective work, and that no privilege is sought to reproduce an entire collective work (for example, an encyclopedia volume, a periodical issue) or a sizable integrated work published as an entity (a novel, treatise, monograph, and so forth). With this limitation, and subject to the other revelant criteria, the requested privilege of making a single copy appears appropriately to be within the scope of fair use.

The educators also sought statutory authority for the privilege of making "a reasonable number of copies or phonorecords for excerpts or quotations * * *, provided such excerpts or quotations are not substantial in length in proportion to their source." In general, and assuming the other necessary factors are present, the copying for classroom purposes of extracts or portions, which are not self-contained and which are relatively "not substantial in length" when compared to the larger, self-contained work from which they are taken, should be considered fair use. Depending on the circumstances, the same would also be true of very short self-contained works such as a brief poem, a map in a newspaper, a "vocabulary builder" from a monthly magazine, and so forth. This should not be construed as permitting a teacher to make multiple copies of the same work on a repetitive basis or for continued use.

Effect of use on potential market for or value of work

This factor must almost always be judged in conjunction with the other three criteria. With certain special exceptions (use in parodies or as evidence in court proceedings might be examples) a use that supplants any part of the normal market for a copyrighted work would ordinarily be considered an infringement. As in any other case, whether this would be the result of reproduction by a teacher for classroom purposes requires an evaluation of the nature and purpose of the use, the type of work involved, and the size and relative importance of the portion taken. Fair use is essentially supplementary by nature, and classroom copying that exceeds the legitimate teaching aims such as filling in missing information or bringing a subject up to date would go beyond the proper bounds of fair use. Isolated instances of minor infringements, when multiplied many times, become in the aggregate a major inroad on copyright that must be prevented.

HOUSE REPORT (Continued)

The next five paragraphs and the two voluntary guidelines which follow did not appear in the SENATE REPORT.

At the Judiciary Subcommittee hearings in June 1975, Chairman Kastenmeier and other members urged the parties to meet together independently in an effort to achieve a meeting of the minds as to permissible educational uses of copyrighted material. The response to these suggestions was positive, and a number of meetings of three groups, dealing respectively with classroom reproduction of printed material, music, and audio-visual material, were held beginning in September 1975.

In a joint letter to Chairman Kastenmeier, dated March 19, 1976, the representatives of the Ad Hoc Committee of Educational Institutions and Organizations on Copyright Law Revision, and of the Authors League of America, Inc., and the Association of American Publishers, Inc., stated:

> You may remember that in our letter of March 8, 1976 we told you that the negotiating teams representing authors and publishers and the Ad Hoc Group had reached tentative agreement on guidelines to insert in the Committee Report covering educational copying from books and periodicals under Section 107 of H.R. 2223 and S. 22, and that as part of that tentative agreement each side would accept the amendments to Sections 107 and 504 which were adopted by your Subcommittee on March 3, 1976.
>
> We are now happy to tell you that the agreement has been approved by the principals and we enclose a copy herewith. We had originally intended to translate the agreement into language suitable for inclusion in the legislative report dealing with Section 107, but we have since been advised by committee staff that this will not be necessary.
>
> As stated above, the agreement refers only to copying from books and periodicals, and it is not intended to apply to musical or audiovisual works.

The full text of the agreement is as follows:

Agreement on Guidelines for Classroom Copying in Not-For-Profit Educational Institutions

with respect to books and periodicals

The purpose of the following guidelines is to state the minimum and not the maximum standards of educational fair use under Section 107 of H.R. 2223. The parties agree that the conditions determining the extent of permissible copying for educational purposes may change in the future; that certain types of copying permitted under these guidelines may not be permissible in the future; and conversely that in the future other types of copying not permitted under these guidelines may be permissible under revised guidelines.

Moreover, the following statement of guidelines is not intended to limit the types of copying permitted under the standards of fair use under judicial decision and which are stated in Section 107 of the Copyright Revision Bill. There may be instances in which copying which does not fall within the guidelines stated below may nonetheless be permitted under the criteria of fair use.

GUIDELINES

I. *Single Copying for Teachers*

A single copy may be made of any of the following by or for a teacher at his or her individual request for his or her scholarly research or use in teaching or preparation to teach a class:

A. A chapter from a book;

B. An article from a periodical or newspaper;

C. A short story, short essay or short poem, whether or not from a collective work;

D. A chart, graph, diagram, drawing, cartoon or picture from a book, periodical, or newspaper;

II. *Multiple Copies for Classroom Use*

Multiple copies (not to exceed in any event more than one copy per pupil in a course) may be made by or for the teacher giving the course for classroom use or discussion; *provided that:*

A. The copying meets the tests of brevity and spontaneity as defined below; *and,*

B. Meets the cumulative effect test as defined below; *and,*

C. Each copy includes a notice of copyright

Definitions

Brevity

(*i*) Poetry: (a) A complete poem if less than 250 words and if printed on not more than two pages or, (b) from a longer poem, an excerpt of not more than 250 words.

(*ii*) Prose: (a) Either a complete article, story or essay of less than 2,500 words, or (b) an excerpt from any prose work of not more than 1,000 words or 10% of the work, whichever is less, but in any event a minimum of 500 words.

[Each of the numerical limits stated in "i" and "ii" above may be expanded to permit the completion of an unfinished line of a poem or of an unfinished prose paragraph.]

(*iii*) Illustration: One chart, graph, diagram, drawing, cartoon or picture per book or per periodical issue.

(*iv*) "Special" works: Certain works in poetry, prose or in "poetic prose" which often combine language with illustrations and which are intended sometimes for children and at other times for a more general audience fall short of 2,500 words in their entirety. Paragraph "ii" above notwithstanding such "special works" may not be reproduced in their entirety; however, an excerpt comprising not more than two of the published pages of such special work and containing not more than 10% of the words found in the text thereof, may be reproduced.

Spontaneity

(*i*) The copying is at the instance and inspiration of the individual teacher, and

(*ii*) The inspiration and decision to use the work and the moment of its use for maximum teaching effectiveness are so close in time that it would be unreasonable to expect a timely reply to a request for permission.

Cumulative Effect

(*i*) The copying of the material is for only one course in the school in which the copies are made.

(*ii*) Not more than one short poem, article, story, essay or two excerpts may be copied from the same author, nor more than three from the same collective work or periodical volume during one class term.

(*iii*) There shall not be more than nine instances of such multiple copying for one course during one class term.

[The limitations stated in "ii" and "iii" above shall not apply to current news periodicals and newspapers and current news sections of other periodicals.]

III. *Prohibitions as to I and II Above*

Notwithstanding any of the above, the following shall be prohibited:

(A) Copying shall not be used to create or to replace or substitute for anthologies, compilations or collective works. Such replacement or substitution may occur whether copies of various works or excerpts therefrom are accumulated or reproduced and used separately.

(B) There shall be no copying of or from works intended to be "consumable" in the course of study or of teaching. These include workbooks, exercises, standardized tests and test booklets and answer sheets and like consumable material.

(C) Copying shall not:

(a) substitute for the purchase of books, publishers' reprints or periodicals;

(b) be directed by higher authority;

(c) be repeated with respect to the same item by the same teacher from term to term.

(D) No charge shall be made to the student beyond the actual cost of the photocopying.

Agreed March 19, 1976.

Ad Hoc Committee on Copyright Law Revision:

By Sheldon Elliott Steinbach.

Author-Publisher Group:

Authors League of America:

By Irwin Karp, *Counsel.*

Association of American Publishers, Inc.:
By ALEXANDER C. HOFFMAN,
Chairman, Copyright Committee.

In a joint letter dated April 30, 1976, representatives of the Music Publishers' Association of the United States, Inc., the National Music Publishers' Association, Inc., the Music Teachers National Association, the Music Educators National Conference, the National Association of Schools of Music, and the Ad Hoc Committee on Copyright Law Revision, wrote to Chairman Kastenmeier as follows:

During the hearings on H.R. 2223 in June 1975, you and several of your subcommittee members suggested that concerned groups should work together in developing guidelines which would be helpful to clarify Section 107 of the bill.

Representatives of music educators and music publishers delayed their meetings until guidelines had been developed relative to books and periodicals. Shortly after that work was completed and those guidelines were forwarded to your subcommittee, representatives of the undersigned music organizations met together with representatives of the Ad Hoc Committee on Copyright Law Revision to draft guidelines relative to music.

We are very pleased to inform you that the discussions thus have been fruitful on the guidelines which have been developed. Since private music teachers are an important factor in music education, due consideration has been given to the concerns of that group.

We trust that this will be helpful in the report on the bill to clarify Fair Use as it applies to music.

The text of the guidelines accompanying this letter is as follows:

GUIDELINES FOR EDUCATIONAL USES OF MUSIC

The purpose of the following guidelines is to state the minimum and not the maximum standards of educational fair use under Section 107 of HR 2223. The parties agree that the conditions determining the extent of permissible copying for educational purposes may change in the future; that certain types of copying permitted under these guidelines may not be permissible in the future, and conversely that in the future other types of copying not permitted under these guidelines may be permissible under revised guidelines.

Moreover, the following statement of guidelines is not intended to limit the types of copying permitted under the standards of fair use under judicial decision and which are stated in Section 107 of the Copyright Revision Bill. There may be instances in which copying which does not fall within the guidelines stated below may nonetheless be permitted under the criteria of fair use.

A. Permissible Uses

1. Emergency copying to replace purchased copies which for any reason are not available for an imminent performance provided purchased replacement copies shall be substituted in due course.

2. (a) For academic purposes other than performance, single or multiple copies of excerpts of works may be made, provided that the excerpts do not comprise a part of the whole which would constitute a performable unit such as a selection, movement or aria, but in no case more than 10% of the whole work. The number of copies shall not exceed one copy per pupil.

(b) For academic purposes other than performance, a single copy of an entire performable unit (section, movement, aria, etc.) that is, (1) confirmed by the copyright proprietor to be out of print or (2) unavailable except in a larger work, may be made by or for a teacher solely for the purpose of his or her scholarly research or in preparation to teach a class.

3. Printed copies which have been purchased may be edited or simplified provided that the fundamental character of the work is not distorted or the lyrics, if any, altered or lyrics added if none exist.

4. A single copy of recordings of performances by students may be made for evaluation or rehearsal purposes and may be retained by the educational institution or individual teacher.

5. A single copy of a sound recording (such as a tape, disc or cassette) of copyrighted music may be made from sound recordings owned by an educatonal institution or an individual teacher for the purpose of constructing aural exercises or examinations and may be retained by the educational institution or individual teacher. (This pertains only to the copyright of the music itself and not to any copyright which may exist in the sound recording.)

B. Prohibitions

1. Copying to create or replace or substitute for anthologies, compilations or collective works.

2. Copying of or from works intended to be "consumable" in the course of study or of teaching such as workbooks, exercises, standardized tests and answer sheets and like material.

3. Copying for the purpose of performance, except as in A(1) above.

4. Copying for the purpose of substituting for the purchase of music, except as in A(1) and A(2) above.

5. Copying without inclusion of the copyright notice which appears on the printed copy.

The next three paragraphs did not appear in the SENATE REPORT.

The problem of off-the-air taping for nonprofit classroom use of copyrighted audiovisual works incorporated in radio and television broadcasts has proved to be difficult to resolve. The Committee believes that the fair use doctrine has some limited application in this area, but it appears that the development of detailed guidelines will require a more thorough exploration than has so far been possible of the needs and problems of a number of different interests affected, and of the various legal problems presented. Nothing in section 107 or elsewhere in the bill is intended to change or prejudge the law on the point. On the other hand, the Committee is sensitive to the importance of the problem, and urges the representatives of the various interests, if possible under the leadership of the Register of Copyrights, to continue their discussions actively and in a constructive spirit. If it would be helpful to a solution, the Committee is receptive to undertaking further consideration of the problem in a future Congress.

The Committee appreciates and commends the efforts and the cooperative and reasonable spirit of the parties who achieved the agreed guidelines on books and periodicals and on music. Representatives of the American Association of University Professors and of the Association of American Law Schools have written to the Committee strongly criticizing the guidelines, particularly with respect to multiple copying, as being too restrictive with respect to classroom situations at the university and graduate level. However, the Committee notes that the Ad Hoc group did include representatives of higher education, that the stated "purpose of the . . . guidelines is to state the minimum and not the maximum standards of educational fair use" and that the agreement acknowledges "there may be instances in which copying which does not fall within the guidelines . . . may nonetheless be permitted under the criteria of fair use."

The Committee believes the guidelines are a reasonable interpretation of the minimum standards of fair use. Teachers will know that copying within the guidelines is fair use. Thus, the guidelines serve the purpose of fulfilling the need for greater certainty and protection for teachers. The Committee expresses the hope that if there are areas where standards other than these guidelines may be appropriate, the parties will continue their efforts to provide additional specific guidelines in the same spirit of good will and give and take that has marked the discussion of this subject in recent months.

Reproduction and uses for other purposes

The concentrated attention given the fair use provision in the context of classroom teaching activities should not obscure its application in other areas. It must be emphasized again that the same general standards of fair use are applicable to all kinds of uses of copyrighted material, although the relative weight to be given them will differ from case to case.

The fair use doctrine would be relevant to the use of excerpts from copyrighted works in educational broadcasting activities not exempted under section 110(2) or 112, and not covered by the licensing provisions of section 118.

The last 10 words of the preceding paragraph did not appear in the SENATE REPORT.

In these cases the factors to be weighed
in applying the criteria of this section would include whether the performers, producers, directors, and others responsible for the broadcast were paid, the size and nature of the audience, the size and number of excerpts taken and, in the case of recordings made for broadcast, the number of copies reproduced and the extent of their reuse or exchange. The availability of the fair use doctrine to educational broadcasters would be narrowly circumscribed in the case of motion pictures and other audiovisual works, but under appropriate circumstances it could apply to the nonsequential showing of an individual still or slide, or to the performance of a short excerpt from a motion picture for criticism or comment.

SENATE REPORT

The following paragraph was omitted in the HOUSE REPORT.

The committee's attention has been directed to the special problems involved in the reception of instructional television programs in remote areas of the country. In certain areas it is currently impossible to transmit such programs by any means other than communications satellites. A particular difficulty exists when such transmissions extend over several time zones within the same state, such as in Alaska. Unless individual schools in such states may make an off-air recording of such transmissions, the programs may not be received by the students during the school's daily schedule. The committee believes that the making by a school located in such a remote area of an off-the-air recording of an instructional television transmission for the purpose of a delayed viewing of the program by students for the same school constitutes a "fair use." The committee does not intend to suggest however, that off-the-air recording for convenience would under any circumstances, be considered "fair use." To meet the requirement of temporary use the school may retain the recording for only a limited period of time after the broadcast.

HOUSE REPORT (Continued)

Another special instance illustrating the application of the fair use doctrine pertains to the making of copies or phonorecords of works in the special forms needed for the use of blind persons. These special forms, such as copies in Braille and phonorecords of oral readings (talking books), are not usually made by the publishers for commercial distribution. For the most part, such copies and phonorecords are made by the Library of Congress' Division for the Blind and Physically Handicapped with permission obtained from the copyright owners, and are circulated to blind persons through regional libraries covering the nation. In addition, such copies and phonorecords are made locally by individual volunteers for the use of blind persons in their communities, and the Library of Congress conducts a program for training such volunteers. While the making of multiple copies or phonorecords of a work for general circulation requires the permission of the copyright owner, a problem addressed in section 710 of the bill,

The last nine words did not appear in the SENATE REPORT.

the making of a single copy or phonorecord by an individual as a free service for a blind persons would properly be considered a fair use under section 107.

A problem of particular urgency is that of preserving for posterity prints of motion pictures made before 1942. Aside from the deplorable fact that in a great many cases the only existing copy of a film has been deliberately destroyed, those that remain are in immediate danger of disintegration; they were printed on film stock with a nitrate base that will inevitably decompose in time. The efforts of the Library of Congress, the American Film Institute, and other organizations to rescue and preserve this irreplaceable contribution to our cultural life are to be applauded, and the making of duplicate copies for purposes of archival preservation certainly falls within the scope of "fair use."

When a copyrighted work contains unfair, inaccurate, or derogatory information concerning an individual or institution, the individual or institution may copy and reproduce such parts of the work as are necessary to permit understandable comment on the statements made in the work.

The following paragraph did not appear in the SENATE REPORT.

The Committee has considered the question of publication, in Congressional hearings and documents, of copyrighted material. Where the length of the work or excerpt published and the number of copies authorized are reasonable under the circumstances, and the work itself is directly relevant to a matter of legitimate legislative concern, the Committee believes that the publication would constitute fair use.

During the consideration of the revision bill in the 94th Congress it was proposed that independent newsletters, as distinguished from house organs and publicity or advertising publications, be given separate treatment. It is argued that newsletters are particularly vulnerable to mass photocopying, and that most newsletters have fairly modest circulations. Whether the copying of portions of a newsletter is an act of infringement or a fair use will necessarily turn on the facts of the individual case. However, as a general principle, it seems clear that the scope of the fair use doctrine should be considerably narrower in the case of newsletters than in that of either mass-circulation periodicals or scientific journals. The commercial nature of the user is a significant factor in such cases: Copying by a profit-making user of even a small portion of a newsletter may have a significant impact on the commercial market for the work.

The Committee has examined the use of excerpts from copyrighted works in the art work of calligraphers. The committee believes that a single copy reproduction of an excerpt from a copyrighted work by a calligrapher for a single client does not represent an infringement of copyright. Likewise, a single reproduction of excerpts from a copyrighted work by a student calligrapher or teacher in a learning situation would be a fair use of the copyrighted work.

The Register of Copyrights has recommended that the committee report describe the relationship between this section and the provisions of section 108 relating to reproduction by libraries and archives. The doctrine of fair use applies to library photocopying, and nothing contained in section 108 "in any way affects the right of fair use." No provision of section 108 is intended to take away any rights existing under the fair use doctrine. To the contrary, section 108 authorizes certain photocopying practices which may not qualify as a fair use.

The criteria of fair use are necessarily set forth in general terms. In the application of the criteria of fair use to specific photocopying practices of libraries, it is the intent of this legislation to provide an appropriate balancing of the rights of creators, and the needs of users.

CONFERENCE REPORT

Fair Use

Senate bill

The Senate bill, in section 107, embodied express statutory recognition of the judicial doctrine that the fair use of a copyrighted work is not an infringement of copyright. It set forth the fair use doctrine, including four criteria for determining its applicability in particular cases, in general terms.

House bill

The House bill amended section 107 in two respects: in the general statement of the fair use doctrine it added a specific reference to multiple copies for classroom use, and it amplified the statement of the first of the criteria to be used in judging fair use (the purpose and character of the use) by referring to the commercial nature or nonprofit educational purpose of the use.

Conference substitute

The conference substitute adopts the House amendments. The conferees accept as part of their understanding of fair use the Guidelines for Classroom Copying in Not-for-Profit Educational Institutions with respect to books and periodicals appearing at pp. 68–70 of the House Report (H. Rept. No 94–1476, as corrected at p. H 10727 of the Congressional Record for September 21, 1976), and for educational uses of music appearing at pp. 70–71 of the House report, as amended in the statement appearing at p. H 10875 of the Congressional Record of September 22, 1976. The conferees also endorse the statement concerning the meaning of the word "teacher" in the guidelines for books and periodicals, and the application of fair use in the case of use of television programs within the confines of a nonprofit educational institution for the deaf and hearing impaired, both of which appear on p. H 10875 of the Congressional Record of September 22, 1976.

CONGRESSIONAL RECORD

The CONFERENCE REPORT, above, mentions Representative Robert Kastenmeier's remarks from the floor of the House. The following are excerpts from that speech, as they appeared in the CONGRESSIONAL RECORD of September 22, 1976, pp. 10874-10875:

Another question involves the reference to "teacher" in the "Agreement on Guidelines for Classroom Copying in Not-for-Profit Educational Institutions" reproduced at pages 68-70 of the committee's report No. 94-1476 in connection with section 107. It has been pointed out that, in planning his or her teaching on a day-to-day basis in a variety of educational situations, an individual teacher will commonly consult with instructional specialists on the staff of the school, such as reading specialists, curriculum specialists, audiovisual directors, guidance counselors, and the like. As long as the copying meets all of the other criteria laid out in the guidelines, including the requirements for spontaneity and the prohibition against the copying being directed by higher authority, the committee regards the concept of "teacher" as broad enough to include instructional specialists working in consultation with actual instructors.

Also in consultation with section 107, the committee's attention has been directed to the unique educational needs and problems of the approximately 50,000 deaf and hearing-impaired students in the United States, and the inadequacy of both public and commercial television to serve their educational needs. It has been suggested that, as long as clear-cut constraints are imposed and enforced, the doctrine of fair use is broad enough to permit the making of an off-the-air fixation of a television program within a nonprofit educational institution for the deaf and hearing impaired, the reproduction of a master and a work copy of a captioned version of the original fixation, and the performance of the program from the work copy within the confines of the institution. In identifying the constraints that would have to be imposed within an institution in order for these activities to be considered as fair use, it has been suggested that the purpose of the use would have to be noncommercial in every respect, and educational in the sense that it serves as part of a deaf or hearing-impaired student's learning environment within the institution, and that the institution would have to insure that the master and work copy would remain in the hands of a limited number of authorized personnel within the institution, would be responsible for assuring against its unauthorized reproduction or distribution, or its performance or retention for other than educational purposes within the institution. Work copies of captioned programs could be shared among institutions for the deaf abiding by the constraints specified. Assuming that these constraints are both imposed and enforced, and that no other factors intervene to render the use unfair, the committee believes that the activities described could reasonably be considered fair use under section 107.

Further, on pages 70 and 71 of the committee report Guidelines for Educational Uses of Music under section 107 are set forth. Those guidelines represent the understanding of the Music Publishers' Association of the United States, Inc., the National Music Publishers Association, Inc., the Music Teachers National Association, the Music Educators National Conference, the National Association of Schools of Music, and the Ad Hoc Committee on Copyright Law Revision as expressed in a joint letter to me dated April 30, 1976.

The report, as printed, does not reflect a subsequent change in the joint guidelines which was described in a subsequent letter to me from a representative of the above named organizations. Subsection A.2. of the guidelines [for educational use of music] should be changed to read as follows: "2. For academic purposes other than performance, single or multiple copies of excerpts of works may be made, provided that the excerpts do not comprise a part of the whole which would constitute a performable unit such as a selection, movement or aria, but in no case more than 10 percent of the whole work. The number of copies shall not exceed one copy per pupil."

HOUSE REPORT 90-83

The fifth paragraph of Section 107 of the HOUSE REPORT refers to the following passages and indicates that "the arguments on the question . . . have not changed materially in the intervening years." House Report 90-83 was published in the spring of 1967.

The controversy over the related problems of fair use and the reproduction of copyrighted material for educational and scholarly purposes began well before the hearings. This problem in copyright law revision received much attention from witnesses at the hearings, and from the committee thereafter.

The fair use provision in H.R. 4347, as introduced, had been reduced to a bare statement that "the fair use of a copyrighted work is not an infringement of copyright." This approach was supported by a wide range of interests on the ground that the doctrine should remain as flexible as possible, and that any attempt at definition could freeze the concept and open the door to massive, unreasonable abuses. On the other side a number of witnesses representing various educational and scholarly organizations criticized the provision as vague and nebulous, and stressed the need of teachers and scholars to be certain whether what they were doing constituted fair use or infringement. They recommended restoration of a part of the provision in the 1964 bill referring to "fair use * * * to the extent reasonably necessary or incidental to a legitimate purpose such as criticism, comment, news reporting, teaching, scholarship, or research."

The group representing educational and scholarly organizations argued further that the doctrine of fair use alone is insufficient to provide the certainty that teachers and other nonprofit educational users of copyrighted material need for their own protection. They emphasized that teachers are not interested in mass copying that actually damages authors and publishers, but that they need to be free to make creative use of all of the resources available to them in the classroom, and that this necessarily involves some reproduction and distribution of copyrighted works such as contemporaneous material in the press, isolated poems and stories for illustrative purposes, and the like. Representatives of the educational group contended that a statute subjecting the use of modern teaching tools to requirements for advance clearance and payment of fees would inhibit use of teachers' imagination and ingenuity, and they proposed adoption of a specific, limited exemption for educational copying that would apply the "not-for-profit" limitation of the present law. They also proposed an amendment of section 504(c) that would allow a court to withhold any award of statutory damages against innocent teachers.

The proposal for a specific educational copying exemption was vigorously opposed by authors and publishers, among a number of others. They characterized the educators' arguments as saying, in effect, that since it is increasingly easy to infringe, violations should be made legal. They maintained that the present "for profit" limitation has nothing to do with copying, and that the argument for exempting educational uses on the ground that they are noncommercial overlooks the serious losses and destruction of incentive that uncompensated educational uses would cause to authors and publishers, particularly in the textbook, reference book, and scientific publishing areas. They stressed that education is the textbook publisher's only market, and that many authors receive their main income from licensing reprints in anthologies and textbooks; if an unlimited number of teachers could prepare and reproduce their own anthologies, the cumulative effect would be disastrous. Because photocopying and other reproducing devices are constantly proliferating and becoming easier and cheaper to use, it was claimed that the future of some kinds of publishing is at stake, and that solutions should be sought through reasonable voluntary licensing or clearance arrangements rather than an outright exemption that would hurt authorship, publishing, and ultimately education itself.

The implications of these opposing positions extend far beneath the surface of the specific arguments and involve fundamental questions of social policy. The fullest possible use of the multitude of technical devices now available to education should be encouraged. But, bearing in mind that the basic constitutional purpose of granting copyright protection is the advancement of learning, the committee also recognizes that the potential destruction of incentives to authorship presents a serious danger.

The sharp exchanges between the representatives of authors and publishers and those of educators and scholars at the hearings did not conceal their recognition of common aims and of the need for reasonable accommodation. Several productive meetings were held in June 1966; while no final agreements were reached, the meetings were generally successful in clarifying the issues and in pointing the way toward constructive solutions.

After full consideration, the committee believes that a specific exemption freeing certain reproductions of copyrighted works for educational and scholarly purposes from copyright control is not justified. As shown by a Copyright Office study dated July 22, 1966, the educational groups are mistaken in their argument that a "for profit" limitation is applicable to educational copying under the present law. Any educational uses that are fair use today would be fair use under the bill.

On the other hand, recognizing the need for greater certainty and protection for teachers, the committee has amended section 504(c), as explained below, to insulate a teacher who honestly and reasonably believes what he was doing constituted a fair use from excessive liability for minimum statutory damages. It has also amended section 107 to restore a statement of the four criteria, quoted above, to indicate that a fair use may include "such use by reproduction in copies or phonorecords or by any other means specified by [section 106]," and to characterize a fair use as generally being "for purposes such as criticism, comment, news reporting, teaching, scholarship, or research."

The intention of the committee with respect to the application of the fair use doctrine in various situations is discussed below. It should be emphasized again that, in those situations or any others, the committee has no purpose of either freezing or changing the doctrine. In particular, the reference to fair use "by reproduction in copies or phonorecords or by any other means" should not be interpreted as sanctioning any reproduction beyond the normal and reasonable limits of fair use. The clause was added in response to arguments by educators that, since the case law on fair use has not yet dealt with photocopying and analogous forms of reproduction, section 107 should contain language making clear that the doctrine has as much application in those areas as in any others.

The above passage appears on pages 30-31 of the report.

COPYRIGHT OFFICE, 1961 REPORT

"The Report of the Register of Copyrights on the General Revision of the U.S. Copyright Law" (1961) contains a significant definition of fair use and examples of its application. The examples are cited in the first paragraph of Section 107 of the HOUSE REPORT. The Register's definition and examples are given in full:

a. What is "fair use"?

Nothing is said in the statute as to the "fair use" of copyrighted works. The doctrine of "fair use," however, has been developed by the courts over a period of many years and is now firmly established as an implied limitation on the exclusive rights of copyright owners.

Copyright does not preclude anyone from using the ideas or information disclosed in a copyrighted work. Beyond that, the work itself is subject to "fair use." That term eludes precise definition; broadly speaking, it means that a reasonable portion of a copyrighted work may be reproduced without permission when necessary for a legitimate purpose which is not competitive with the copyright owner's market for his work.

The general scope of fair use can be indicated by the following examples of the kinds of uses that may be permitted under that concept:

- Quotation of excerpts in a review or criticism for purposes of illustration or comment.
- Quotation of short passages in a scholarly or technical work, for illustration or clarification of the author's observations.
- Use in a parody of some of the content of the work parodied.
- Summary of an address or article, with brief quotations, in a news report.
- Reproduction by a library of a portion of a work to replace part of a damaged copy.
- Reproduction by a teacher or student of a small part of a work to illustrate a lesson.
- Reproduction of a work in legislative or judicial proceedings or reports.
- Incidental and fortuitous reproduction, in a newsreel or broadcast, of a work located at the scene of an event being reported.

Whether any particular use of a copyrighted work constitutes a fair use rather than an infringement of copyright has been said to depend upon (1) the purpose of the use, (2) the nature of the copyrighted work, (3) the amount and substantiality of the material used in relation to the copyrighted work as a whole, and (4) the effect of the use on the copyright owner's potential market for his work. These criteria are interrelated and their relative significance may vary, but the fourth one—the competitive character of the use—is often the most decisive.

The above passage appears on pp. 24-25 of the report.

LAW

§ 108. Limitations on exclusive rights: Reproduction by libraries and archives

(a) Notwithstanding the provisions of section 106, it is not an infringement of copyright for a library or archives, or any of its employees acting within the scope of their employment, to reproduce no more than one copy or phonorecord of a work, or to distribute such copy or phonorecord, under the conditions specified by this section, if—

(1) the reproduction or distribution is made without any purpose of direct or indirect commercial advantage;

(2) the collections of the library or archives are (i) open to the public, or (ii) available not only to researchers affiliated with the library or archives or with the institution of which it is a part, but also to other persons doing research in a specialized field; and

(3) the reproduction or distribution of the work includes a notice of copyright.

A notice which meets this requirement appears on page 58.

(b) The rights of reproduction and distribution under this section apply to a copy or phonorecord of an unpublished work duplicated in facsimile form solely for purposes of preservation and security or for deposit for research use in another library or archives of the type described by clause (2) of subsection (a), if the copy or phonorecord reproduced is currently in the collections of the library or archives.

(c) The right of reproduction under this section applies to a copy or phonorecord of a published work duplicated in facsimile form solely for the purpose of replacement of a copy or phonorecord that is damaged, deteriorating, lost, or stolen, if the library or archives has, after a reasonable effort, determined that an unused replacement cannot be obtained at a fair price.

(d) The rights of reproduction and distribution under this section apply to a copy, made from the collection of a library or archives where the user makes his or her request or from that of another library or archives, of no more than one article or other contribution to a copyrighted collection or periodical issue, or to a copy or phonorecord of a small part of any other copyrighted work, if—

(1) the copy or phonorecord becomes the property of the user, and the library or archives has had no notice that the copy or phonorecord would be used for any purpose other than private study, scholarship, or research; and

(2) the library or archives displays prominently, at the place where orders are accepted, and includes on its order form, a warning of copyright in accordance with requirements that the Register of Copyrights shall prescribe by regulation.

The required notice is found under REGISTER OF COPYRIGHTS, on pages 119-20.

(e) The rights of reproduction and distribution under this section apply to the entire work, or to a substantial part of it, made from the collection of a library or archives where the user makes his or her request or from that of another library or archives, if the library or archives has first determined, on the basis of a reasonable investigation, that a copy or phonorecord of the copyrighted work cannot be obtained at a pair price, if—

(1) the copy or phonorecord becomes the property of the user, and the library or archives has had no notice that the copy or phonorecord would be used for any purpose other than private study, scholarship, or research; and

(2) the library or archives displays prominently, at the place where orders are accepted, and includes on its order form, a warning of copyright in accordance with requirements that the Register of Copyrights shall prescribe by regulation.

The required notice is found under REGISTER OF COPYRIGHTS, on pages 119-20.

(f) Nothing in this section—

(1) shall be construed to impose liability for copyright infringement upon a library or archives or its employees for the unsupervised use of reproducing equipment located on its premises: *Provided*, That such equipment displays a notice that the making of a copy may be subject to the copyright law;

A notice which meets this requirement appears on page 58.

(2) excuses a person who uses such reproducing equipment or who requests a copy or phonorecord under subsection (d) from liability for copyright infringement for any such act, or for any later use of such copy or phonorecord, if it exceeds fair use as provided by section 107;

(3) shall be construed to limit the reproduction and distribution by lending of a limited number of copies and excerpts by a library or archives of an audiovisual news program, subject to clauses (1), (2), and (3) of subsection (a); or

(4) in any way affects the right of fair use as provided by section 107, or any contractual obligations assumed at any time by the library or archives when it obtained a copy or phonorecord of a work in its collections.

(g) The rights of reproduction and distribution under this section extend to the isolated and unrelated reproduction or distribution of a single copy or phonorecord of the same material on separate occasions, but do not extend to cases where the library or archives, or its employee—

(1) is aware or has substantial reason to believe that it is engaging in the related or concerted reproduction or distribution of multiple copies or phonorecords of the same material, whether made on one occasion or over a period of time, and whether intended for aggregate use by one or more individuals or for separate use by the individual members of a group; or

(2) engages in the systematic reproduction or distribution of single or multiple copies or phonorecords of material described in subsection (d): *Provided*, That nothing in this clause prevents a library or archives from participating in interlibrary arrangements that do not have, as their purpose or effect, that the library or archives receiving such copies or phonorecords for distribution

does so in such aggregate quantities as to substitute for a subscription to or purchase of such work.

(h) The rights of reproduction and distribution under this section do not apply to a musical work, a pictorial, graphic or sculptural work, or a motion picture or other audiovisual work other than an audiovisual work dealing with news, except that no such limitation shall apply with respect to rights granted by subsections (b) and(c), or with respect to pictorial or graphic works published as illustrations, diagrams, or similar adjuncts to works of which copies are reproduced or distributed in accordance with subsections (d) and (e).

(i) Five years from the effective date of this Act, and at five-year intervals thereafter, the Register of Copyrights, after consulting with representatives of authors, book and periodical publishers, and other owners of copyrighted materials, and with representatives of library users and librarians, shall submit to the Congress a report setting forth the extent to which this section has achieved the intended statutory balancing of the rights of creators, and the needs of users. The report should also describe any problems that may have arisen, and present legislative or other recommendations, if warranted.

The Register's first report on Section 108 is due on January 1, 1983.

HOUSE REPORT

Notwithstanding the exclusive rights of the owners of copyright, section 108 provides that under certain conditions it is not an infringement of copyright for a library or archives, or any of its employees acting within the scope of their employment, to reproduce or distribute not more than one copy or phonorecord of a work, provided (1) the reproduction or distribution is made without any purpose of direct or indirect commercial advantage and (2) the collections of the library or archives are open to the public or available not only to researchers affiliated with the library or archives, but also to other persons doing research in a specialized field, and (3) the reproduction or distribution of the work includes a notice of copyright.

The next four paragraphs did not appear in the SENATE REPORT.

Under this provision, a purely commercial enterprise could not establish a collection of copyrighted works, call itself a library or archive, and engage in for-profit reproduction and distribution of photocopies. Similarly, it would not be possible for a non-profit institution, by means of contractual arrangements with a commercial copying enterprise, to authorize the enterprise to carry out copying and distribution functions that would be exempt if conducted by the non-profit institution itself.

The reference to "indirect commercial advantage" has raised questions as to the status of photocopying done by or for libraries or archival collections within industrial, profitmaking, or proprietary institutions (such as the research and development departments of chemical, pharmaceutical, automobile, and oil corporations, the library of a propritary hospital, the collections owned by a law or medical partnership, etc.).

There is a direct interrelationship between this problem and the prohibitions against "multiple" and "systematic" photocopying in section 108(g) (1) and (2). Under section 108, a library in a profit-making organization would not be authorized to:

(a) use a single subscription or copy to supply its employees with multiple copies of material relevant to their work; or

(b) use a single subscription or copy to supply its employees, on request, with single copies of material relevant to their work, where the arrangement is "systematic" in the sense of deliberately substituting photocopying for subscription or purchase; or

(c) use "interlibrary loan" arrangements for obtaining photocopies in such aggregate quantities as to substitute for subscriptions or purchase of material needed by employees in their work.

Moreover, a library in a profit-making organization could not evade these obligations by installing reproducing equipment on its premises for unsupervised use by the organization's staff.

Isolated, spontaneous making of single photocopies by a library in a for-profit organization, without any systematic effort to substitute photocopying for subscriptions or purchases, would be covered by section 108, even though the copies are furnished to the employees of the organization for use in their work. Similarly, for-profit libraries could participate in interlibrary arrangements for exchange of photocopies, as long as the reproduction or distribution was not "systematic." These activities, by themselves, would ordinarily not be considered "for direct or indirect commercial advantage," since the "advantage" referred to in this clause must attach to the immediate commercial motivation behind the reproduction or distribution itself, rather than to the ultimate profit-making motivation behind the enterprise in which the library is located. On the other hand, section 108 would not excuse reproduction or distribution if there were a commercial motive behind the actual making or distributing of the copies, if multiple copies were made or distributed, or if the photocopying activities were "systematic" in the sense that their aim was to substitute for subscriptions or purchases.

SENATE REPORT

The four preceding paragraphs in the HOUSE REPORT were briefly stated as follows:

The limitation of section 108 to reproduction and distribution by libraries and archives "without any purpose of direct or indirect commercial advantage" is intended to preclude a library or archives in a profit-making organization from providing photocopies of copyrighted materials to employees engaged in furtherance of the organization's commercial enterprise, unless such copying qualifies as a fair use, or the organization has obtained the necessary copyright licenses. A commercial organization should purchase the number of copies of a work that it requires, or obtain the consent of the copyright owner to the making of the photocopies.

HOUSE REPORT (Continued)

The rights of reproduction and distribution under section 108 apply in the following circumstances:

Archival reproduction

Subsection (b) authorizes the reproduction and distribution of a copy or phonorecord of an unpublished work duplicated in facsimile form solely for purposes of preservation and security, or for deposit for research use in another library or archives, if the copy or phonorecord reproduced is currently in the collections of the first library or archives. Only unpublished works could be reproduced under this exemption, but the right would extend to any type of work, including photographs, motion pictures and sound recordings. Under this exemption, for example, a repository could make photocopies of manuscripts by microfilm or electrostatic process, but could not reproduce the work in "machine-readable" language for storage in an information system.

Replacement of damaged copy

Subsection (c) authorizes the reproduction of a published work duplicated in facsimile form solely for the purpose of replacement of a copy or phonorecord that is damaged, deteriorating, lost or stolen, if the library or archives has, after a reasonable effort, determined that an unused replacement cannot be obtained at a fair price. The scope and nature of a reasonable investigation to determine that an unused replacement cannot be obtained will vary according to the circumstances of a particular situation. It will always require recourse to commonly-known trade sources in the United States, and in the normal situation also to the publisher or other copyright owner (if such owner can be located at the address listed in the copyright registration), or an authorized reproducing service.

Articles and small excerpts

Subsection (d) authorizes the reproduction and distribution of a copy of not more than one article or other contribution to a copyrighted collection or periodical issue, or of a copy or phonorecord of a small part of any other copyrighted work. The copy or phonorecord may be made by the library where the user makes his request or by another library pursuant to an interlibrary loan. It is further required that the copy become the property of the user, that the library or archives have no notice that the copy would be used for any purposes other than private study, scholarship or research, and that the library or archives display prominently at the place where reproduction requests are accepted, and includes in its order form, a warning of copyright in accordance with requirements that the Register of Copyrights shall prescribe by regulation.

Out-of-print works

Subsection (e) authorizes the reproduction and distribution of a copy or phonorecord of an entire work under certain circumstances, if it has been established that a copy cannot be obtained at a fair price. The copy may be made by the library where the user makes his request or by another library pursuant to an interlibrary loan. The scope and nature of a reasonable investigation to determine that an unused copy cannot be obtained will vary according to the circumstances of a particular situation. It will always require recourse to commonly-known trade sources in the United States, and in the normal situation also to the publisher or other copyright owner (if the owner can be located at the address listed in the copyright registration), or an authorized reproducing service. It is further required that the copy become the property of the user, that the library or archives have no notice that the copy would be used for any purpose other than private study, scholarship, or research, and that the library or archives display prominently at the place where reproduction requests are accepted, and include on its order form, a warning of copyright in accordance with requirements that the Register of Copyrights shall prescribe by regulation.

SENATE REPORT

The first sentence in the subsection on "Out-of-print works" reads:

Subsection (e) authorizes the reproduction and distribution of a copy of a work, with certain exceptions, at the request of the user of the collection if the user has established that an unused copy cannot be obtained at a fair price.

This passage was superseded by the passage in the HOUSE REPORT, above, which removes the searching responsibility from the library patron.

HOUSE REPORT (Continued)

General exemptions

Clause (1) of subsection (f) specifically exempts a library or archives or its employees from liability for the unsupervised use of reproducing equipment located on its premises, provided that the reproducing equipment displays a notice that the making of a copy may be subject to the copyright law. Clause (2) of subsection (f) makes clear that this exemption of the library or archives does not extend to the person using such equipment or requesting such copy if the use exceeds fair use. Insofar as such person is concerned the copy or phonorecord made is not considered "lawfully" made for purposes of sections 109, 110 or other provisions of the title.

Clause (3) provides that nothing in section 108 is intended to limit the reproduction and distribution by lending of a limited number of copies and excerpts of an audiovisual news program. This exemption is intended to apply to the daily newscasts of the national television networks, which report the major events of the day. It does not apply to documentary (except documentary programs involving news reporting as that term is used in section 107), magazine-format or other public affairs broadcasts dealing with subjects of general interest to the viewing public.

The last two sentences did not appear in the SENATE REPORT.

The clause was first added to the revision bill in 1974 by the adoption of an amendment proposed by Senator Baker. It is intended to permit libraries and archives, subject to the general conditions of this section, to make off-the-air videotape recordings of daily network newscasts*for limited distribution to scholars and researchers for use in research purposes. As such, it is an adjunct to the American Television and Radio Archive established in Section 113 of the Act which will be the principal repository for television broadcast material, including news broadcasts. The inclusion of language indicating that such material may only be distributed by lending by the library or archive is intended to preclude performance, copying, or sale, whether or not for profit, by the recipient of a copy of a television broadcast taped off-the-air pursuant to this clause.

The text following the asterisk did not appear in the SENATE REPORT.

SENATE REPORT

The following sentence was omitted in the HOUSE REPORT.

Despite the importance of preserving television news, the United States currently has no institution performing this function on a systematic basis.

This omission was remedied in Section 407(e) and Section 113 of the Transitional and Supplementary Provision, authorizing the creation of an American television and radio archives in the Library of Congress and authorizing the archives to reproduce or purchase radio and television programs.

The following three paragraphs were omitted in the HOUSE REPORT.

The purpose of the clause is to prevent the copyright law from precluding such operations as the Vanderbilt University Television News Archive, which makes videotape recordings of television news programs, prepares indexes of the contents, and leases copies of complete broadcasts or compilations of coverage of specified subjects for limited periods upon request from scholars and researchers.

Because of the important copyright policy issues inherent in this issue, the exemption has been narrowly drafted. The Register of Copyrights in 1974 advised that the language of this clause was technically appropriate for its purpose and not "broader than is necessary to validate the Vanderbilt operation."

The Copyright Office recommended that if the Congress desires a news videotape exemption it should be incorporated in section 108. The Copyright Office stated that the inclusion of such a clause in section 108 would be adequate "to enable the Vanderbilt operation to continue."

HOUSE REPORT (Continued)

Clause (4), in addition to asserting that nothing contained in section 108 "affects the right of fair use as provided by section 107," also provides that the right of reproduction granted by this section does not override any contractual arrangements assumed by a library or archives when it obtained a work for its collections. For example, if there is an express contractual prohibition against reproduction for any purpose, this legislation shall not be construed as justifying a violation of the contract. This clause is intended to encompass the situation where an individual makes papers, manuscripts or other works available to a library with the understanding that they will not be reproduced.

It is the intent of this legislation that a subsequent unlawful use by a user of a copy or phonorecord of a work lawfully made by a library, shall not make the library liable for such improper use.

Multiple copies and systematic reproduction

Subsection (g) provides that the rights granted by this section extend only to the "isolated and unrelated reproduction of a single copy or phonorecord of the same material on separate occasions." However, this section does not authorize the related or concerted reproduction of multiple copies or phonorecords of the same material, whether made on one occasion or over a period of time, and whether intended for aggregate use by one individual or for separate use by the individual members of a group.

With respect to material described in subsection (d)—articles or other contributions to periodicals or collections, and small parts of other copyrighted works—subsection (g) (2) provides that the exemptions of section 108 do not apply if the library or archive engages in "systematic reproduction or distribution of single or multiple copies or phonorecords." This provision in S. 22 provoked a storm of controversy, centering around the extent to which the restrictions on "systematic" activities would prevent the continuation and development of interlibrary networks and other arrangements involving the exchange of photocopies. After thorough consideration, the Committee amended section 108(g) (2) to add the following proviso:

> *Provided*, that nothing in this clause prevents a library or archives from participating in interlibrary arrangements that do not have, as their purpose or effect, that the library or archives receiving such copies or phonorecords for distribution does so in such aggregate quantities as to substitute for a subscription to or purchase of such work.

In addition, the Committee added a new subsection (i) to section 108, requiring the Register of Copyrights, five years from the effective date of the new Act and at five-year intervals thereafter, to report to Congress upon "the extent to which this section has achieved the intended statutory balancing of the rights of creators, and the needs of users," and to make appropriate legislative or other recommendations. As noted in connection with section 107, the Committee also amended section 504(c) in a way that would insulate librarians from unwarranted liability for copyright infringement; this amendment is discussed below.

The key phrases in the Committee's amendment of section 108(g) (2) are "aggregate quantities" and "substitute for a subscription to or purchase of" a work. To be implemented effectively in practice, these provisions will require the development and implementation of more-or-less specific guidelines establishing criteria to govern various situations.

The National Commission on New Technological Uses of Copyrighted Works (CONTU) offered to provide good offices in helping to develop these guidelines. This offer was accepted and, although the final text of guidelines has not yet been achieved, the Committee has reason to hope that, within the next month, some agreement can be reached on an initial set of guidelines covering practices under section 108(g)(2).

SENATE REPORT

The subsections on "Multiple copies and systematic reproduction" are quite different. The House version appears above; the Senate version follows.

Multiple copies and systematic reproduction

Subsection (g) provides that the rights granted by this section extend only to the "isolated and unrelated reproduction of a single copy", but this section does not authorize the related or concerted reproduction of multiple copies of the same material whether made on one occasion or over a period of time, and whether intended for aggregate use by one individual or for separate use by the individual members of a group. For example, if a college professor instructs his class to read an article from a copyrighted journal, the school library would not be permitted, under subsection (g), to reproduce copies of the article for the members of the class.

Subsection (g) also provides that section 108 does not authorize the systematic reproduction or distribution of copies or phonorecords of articles or other contributions to copyrighted collections or periodicals or of small parts of other copyrighted works whether or not multiple copies are reproduced or distributed. Systematic reproduction or distribution occurs when a library makes copies of such materials available to other libraries or to groups of users under formal or informal arrangements whose purpose or effect is to have the reproducing library serve as their source of such material. Such systematic reproduction and distribution, as distinguished from isolated and unrelated reproduction or distribution, may substitute the copies reproduced by the source library for subscriptions or reprints or other copies which the receiving libraries or users might otherwise have purchased for themselves, from the publisher or the licensed reproducing agencies.

While it is not possible to formulate specific definitions of "systematic copying", the following examples serve to illustrate some of the copying prohibited by subsection (g).

(1) A library with a collection of journals in biology informs other libraries with similar collections that it will maintain and build its own collection and will make copies of articles from these journals available to them and their patrons on request. Accordingly, the other libraries discontinue or refrain from purchasing subscriptions to these journals and fulfill their patrons' requests for articles by obtaining photocopies from the source library.

(2) A research center employing a number of scientists and technicians subscribes to one or two copies of needed periodicals. By reproducing photocopies of articles the center is able to make the material in these periodicals available to its staff in the same manner which otherwise would have required multiple subscriptions.

(3) Several branches of a library system agree that one branch will subscribe to particular journals in lieu of each branch purchasing its own subscriptions, and the one subscribing branch will reproduce

copies of articles from the publication for users of the other branches.

The committee believes that section 108 provides an appropriate statutory balancing of the rights of creators, and the needs of users. However, neither a statute nor legislative history can specify precisely which library photocopying practices constitute the making of "single copies" as distinguished from "systematic reproduction". Isolated single spontaneous requests must be distinguished from "systematic reproduction". The photocopying needs of such operations as multi-county regional systems must be met. The committee therefore recommends that representatives of authors, book and periodical publishers and other owners of copyrighted material meet with the library community to formulate photocopying guidelines to assist library patrons and employees. Concerning library photocopying practices not authorized by this legislation, the committee recommends that workable clearance and licensing procedures be developed.

It is still uncertain how far a library may go under the Copyright Act of 1909 in supplying a photocopy of copyrighted material in its collection. The recent case of *The Williams and Wilkins Company* v. *The United States* failed to significantly illuminate the application of the fair use doctrine to library photocopying practices. Indeed, the opinion of the Court of Claims said the Court was engaged in "a 'holding operation' in the interim period before Congress enacted its preferred solution."

While the several opinions in the *Wilkins* case have given the Congress little guidance as to the current state of the law on fair use, these opinions provide additional support for the balanced resolution of the photocopying issue adopted by the Senate last year in S. 1361 and preserved in section 108 of this legislation. As the Court of Claims opinion succinctly stated "there is much to be said on all sides."

In adopting these provisions on library photocopying, the committee is aware that through such programs as those of the National Commission on Libraries and Information Science there will be a significant evolution in the functioning and services of libraries. To consider the possible need for changes in copyright law and procedures as a result of new technology, a National Commission on New Technological Uses of Copyrighted Works has been established (Public Law 93–573).

HOUSE REPORT (Continued)

Works excluded

Subsection (h) provides that the rights of reproduction and distribution under this section do not apply to a musical work, a pictorial, graphic or sculptural work, or a motion picture or other audiovisual work* other than "an audiovisual work dealing with news." The latter term is intended as the equivalent in meaning of the phrase "audiovisual news program" in section 108(f)(3). The exclusions under subsection (h) do not apply to archival reproduction under subsection (b), to replacement of damaged or lost copies or phonorecords under subsection (c), or to "pictorial or graphic works published as illustrations, diagrams, or similar adjuncts to works of which copies are reproduced or distributed in accordance with subsections (d) and (e)."

Although subsection (h) generally removes musical, graphic, and audiovisual works from the specific exemptions of section 108, it is important to recognize that the doctrine of fair use under section 107 remains fully applicable to the photocopying or other reproduction of such works. In the case of music, for example, it would be fair use for a scholar doing musicological research to have a library supply a copy of a portion of a score or to reproduce portions of a phonorecord of a work. Nothing in section 108 impairs the applicability of the fair use doctrine to a wide variety of situations involving photocopying or other reproduction by a library of copyrighted material in its collections, where the user requests the reproduction for legitimate scholarly or research purposes.

The text following the asterisk did not appear in the SENATE REPORT.

SENATE REPORT

The following sentence did not appear in the HOUSE REPORT. It was replaced by the expanded statement following the asterisk, above.

Such limitation does not apply to archival reproduction and replacement of a damaged copy.

CONFERENCE REPORT

Senate bill

Section 108 of the Senate bill dealt with a variety of situations involving photocopying and other forms of reproduction by libraries and archives. It specified the conditions under which single copies of copyrighted material can be noncommercially reproduced and distributed, but made clear that the privileges of a library or archives under the section do not apply where the reproduction or distribution is of multiple copies or is "systematic." Under subsection (f), the section was not to be construed as limiting the reproduction and distribution, by a library or archive meeting the basic criteria of the section, of a limited number of copies and excerpts of an audiovisual news program.

House bill

The House bill amended section 108 to make clear that, in cases involving interlibrary arrangements for the exchange of photocopies, the activity would not be considered "systematic" as long as the library or archives receiving the reproductions for distribution does not do so in such aggregate quantities as to substitute for a subscription to or purchase of the work. A new subsection (i) directed the Register of Copyrights, by the end of 1982 and at five-year intervals thereafter, to report on the practical success of the section in balancing the various interests, and to make recommendations for any needed changes. With respect to audiovisual news programs, the House bill limited the scope of the distribution privilege confirmed by section 108(f)(3) to cases where the distribution takes the form of a loan.

Conference substitute

The conference substitute adopts the provisions of section 108 as amended by the House bill. In doing so, the conferees have noted two letters dated September 22, 1976, sent respectively to John L. McClellan, Chairman of the Senate Judiciary Subcommittee on Patents, Trademarks, and Copyrights, and to Robert W. Kastenmeier, Chairman of the House Judiciary Subcommittee on Courts, Civil Liberties, and the Administration of Justice. The letters, from the Chairman of the National Commission on New Technological Uses of Copyrighted Works (CONTU), Stanley H. Fuld, transmitted a document consisting of "guidelines interpreting the provision in subsection 108(g)(2) of S. 22, as approved by the House Committee on the Judiciary." Chairman Fuld's letters explain that, following lengthy consultations with the parties concerned, the Commission adopted these guidelines as fair and workable and with the hope that the conferees on S. 22 may find that they merit inclusion in the conference report. The letters add that, although time did not permit securing signatures of the representatives of the principal library organizations or of the organizations representing publishers and authors on these guidelines, the Commission had received oral assurances from these representatives that the guidelines are acceptable to their organizations.

The conference committee understands that the guidelines are not intended as, and cannot be considered, explicit rules or directions governing any and all cases, now or in the future. It is recognized that their purpose is to provide guidance in the most commonly-encountered interlibrary photocopying situations, that they are not intended to be limiting or determinative in themselves or with respect to other situations, and that they deal with an evolving situation that will undoubtedly require their continuous reevaluation and adjustment. With these qualifications, the conference committee agrees that the guidelines are a reasonable interpretation of the proviso of section 108(g)(2) in the most common situations to which they apply today.

The text of the guidelines follows:

Photocopying—Interlibrary Arrangements

INTRODUCTION

Subsection 108(g)(2) of the bill deals, among other things, with limits on interlibrary arrangements for photocopying. It prohibits systematic photocopying of copyrighted materials but permits interlibrary arrangements "that do not have, as their purpose or effect, that the library or archives receiving such copies or phonorecords for distribution does so in such aggregate quantities as to substitute for a subscription to or purchase of such work."

The National Commission on New Technological Uses of Copyrighted Works offered its good offices to the House and Senate subcommittees in bringing the interested parties together to see if agreement could be reached on what a realistic definition would be of "such aggregate quantities." The Commission consulted with the parties and suggested the interpretation which follows, on which there has been substantial agreement by the principal library, publisher, and author organizations. The Commission considers the guidelines which follow to be a workable and fair interpretation of the intent of the proviso portion of subsection 108(g)(2).

These guidelines are intended to provide guidance in the application of section 108 to the most frequently encountered interlibrary case: a library's obtaining from another library, in lieu of interlibrary loan, copies of articles from relatively recent issues of periodicals—those published within five years prior to the date of the request. The guidelines do not specify what aggregate quantity of copies of an article or articles published in a periodical, the issue date of which is more than five years prior to the date when the request for the copy thereof is made, constitutes a substitute for a subscription to such periodical. The meaning of the proviso to subsection 108(g)(2) in such case is left to future interpretation.

The point has been made that the present practice on interlibrary loans and use of photocopies in lieu of loans may be supplemented or even largely replaced by a system in which one or more agences or institutions, public or private, exist for the specific purpose of providing a central source for photocopies. Of course, these guidelines would not apply to such a situation.

GUIDELINES FOR THE PROVISO OF SUBSECTION 108(G)(2)

1. As used in the proviso of subsection 108(g)(2), the words "... such aggregate quantities as to substitute for a subscription to or purchase of such work" shall mean:

(a) with respect to any given periodical (as opposed to any given issue of a periodical), filled requests of a library or archives (a "requesting entity") within any calendar year for a total of six or more copies of an article or articles published in such periodical within five years prior to the date of the request. These guidelines specifically shall not apply, directly or indirectly, to any request of a requesting entity for a copy or copies of an article or articles published in any issue of a periodical, the publication date of which is more than five years prior to the date when the request is made. These guidelines do not define the meaning, with respect to such a request, of "... such aggregate quantities as to substitute for a subscription to [such periodical]".

(b) With respect to any other material described in subsection 108(d), (including fiction and poetry), filled requests of a requesting entity within any calendar year for a total of six or more copies or phonorecords of or from any given work (including a collective work) during the entire period when such material shall be protected by copyright.

2. In the event that a requesting entity—

(a) shall have in force or shall have entered an order for a subscription to a periodical, or

(b) has within its collection, or shall have entered an order for, a copy or phonorecord of any other copyrighted work,

material from either category of which it desires to obtain by copy from another library or archives (the "supplying entity"), because the material to be copied is not reasonably available for use by the requesting entity itself, then the fulfillment of such request shall be treated as though the requesting entity made such copy from its own collection. A library or archives may request a copy or phonorecord from a supplying entity only under those circumstances where the requesting entity would have been able, under the other provisions of section 108, to supply such copy from materials in its own collection.

3. No request for a copy or phonorecord of any material to which these guidelines apply may be fulfilled by the supplying entity unless such request is accompanied by a representation by the requesting entity that the request was made in conformity with these guidelines.

4. The requesting entity shall maintain records of all requests made by it for copies or phonorecords of any materials to which these guidelines apply and shall maintain records of the fulfillment of such requests, which records shall be retained until the end of the third complete calendar year after the end of the calendar year in which the respective request shall have been made.

5. As part of the review provided for in subsection 108(i), these guidelines shall be reviewed not later than five years from the effective date of this bill.

The conference committee is aware that an issue has arisen as to the meaning of the phrase "audiovisual news program" in section 108 (f)(3). The conferees believe that, under the provision as adopted in the conference substitute, a library or archives qualifying under section 108(a) would be free, without regard to the archival activities of the Library of Congress or any other organization, to reproduce, on videotape or any other medium of fixation or reproduction, local, regional, or network newscasts, interviews concerning current news events, and on-the-spot coverage of news events, and to distribute a limited number of reproductions of such a program on a loan basis.

Another point of interpretation involves the meaning of "indirect commercial advantage," as used in section 108(a)(1), in the case of libraries or archival collections within industrial, profit-making, or proprietary institutions. As long as the library or archives meets the criteria in section 108(a) and the other requirements of the section, including the prohibitions against multiple and systematic copying in subsection (g), the conferees consider that the isolated, spontaneous making of single photocopies by a library or archives in a for-profit organization without any commercial motivation, or participation by such a library or archives in interlibrary arrangements, would come within the scope of section 108.

CONTU FINAL REPORT

The National Commission on the New Technological Uses of Copyrighted Works (CONTU) offered the following recommendations for the revision of Section 108:

Recommendation for Congressional Action

Any legislation enacted as a result of these recommendations should be subject to a periodic review to determine its adequacy in the light of continuing technological change. This review should especially consider the impact of such legislation on competition and consumer prices in the computer and information industries and the effect on cultural values of including computer programs within the ambit of copyright.

PHOTOCOPYING

Recommendation for Legislation

The Act of 1976 should be amended at this time only to provide specific guidance for situations in which photocopying is done by commercial organizations on demand and for profit.

Recommendation to the Copyright Office

In conducting the five-year review of photocopying practices required by section 108(i) of the Act of 1976, the Register of Copyrights should begin immediately to plan and implement a study of the overall impact of all photoduplication practices on both proprietors' rights and the public's access to published information.

Recommendation to Other Government Agencies

Publishers, libraries and government agencies should cooperate in making information about the copyright status of all published works, both current and older publications, more readily available to the public.

COPYRIGHT OFFICE

Warnings of Copyright for Use by Certain Libraries and Archives

(a) *Definitions*. (1) A "Display Warning of Copyright" is a notice under paragraphs (d)(2) and (e)(2) of section 108 of Title 17 of the United States Code as amended by Pub. L. 94-553. As required by those sections the "Display Warning of Copyright" is to be displayed at the place where orders for copies or phonorecords are accepted by certain libraries and archives.

(2) An "Order Warning of Copyright" is a notice under paragraphs (d)(2) and (e)(2) of section 108 of Title 17 of the United States Code as amended by Pub. L. 94-553. As required by those sections the "Order Warning of Copyright" is to be included on printed forms supplied by certain libraries and archives and used by their patrons for ordering copies or phonorecords.

(b) *Contents*. A Display Warning of Copyright and an Order Warning of Copyright shall consist of verbatim reproduction of the following notice, printed in such size and form and displayed in such manner as to comply with paragraph (c) of this section:

NOTICE

WARNING CONCERNING COPYRIGHT RESTRICTIONS

The copyright law of the United States (Title 17, United States Code) governs the making of photocopies or other reproductions of copyrighted material.

Under certain conditions specified in the law, libraries and archives are authorized to furnish a photocopy or other reproduction. One of these specified conditions is that the photocopy or reproduction is not to be "used for any purpose other than private study, scholarship, or research." If a user makes a request for, or later uses, a photocopy or reproduction for purposes in excess of "fair use," that user may be liable for copyright infringement.

This institution reserves the right to refuse to accept a copying order if, in its judgment, fulfillment of the order would involve violation of copyright law.

(c) *Form and Manner of Use.* (1) A Display Warning of Copyright shall be printed on heavy paper or other durable material in type at least 18 points in size, and shall be displayed prominently, in such manner and location as to be clearly visible, legible, and comprehensible to a casual observer within the immediate vicinity of the place where orders are accepted.

(2) An Order Warning of Copyright shall be printed within a box located prominently on the order form itself, either on the front side of the form or immediately adjacent to the space calling for the name or signature of the person using the form. The notice shall be printed in type size no smaller than that used predominantly throughout the form, and in no case shall the type size be smaller than 8 points. The notice shall be printed in such manner as to be clearly legible, comprehensible, and readily apparent to a casual reader of the form.

Source: *U.S. Code of Federal Regulations*, Title 37, Sec. 201.14 (Washington: Office of the Federal Register, 1979).

AMERICAN LIBRARY ASSOCIATION

Record Maintenance and Retention Guidelines for Interlibrary Loan Departments

This statement deals only with recommended RECORD MAINTENANCE AND RETENTION GUIDELINES. Interlibrary Loan librarians have a responsibility to familiarize themselves thoroughly with the provisions of the Copyright Revision Act of 1976 (P.L. 94-553), particularly Sections 107 and 108, and the provisions of the Guidelines drafted by the National Commission on New Technological Uses of Copyrighted Works (CONTU). Guideline #4 states:

> The requesting entity shall maintain records of all requests made by it for copies or phonorecords of any materials to which these guidelines apply and shall maintain records of the fulfillment of such requests, which records shall be retained until the end of the third complete calendar year after the end of the calendar year in which the respective request shall have been made.

Most libraries already keep some kind of record of *all* interlibrary loan requests. That record should continue. However, it must be supplemented by the kind of record described below *for certain kinds of requests.* (See Subsection 108(d) of the law and CONTU Guideline #1)

1. *Form of Record.*

   It is recommended that records for periodicals be kept by title. Two possibilities seem workable: 1) a copy of the ALA Request for Loan or Photocopy form, a copy of the teletype request, etc. could be kept; or 2) a card could be set up for each title requested containing essential information including whatever is necessary to link this card to the library's file of request forms.

   N.B.: A library may choose one of these methods or develop its own. Whatever is done it is essential that the library keep a file of requests for these materials, that the file be accessible by title and that the date of the request be noted.

2. *Creation of Record.*
   a. For periodical material: Beginning on January 1, 1978, when a request is made for a copy of an article or articles published in a copyrighted periodical *within five years prior to the date of the request,* the library will either: a) set up a card for the title of that periodical or b) enter a copy of the request form in a file of forms arranged by title. If a card is set up it should include the date of the request and either the name of the requester or the requester's order number so that reference may be made to the complete form if necessary. All later requests for the same periodical title will be recorded in like manner.
   b. For material in any other copyrighted work: Beginning on January 1, 1978, when a request is made for a contribution to a collection or for a small part of any copyrighted work, the library will follow procedures based on those described above. The record may be kept by title or main entry.
3. *Use of Record.*
   a. Making requests: Before requesting a photocopy, the record will be checked. If a library is using the card system and no card exists, one will be created. If a card does exist, and the number of previous requests filled complies with the CONTU Guidelines, the date and name of requester will be entered. If a library is using the copy system and the number of previous requests complies with the CONTU Guidelines, the request will be made and a copy filed.
   b. Receiving material: When a request is filled, this will be noted on the card or copy. If a request is not filled, a line will be drawn through the entry on the card or the copy will be marked "not filled."

4. *Contingencies.*
   When a request is made for loan of material rather than a copy, but the supplying library sends a photocopy, a record will be made either by marking on a card or by filing a copy of the form, at the time when the material is *received.*
5. *Retention of Records.*
   a. Items in this file of cards or copies of forms must be kept until the end of the third complete calendar year after the end of the calendar year in which a request shall have been made. Thus, for a request made on any date in 1978, the record must be retained until 31 December 1981.
   b. If a library uses the card method, copies of the form on which an interlibrary loan has been requested must also be kept, in whatever order the library wishes, until the end of the third complete calendar year after the end of the calendar year in which a request is made.
   c. Information contained in the records should be summarized before records are destroyed. The summary may be useful for the five-year review mandated by Subsection 108(i) of the copyright law as well as for internal management purposes. Suggestions for the form of the five-year review summary will be made at a later time.

American Library Association
Reference and Adult Services Division
Interlibrary Loan Committee
September, 1977

AMERICAN LIBRARY ASSOCIATION

Guidelines for Seeking or Making a Copy of an Entire Copyrighted Work for a Library, Archives, or User

A library or archives which wishes to make a single photocopy or sound recording copy of a published copyrighted work for a user or to replace a copy or phonorecord in its collection which is damaged, deteriorating, lost, or stolen, must first make a reasonable effort to obtain a copy in its original form at a fair price, in accordance with Subsections 108(c) and 108(e) of Public Law 94-553, the 1976 omnibus copyright revision act.

"Reasonable Effort"

A reasonable effort requires that the library or archives take the following steps:

1. Attempt to determine whether the work is in print by consulting commonly-known trade bibliographic sources, e.g., *Publishers' Trade List Annual, Books in Print* for printed books, *Schwann Catalog, Phonolog* for phonorecords.
2. If the work is in print, attempt to acquire it from a library wholesaler or retail outlet, or from the publisher of the work.

3. If the work is out of print and unavailable in its original form from these sources, attempt to acquire the work or a photocopy or sound recording copy from the publisher or other copyright owner (if such owner can be located readily at the address listed in the copyright registration) or from an authorized reproducing service.
4. If the publisher, other copyright owner, or authorized reproducing service is unable or unwilling to supply a copy of the work, or if the requesting library receives no reply to its request within thirty days of the date it is sent, then it may place an order for a photocopy or sound recording copy with a library or archives which has a copy. The "Revised Interlibrary Loan Form," which has been prepared by the ALA-RASD Interlibrary Loan Committee, may be used for this purpose, in which case the appropriate box on the form should be checked, to indicate that all of the above-mentioned steps have been taken. An order form used in its stead should also indicate compliance with these guidelines.

"Fair Price"

1. *Original format*
   In order to meet the requirement of fair price, an unused copy of a published copyrighted work should be available at a price as close as possible to the latest suggested retail price.
2. *Reproductions* (photocopy, microform, sound recording copy)
   To meet the requirement of fair price, a reproduction of a copyrighted work should be available on a timely basis (within thirty days) at a price which is as close as possible to actual manufacturing costs plus royalty payments.

The requesting library or archives shall maintain records on all requests it has made for photocopies or sound recording copies to which these guidelines apply, together with records of the fulfillment of these requests, which records shall be retained until the end of the third complete calendar year after the end of the calendar year in which the respective request shall have been made.

Authorized Reproducing Services

The House Judiciary Committee Report on the New Copyright Law (H. Rept. 94-1476) in discussing Subsections 108(c) and 108(e) of the copyright law, specifies that a reasonable investigation to determine that an unused replacement or copy cannot be obtained at a fair price will, in the normal situation, involve recourse to the publisher or other copyright owner, or an authorized reproducing service.

The RTSD [Resources and Technical Services Division of the American Library Association] Copyright Revision Act Committee has prepared a set of criteria which authorized reproducing services should meet in providing adequate services to the library community.

Publishers, other copyright owners, and authorized reproducing services which receive requests for photocopies or sound recording copies should all be required to meet the following conditions:

1. The copy supplied should be of sufficiently good quality to meet the needs of the user, or of as good quality as that which the requesting library or archives could ordinarily expect to receive from any supplier.
2. The copy should be supplied, or notification given to the requestor that such copy cannot be supplied, within thirty days of the date of receipt of the request.
3. The price of the copy should be as close as possible to actual manufacturing costs plus royalty payments.

If any of these conditions are not met, the requestor may be considered to have complied with the provisions of Subsections 108(c) and 108(e) of PL 94-553 and may order a photocopy or sound recording of a work from a library or archives which possesses one without further authorization.

While authorized reproducing services should be required to meet the same criteria of quality, service and price as publishers and other copyright owners, there is a great need for better bibliographic information about what titles are available from such reproducing services. This could be done in the following way:

1. Publishers should include in their catalogs in *PTLA* a list of titles which are available from reproducing services and their prices, together with the names and addresses of these services.
2. *Books in Print* should include these titles in their regular listing, together with the names of the reproducing services, or they could have a separate listing of these titles.

Prepared by Implementation of the Copyright Revision Act Committee
Resources and Technical Services Division
American Library Association

SOCIETY OF AMERICAN ARCHIVISTS

Statement on the Reproduction of Manuscripts and Archives for Reference Use

1. It is the responsibility of a library, archives, or manuscript repository to assist researchers by making or having made reproductions of any material in its possession, for research purposes, subject to certain conditions. Manuscript and archival materials may be reproduced if: (a) The condition of the originals will permit such reproduction. (b) The originals have no gift, purchase, or legal restrictions on reproduction.

2. In the interest of making research collections more generally available, the orderly microfilming of archives and entire manuscript collections, together with appropriate guides, is to be encouraged, within the available resources of the repository.

3. The price of reproductions shall be set by the repository, which should endeavor to keep charges to a minimum.

4. Copies should be made for reference use as follows: (a) Repositories which permit their manuscript and archival holdings to be reproduced in whole or in part must specify before the copies are made what restrictions, if any, have been placed on the use or further reproduction of copies. (b) Repositories may require that purchasers agree in writing to abide by any restrictions. (c) All reproductions should identify the source of the original manuscript collection or archival record group.

5. The repository should inform the researcher: (a) When and under what conditions permission to make extensive direct quotation from or to print in full any reproduction must be obtained from the institution owning the originals. (b) That in the case of material under copyright, the right to quote or print, beyond fair use, must also be obtained by the researcher from the copyright owner. (c) That the researcher assumes legal responsibility for observing common law literary rights, property rights, and libel laws. (d) Of known retention of literary rights.

6. A repository may decline to furnish reproductions when fulfilling mail requests requires subjective criteria for selection of material to be duplicated or the commitment of an unreasonable amount of staff time for extended research to identify the material.

7. In cases when researchers request the reproduction of large amounts of material which they have identified in the course of their research, the repository may prescribe a preferred method of copying (i.e., microfilm vs. xerox) and may provide for a reasonable time period in which to produce the copies.

Prepared by the Society of American Archivists Committee on Reference and Access Policies and approved by the Council of the Society in April, 1976. Copyright, 1976, Society of American Archivists; reprinted by permission of the Society.

LAW

§ 109. Limitations on exclusive rights: Effect of transfer of particular copy or phonorecord

(a) Notwithstanding the provisions of section 106(3), the owner of a particular copy or phonorecord lawfully made under this title, or any person authorized by such owner, is entitled, without the authority of the copyright owner, to sell or otherwise dispose of the possession of that copy or phonorecord.

(b) Notwithstanding the provisions of section 106(5), the owner of a particular copy lawfully made under this title, or any person authorized by such owner, is entitled, without the authority of the copyright owner, to display that copy publicly, either directly or by the projection of no more than one image at a time, to viewers present at the place where the copy is located.

(c) The privileges prescribed by subsections (a) and (b) do not, unless authorized by the coyright owner, extend to any person who has acquired possession of the copy or phonorecord from the copyright owner, by rental, lease, loan, or otherwise, without acquiring ownership of it.

HOUSE REPORT

Effect on further disposition of copy or phonorecord

Section 109(a) restates and confirms the principle that, where the copyright owner has transferred ownership of a particular copy or phonorecord of a work, the person to whom the copy or phonorecord is transferred is entitled to dispose of it by sale, rental, or any other means. Under this principle, which has been established by the court decisions and section 27 of the present law, the copyright owner's exclusive right of public distribution would have no effect upon anyone who owns "a particular copy or phonorecord lawfully made under this title" and who wishes to transfer it to someone else or to destroy it.

Thus, for example, the outright sale of an authorized copy of a book frees it from any copyright control over its resale price or other conditions of its future disposition. A library that has acquired ownership of a copy is entitled to lend it under any conditions it chooses to impose. This does not mean that conditions on future disposition of copies or phonorecords, imposed by a contract between their buyer and seller, would be unenforceable between the parties as a breach of contract, but it does mean that they could not be enforced by an action for infringement of copyright. Under section 202 however, the owner of the physical copy or phonorecord cannot reproduce or perform the copyrighted work publicly without the copyright owner's consent.

To come within the scope of section 109(a), a copy or phonorecord must have been "lawfully made under this title," though not necessarily with the copyright owner's authorization. For example, any resale of an illegally "pirated" phonorecord would be an infringement, but the disposition of a phonorecord legally made under the compulsory licensing provisions of section 115 would not.

Effect on display of copy

Subsection (b) of section 109 deals with the scope of the copyright owner's exclusive right to control the public display of a particular "copy" of a work (including the original or prototype copy in which the work was first fixed). Assuming, for example, that a painter has sold the only copy of an original work of art without restrictions, would it be possible for him to restrain the new owner from displaying it publicly in galleries, shop windows, on a projector, or on television?

Section 109(b) adopts the general principle that the lawful owner of a copy of a work should be able to put his copy on public display without the consent of the copyright owner. As in cases arising under section 109(a), this does not mean that contractual restrictions on display between a buyer and seller would be unenforceable as a matter of contract law.

The last sentence does not appear in the SENATE REPORT.

The exclusive right of public display granted by section 106(5) would not apply where the owner of a copy wishes to show it directly to the public, as in a gallery or display case, or indirectly, as through an opaque projector. Where the copy itself is intended for projection, as in the case of a photographic slide, negative, or transparency, the public projection of a single image would be permitted as long as the viewers are "present at the place where the copy is located."

The following paragraph does not appear in the SENATE REPORT.

On the other hand, section 109(b) takes account of the potentialities of the new communications media, notably television, cable and optical transmission devices, and information storage and retrieval devices, for replacing printed copies with visual images. First of all, the public display of an image of a copyrighted work would not be exempted from copyright control if the copy from which the image was derived were outside the presence of the viewers. In other words, the display of a visual image of a copyrighted work would be an infringement if the image were transmitted by any method (by closed or open circuit television, for example, or by a computer system) from one place to members of the public located elsewhere.

Moreover, the exemption would extend only to public displays that are made "either directly or by the projection of no more than one image at a time." Thus, even where the copy and the viewers are located at the same place, the simultaneous projection of multiple images of the work would not be exempted. For example, where each person in a lecture hall is supplied with a separate viewing apparatus, the copyright owner's permission would generally be required in order to project an image of a work on each individual screen at the same time.

The committee's intention is to preserve the traditional privilege of the owner of a copy to display it directly, but to place reasonable restrictions on the ability to display it indirectly in such a way that the copyright owner's market for reproduction and distribution of copies would be affected. Unless it constitutes a fair use under section 107, or unless one of the special provisions of section 110 or 111 is applicable, projection of more than one image at a time, or transmission of an image to the public over television or other communication channels, would be an infringement for the same reasons that reproduction in copies would be. The concept of "the place where the copy is located" is generally intended to refer to a situation in which the viewers are present in the same physical surroundings as the copy, even though they cannot see the copy directly.

The last sentence does not appear in the SENATE REPORT.

Effect of mere possession of copy or phonorecord

Subsection (c) of section 109 qualifies the privileges specified in subsections (a) and (b) by making clear that they do not apply to someone who merely possesses a copy or phonorecord without having acquired ownership of it. Acquisition of an object embodying a copyrighted work by rental, lease, loan, or bailment carries with it no privilege to dispose of the copy under section 109(a) or to display it publicly under section 109(b). To cite a familiar example, a person who has rented a print of a motion picture from the copyright owner would have no right to rent it to someone else without the owner's permission.

In the preceding sentence, the SENATE REPORT uses the phrase "modern picture" instead of "motion picture."

The following paragraph does not appear in the SENATE REPORT.

Burden of proof in infringement actions

During the course of its deliberations on this section, the Committee's attention was directed to a recent court decision holding that the plaintiff in an infringement action had the burden of establishing that the allegedly infringing copies in the defendant's possession were not lawfully made or acquired under section 27 of the present law. *American International Pictures, Inc.* v. *Foreman*, 400 F. Supp. 928 (S.D. Alabama 1975). The Committee believes that the court's decision, if followed, would place a virtually impossible burden on copyright owners. The decision is also inconsistent with the established legal principle that the burden of proof should not be placed upon a litigant to establish facts particularly within the knowledge of his adversary. The defendant in such actions clearly has the particular knowledge of how possession of the particular copy was acquired, and should have the burden of providing this evidence to the court. It is the intent of the Committee, therefore, that in an action to determine whether a defendant is entitled to the privilege established by section 109 (a) and (b), the burden of proving whether a particular copy was lawfully made or acquired should rest on the defendant.

LAW

§ 110. Limitations on exclusive rights: Exemption of certain performances and displays

Notwithstanding the provisions of section 106, the following are not infringements of copyright:

(1) performance or display of a work by instructors or pupils in the course of face-to-face teaching activities of a nonprofit educational institution, in a classroom or similar place devoted to instruction, unless, in the case of a motion picture or other audiovisual work, the performance, or the display of individual images, is given by means of a copy that was not lawfully made under this title, and that the person responsible for the performance knew or had reason to believe was not lawfully made;

(2) performance of a nondramatic literary or musical work or display of a work, by or in the course of a transmission, if—

(A) the performance or display is a regular part of the systematic instructional activities of a governmental body or a nonprofit educational institution; and

(B) the performance or display is directly related and of material assistance to the teaching content of the transmission; and

(C) the transmission is made primarily for—

(i) reception in classrooms or similar places normally devoted to instruction, or

(ii) reception by persons to whom the transmission is directed because their disabilities or other special circumstances prevent their attendance in classrooms or similar places normally devoted to instruction, or

(iii) reception by officers or employees of governmental bodies as a part of their official duties or employment;

(3) performance of a nondramatic literary or musical work or of a dramatico-musical work of a religious nature, or display of a work, in the course of services at a place of worship or other religious assembly;

(4) performance of a nondramatic literary or musical work otherwise than in a transmission to the public, without any purpose of direct or indirect commercial advantage and without

payment of any fee or other compensation for the performance to any of its performers, promoters, or organizers, if—

(A) there is no direct or indirect admission charge; or

(B) the proceeds, after deducting the reasonable costs of producing the performance, are used exclusively for educational, religious, or charitable purposes and not for private financial gain, except where the copyright owner has served notice of objection to the performance under the following conditions;

(i) the notice shall be in writing and signed by the copyright owner or such owner's duly authorized agent; and

(ii) the notice shall be served on the person responsible for the performance at least seven days before the date of the performance, and shall state the reasons for the objection; and

(iii) the notice shall comply, in form, content, and manner of service, with requirements that the Register of Copyrights shall prescribe by regulation;

(5) communication of a transmission embodying a performance or display of a work by the public reception of the transmission on a single receiving apparatus of a kind commonly used in private homes, unless—

(A) a direct charge is made to see or hear the transmission; or

(B) the transmission thus received is further transmitted to the public;

(6) performance of a nondramatic musical work by a governmental body or a nonprofit agricultural or horticultural organization, in the course of an annual agricultural or horticultural fair or exhibition conducted by such body or organization; the exemption provided by this clause shall extend to any liability for copyright infringement that would otherwise be imposed on such body or organization, under doctrines of vicarious liability or related infringement, for a performance by a concessionnaire, business establishment, or other person at such fair or exhibition, but shall not excuse any such person from liability for the performance;

(7) performance of a nondramatic musical work by a vending establishment open to the public at large without any direct or indirect admission charge, where the sole purpose of the performance is to promote the retail sale of copies or phonorecords of the work, and the performance is not transmitted beyond the place where the establishment is located and is within the immediate area where the sale is occurring;

(8) performance of a nondramatic literary work, by or in the course of a transmission specifically designed for and primarily directed to blind or other handicapped persons who are unable to read normal printed material as a result of their handicap, or deaf or other handicapped persons who are unable to hear the aural signals accompanying a transmission of visual signals, if the performance is made without any purpose of direct or indirect commercial advantage and its transmission is made through the facilities of: (i) a governmental body; or (ii) a noncommercial educational broadcast station (as defined in section 397 of title 47); or (iii) a radio subcarrier authorization (as defined in 47 CFR 73.293–73.295 and 73.593–73.595); or (iv) a cable system (as defined in section 111(f)).

(9) performance on a single occasion of a dramatic literary work published at least ten years before the date of the performance, by or in the course of a transmission specifically designed for and primarily directed to blind or other handicapped persons who are unable to read normal printed material as a result of their handicap, if the performance is made without any purpose of direct or indirect commercial advantage and its transmission is made through the facilities of a radio subcarrier authorization referred to in clause (8)(iii), *Provided*, That the provisions of this clause shall not be applicable to more than one performance of the same work by the same performers or under the auspices of the same organization.

HOUSE REPORT

Clauses (1) through (4) of section 110 deal with performances and exhibitions that are now generally exempt under the "for profit" limitation or other provisions of the copyright law, and that are specifically exempted from copyright liability under this legislation. Clauses (1) and (2) between them are intended to cover all of the various methods by which performances or displays in the course of systematic instruction take place.

Face-to-face teaching activities

Clause (1) of section 110 is generally intended to set out the conditions under which performances or displays, in the course of instructional activities other than educational broadcasting, are to be exempted from copyright control. The clause covers all types of copyrighted works, and exempts their performance or display "by instructors or pupils in the course of face-to-face teaching activities of a nonprofit educational institution," where the activities take place "in a classroom or similar place devoted to instruction."

There appears to be no need for a statutory definition of "face-to-face" teaching activities to clarify the scope of the provision. "Face-to-face teaching activities" under clause (1) embrace instructional performances and displays that are not "transmitted." The concept does not require that the teacher and students be able to see each other, although it does require their simultaneous presence in the same general place. Use of the phrase "in the course of face-to-face teaching activities" is intended to exclude broadcasting or other transmissions from an outside location into classrooms, whether radio or television and whether open or closed circuit. However, as long as the instructor and pupils are in the same building or general area, the exemption would extend to the use of devices for amplifying or reproducing sound and for projecting visual images. The "teaching activities" exempted by the clause encompass systematic instruction of a very wide variety of subjects, but they do not include performances or displays, whatever their cultural value or intellectual appeal, that are given for the recreation or entertainment of any part of their audience.

Works affected.—Since there is no limitation on the types of works covered by the exemption, teachers or students would be free to perform or display anything in class as long as the other conditions of the clause are met. They could read aloud from copyrighted text material, act out a drama, play or sing a musical work, perform a motion picture or filmstrip, or display text or pictorial material to the class by means of a projector. However, nothing in this provision is intended to sanction the unauthorized reproduction of copies or phonorecords for the purpose of classroom performance or display, and the clause contains a special exception dealing with performances from unlawfully made copies of motion pictures and other audiovisual works, to be discussed below.

Instructors or pupils.—To come within clause (1), the performance or display must be "by instructors or pupils," thus ruling out performances by actors, singers, or instrumentalists brought in from outside the school to put on a program. However, the term "instructors" would be broad enough to include guest lecturers if their instructional activities remain confined to classroom situations. In general, the term "pupils" refers to the enrolled members of a class.

Nonprofit educational institution.—Clause (1) makes clear that it applies only to the teaching activities "of a nonprofit educational institution," thus excluding from the exemption performances or displays in profit-making institutions such as dance studios and language schools.

Classroom or similar place.—The teaching activities exempted by the clause must take place "in a classroom or similar place devoted to instruction." For example, performances in an auditorium or stadium during a school assembly, graduation ceremony, class play, or sporting event, where the audience is not confined to the members of a particular class, would fall outside the scope of clause (1), although in some cases they might be exempted by clause (4) of section 110. The "similar place" referred to in clause (1) is a place which is "devoted to instruction" in the same way a classroom is; common examples would include a studio, a workshop, a gymnasium, a training field, a library, the stage of an auditorium, or the auditorium itself, if it is actually used as a classroom for systematic instructional activities.

Motion pictures and other audiovisual works.—The final provision of clause (1) deals with the special problem of performances from unlawfully-made copies of motion pictures and other audiovisual works. The exemption is lost where the copy being used for a classroom performance was "not lawfully made under this title" and the person responsible for the performance knew or had reason to suspect as much. This special exception to the exemption would not apply to performances from lawfully-made copies, even if the copies were acquired from someone who had stolen or converted them, or if the performances were in violation of an agreement. However, though the performance would be exempt under section 110(1) in such cases, the copyright owner might have a cause of action against the unauthorized distributor under section 106(3), or against the person responsible for the performance, for breach of contract.

Projection devices.—As long as there is no transmission beyond the place where the copy is located, both section 109(b) and section 110(1) would permit the classroom display of a work by means of any sort of projection device or process.

Instructional broadcasting

Works affected.—The exemption for instructional broadcasting provided by section 110(2) would apply only to "performance of a nondramatic literary or musical work or display of a work." Thus, the copyright owner's permission would be required for the performance on educational television or radio of a dramatic work, of a dramatico-musical work such as an opera or musical comedy, or of a motion picture. Since, as already explained, audiovisual works such as filmstrips are equated with motion pictures, their sequential showing would be regarded as a performance rather than a display and would not be exempt under section 110(2). The clause is not intended to limit in any way the copyright owner's exclusive right to make dramatizations, adaptations, or other derivative works under section 106(2). Thus, for example, a performer could read a nondramatic literary work aloud under section 110(2), but the copyright owner's permission would be required for him to act it out in dramatic form.

Systematic instructional activities.—Under section 110(2) a transmission must meet three specified conditions in order to be exempted from copyright liability. The first of these, as provided by subclause (A), is that the performance or display must be "a regular part of the systematic instructional activities of a governmental body or a nonprofit educational institution." The concept of "systematic instructional activities" is intended as the general equivalent of "curriculums," but it could be broader in a case such as that of an institution using systematic teaching methods not related to specific course work. A transmission would be a regular part of these activities if it is in accordance with the pattern of teaching established by the governmental body or institution. The use of commercial facilities, such as those of a cable service, to transmit the performance or display, would not affect the exemption as long as the actual performance or display was for nonprofit purposes.

Content of transmission.—Subclause (B) requires that the performance or display be directly related and of material assistance to the teaching content of the transmission.

Intended recipients.—Subclause (C) requires that the transmission is made primarily for:

(*i*) Reception in classrooms or similar places normally devoted to instruction, or

(*ii*) Reception by persons to whom the transmission is directed because their disabilities or other special circumstances prevent their attendance in classrooms or similar places normally devoted to instruction, or

(*iii*) Reception by officers or employees of governmental bodies as a part of their official duties or employment.

In all three cases, the instructional transmission need only be made "primarily" rather than "solely" to the specified recipients to be exempt. Thus, the transmission could still be exempt even though it is capable of reception by the public at large. Conversely, it would not be regarded as made "primarily" for one of the required groups of recipients if the principal purpose behind the transmission is reception by the public at large, even if it is cast in the form of instruction and is also received in classrooms. Factors to consider in determining the "primary" purpose of a program would include its subject matter, content, and the time of its transmission.

Paragraph (i) of subclause (C) generally covers what are known as "in-school" broadcasts, whether open- or closed-circuit. The reference to "classrooms or similar places" here is intended to have the same meaning as that of the phrase as used in section 110(1). The exemption in paragraph (ii) is intended to exempt transmissions providing systematic instuction to individuals who cannot be reached in classrooms because of "their disabilities or other special circumstances." Accordingly, the exemption is confined to instructional broadcasting that is an adjunct to the actual classwork of nonprofit schools or is primarily for people who cannot be brought together in classrooms such as preschool children, displaced workers, illiterates, and shut-ins.

There has been some question as to whether or not the language in this section of the bill is intended to include instructional television college credit courses. These telecourses are aimed at undergraduate and graduate students in earnest pursuit of higher educational degrees who are unable to attend daytime classes because of daytime employment, distance from campus, or some other intervening reason. So long as these broadcasts are aimed at regularly enrolled students and conducted by recognized higher educational institutions, the committee believes that they are clearly within the language of section 110 (2(C)(ii). Like night school and correspondence courses before them, these telecourses are fast becoming a valuable adjunct of the normal college curriculum.

The third exemption in subclause (C) is intended to permit the use of copyrighted material, in accordance with the other conditions of section 110(2), in the course of instructional transmissions for Government personnel who are receiving training "as a part of their official duties or employment."

Religious services

[This section has been omitted to save space.]

Certain other nonprofit performances

In addition to the educational and religious exemptions provided by clauses (1) through (3) of section 110, clause (4) contains a general exception to the exclusive right of public performance that would cover some, though not all, of the same ground as the present "for profit" limitation.

Scope of exemption.—The exemption in clause (4) applies to the same general activities and subject matter as those covered by the "for profit" limitation today: public performances of nondramatic literary and musical works. However, the exemption would be limited to public performances given directly in the presence of an audience whether by means of living performers, the playing of phonorecords, or the operation of a receiving apparatus, and would not include a "transmission to the public." Unlike the clauses (1) through (3) and (5) of section 110, but like clauses (6) through (8), clause (4) applies only to performing rights in certain works, and does not affect the exclusive right to display a work in public.

SENATE REPORT

The last sentence in the above paragraph reads:

Unlike the other clauses of section 110, clause (4) applies only to performing rights in certain works and does not affect the exclusive right to display a work in public.

HOUSE REPORT (Continued)

No profit motive.—In addition to the other conditions specified by the clause, the performance must be "without any purpose of direct or indirect commercial advantage." This provision expressly adopts the principle established by the court decisions construing the "for profit" limitation: that public performances given or sponsored in connection with any commercial or profit-making enterprises are subject to the exclusive rights of the copyright owner even though the public is not charged for seeing or hearing the performance.

No payment for performance.—An important condition for this exemption is that the performance be given "without payment of any fee or other compensation for the performance to any of its performers, promoters, or organizers." The basic purpose of this requirement is to prevent the free use of copyrighted material under the guise of charity where fees or percentatges are paid to performers, promoters, producers, and the like. However, the exemption would not be lost if the performers, directors, or producers of the performance, instead of being paid directly "for the performance," are paid a salary for duties encompassing the performance. Examples are performances by a school orchestra conducted by a music teacher who receives an annual salary, or by a service band whose members and conductors perform as part of their assigned duties and who receive military pay. The committee believes that performances of this type should be exempt, assuming the other conditions in clause (4) are met, and has not adopted the suggestion that the word "salary" be added to the phrase referring to the "payment of any fee or other compensation."

Admission charge.—Assuming that the performance involves no profit motive and no one responsible for it gets paid a fee, it must still meet one of two alternative conditions to be exempt. As specified in subclauses (A) and (B) of section 110(4), these conditions are: (1) that no direct or indirect admission charge is made, or (2) that the net proceeds are "used exclusively for educational, religious, or charitable purposes and not for private financial gain."

Under the second of these conditions, a performance meeting the other conditions of clause (4) would be exempt even if an admission fee is charged, provided any amounts left "after deducting the reasonable costs of producing the performance" are used solely for bona fide educational, religious, or charitable purposes.

The remaining text of Section 110 of the HOUSE REPORT did not appear in the SENATE REPORT:

In cases arising under this second condition and as provided in subclause (B), where there is an admission charge, the copyright owner is given an opportunity to decide whether and under what conditions the copyrighted work should be performed; otherwise, owners could be compelled to make involuntary donations to the fund-raising activities of causes to which they are opposed. The subclause would thus permit copyright owners to prevent public performances of their works under section 110(4)(B) by serving notice of objection, with the reasons therefor, at least seven days in advance.

Mere reception in public

Unlike the first four clauses of section 110, clause (5) is not to any extent a counterpart of the "for profit" limitation of the present statute. It applies to performances and displays of all types of works, and its purpose is to exempt from copyright liability anyone who merely turns on, in a public place, an ordinary radio or television receiving apparatus of a kind commonly sold to members of the public for private use.

The basic rationale of this clause is that the secondary use of the transmission by turning on an ordinary receiver in public is so remote and minimal that no further liability should be imposed. In the vast majority of these cases no royalties are collected today, and the exemption should be made explicit in the statute. This clause has nothing to do with cable television systems and the exemptions would be denied in any case where the audience is charged directly to see or hear the transmission.

On June 17, 1975, the Supreme Court handed down a decision in *Twentieth Century Music Corp.* v. *Aiken*, 95 S.Ct. 2040, that raised fundamental questions about the proper interpretation of section 110(5). The defendant, owner and operator of a fast-service food shop in downtown Pittsburgh, had "a radio with outlets to four speakers in the ceiling," which he apparently turned on and left on throughout the business day. Lacking any performing license, he was sued for copyright infringement by two ASCAP members. He lost in the District Court, won a reversal in the Third Circuit Court of Appeals, and finally prevailed, by a margin of 7–2, in the Supreme Court.

The *Aiken* decision is based squarely on the two Supreme Court decisions dealing with cable television. In *Fortnightly Corp.* v. *United Artists*, 392 U.S. 390, and again in *Teleprompter Corp.* v. *CBS*, 415 U.S. 394, the Supreme Court has held that a CATV operator was not "performing" within the meaning of the 1909 statute, when it picked up broadcast signals off the air and retransmitted them to subscribers by cable. The *Aiken* decision extends this interpretation of the scope of the 1909 statute's right of "public performance for profit" to a situation outside the CATV context and, without expressly overruling the decision in *Buck* v. *Jewell-LaSalle Realty Co.*, 283 U.S. 191 (1931), effectively deprives it of much meaning under the present law. For more than forty years the *Jewell-LaSalle* rule was thought to require a business establishment to obtain copyright licenses before it could legally pick up any broadcasts off the air and retransmit them to its guests and patrons. As reinterpreted by the *Aiken* decision, the rule of *Jewell-LaSalle* applies only if the broadcast being retransmitted was itself unlicensed.

The majority of the Supreme Court in the *Aiken* case based its decision on a narrow construction of the word "perform" in the 1909 statute. This basis for the decision is completely overturned by the present bill and its broad definition of "perform" in section 101. The Committee has adopted the language of section 110(5), with an amendment expressly denying the exemption in situations where "the performance or display is further transmitted beyond the place where the receiving apparatus is located"; in doing so, it accepts the traditional, pre-*Aiken*, interpretation of the *Jewell-LaSalle* decision, under which public communication by means other than a home receiving set, or further transmission of a broadcast to the public, is considered an infringing act.

Under the particular fact situation in the *Aiken* case, assuming a small commercial establishment and the use of a home receiver with four ordinary loudspeakers grouped within a relatively narrow circumference from the set, it is intended that the performances would be exempt under clause (5). However, the Committee considers this fact situation to represent the outer limit of the exemption, and believes that the line should be drawn at that point. Thus, the clause would exempt small commercial establishments whose proprietors merely bring onto their premises standard radio or television equipment and turn it on for their customers' enjoyment, but it would impose liability where the proprietor has a commercial "sound system" installed or converts a standard home receiving apparatus (by agumenting it with sophisticated or extensive amplification equipment) into the equivalent of a commercial sound system. Factors to consider in particular cases would include the size, physical arrangement, and noise level of the areas within the establishment where the transmissions are made audible or visible, and the extent to which the receiving apparatus is altered or augmented for the purpose of improving the aural or visual quality of the performance for individual members of the public using those areas.

Agricultural fairs

[This section was omitted to save space.]

Retail sale of phonorecords

[This section applies only to the playing of phonograph records at retail record shops. It was omitted to save space.]

Transmission to handicapped audiences

The new clause (8) of subsection 110, which had been added to S. 22 by the Senate Judiciary Committee when it reported the bill on November 20, 1975, and had been adopted by the Senate on February 19, 1976, was substantially amended by the Committee. Under the amendment, the exemption would apply only to performances of "nondramatic literary works" by means of "a transmission specifically designed for and primarily directed to" one or the other of two defined classes of handicapped persons: (1) "blind or other handicapped persons who are unable to read normal printed material as a result of their handicap" or (2) "deaf or other handicapped persons who are unable to hear the aural signals accompanying a transmission." Moreover, the exemption would be applicable only if the performance is "without any purpose of direct or indirect commercial advantage," and if the transmission takes place through government facilities or through the facilities of a noncommercial educational broadcast station, a radio subcarrier authorization (SCA), or a cable system.

CONFERENCE REPORT

LIMITATIONS ON RIGHTS OF PERFORMANCE AND DISPLAY

Senate bill

Section 110 of the Senate bill set forth eight specific exceptions to the exclusive rights to perform and display copyrighted works. The first four exceptions were roughly the equivalent of the "for profit" limitations on performing rights under the present law. Section 110(5) provided an exemption for public communication of a transmission received on an ordinary receiving set unless a direct charge is made or the transmission "is further transmitted to the public." Section 110(6) exempted performances of nondramatic music at nonprofit annual agricultural or horticultural fairs, and section 110(7) dealt with performances in connection with the retail sale of copies or records of musical works. Clause (8) of section 110 provided an exemption for performances of literary works "in the course of a broadcast service specifically designed for broadcast on noncommercial educational radio and television stations to a print or aural handicapped audience," but did not contain, in section 112 or elsewhere, a provision allowing the making of copies or phonorecords for the purpose of such broadcasts to the blind or deaf.

House bill

The House bill amended the last four clauses of section 110. With respect to clause (5), it made the exemption inapplicable to cases where there is a further transmission "beyond the place where the receiving apparatus is located." Clause (6) was amended to make the exemption applicable only to the governmental body or nonprofit organization sponsoring the fair, and the amendment of clause (7) was merely for purposes of clarification. The House bill amended clause (8) by limiting its application to nondramatic literary works, by clarifying the audiences to which the transmissions are directed, and by more narrowly defining the types of nonprofit transmissions within the exemptions. The House bill also added a new subsection (d) to section 112 to permit the making of ten recordings of performances exempted under section 110(8), their retention for an unlimited period, and their exchange with other nonprofit organizations.

Conference substitute

The conference substitute adopts the House amendments of clauses (6), (7), and (8) of section 110, and of section 112. It adds a new clause (9) to section 110 exempting nonprofit performances of dramatic works transmitted to audiences of the blind by radio subcarrier authorization, but only for a single performance of a dramatic work published at least ten years earlier.

With respect to section 110(5), the conference substitute conforms to the language in the Senate bill. It is the intent of the conferees that a small commercial establishment of the type involved in *Twentieth Century Music Corp.* v. *Aiken*, 422 U.S. 151 (1975), which merely augmented a home-type receiver and which was not of sufficient size to justify, as a practical matter, a subscription to a commercial background music service, would be exempt. However, where the public communication was by means of something other than a home-type receiving apparatus, or where the establishment actually makes a further transmission to the public, the exemption would not apply.

COPYRIGHT OFFICE

Section 110(4)(B) of the LAW permits the owner of a copyrighted nondramatic literary or musical work to serve notice that the work(s) may not be used in a benefit performance. The provisions for giving such a notice appear in Copyright Office Regulation 201.13. The regulation also appears in the Federal Register, Vol. 42, No. 249 (December 28, 1977), pp. 64682-64684. It has not been reproduced here because of its length.

LAW

§ 111. Limitations on exclusive rights: Secondary transmissions

(a) CERTAIN SECONDARY TRANSMISSIONS EXEMPTED.—The secondary transmission of a primary transmission embodying a performance or display of a work is not an infringement of copyright if—

(1) the secondary transmission is not made by a cable system, and consists entirely of the relaying, by the management of a hotel, apartment house, or similar establishment, of signals transmitted by a broadcast station licensed by the Federal Communications Commission, within the local service area of such station, to the private lodgings of guests or residents of such establishment, and no direct charge is made to see or hear the secondary transmission; or

(2) the secondary transmission is made solely for the purpose and under the conditions specified by clause (2) of section 110; or

(3) the secondary transmission is made by any carrier who has no direct or indirect control over the content or selection of the primary transmission or over the particular recipients of the secondary transmission, and whose activities with respect to the secondary transmission consist solely of providing wires, cables, or other communications channels for the use of others: *Provided*, That the provisions of this clause extend only to the activities of said carrier with respect to secondary transmissions and do not exempt from liability the activities of others with respect to their own primary or secondary transmissions; or

(4) the secondary transmission is not made by a cable system but is made by a governmental body, or other nonprofit organization, without any purpose of direct or indirect commercial advantage, and without charge to the recipients of the secondary transmission other than assessments necessary to defray the actual and reasonable costs of maintaining and operating the secondary transmission service.

(b) SECONDARY TRANSMISSION OF PRIMARY TRANSMISSION TO CONTROLLED GROUP.—Notwithstanding the provisions of subsections (a) and (c), the secondary transmission to the public of a primary transmission embodying a performance or display of a work is actionable as an act of infringement under section 501, and is fully subject to the remedies provided by sections 502 through 506 and 509, if the primary transmission is not made for reception by the public at large but is controlled and limited to reception by particular members of the public: *Provided*, however, That such secondary transmission is not actionable as an act of infringement if—

(1) the primary transmission is made by a broadcast station licensed by the Federal Communications Commission; and

(2) the carriage of the signals comprising the secondary transmission is required under the rules, regulations, or authorizations of the Federal Communications Commission; and

(3) the signal of the primary transmitter is not altered or changed in any way by the secondary transmitter.

(c) Secondary Transmissions by Cable Systems.—

(1) Subject to the provisions of clauses (2), (3), and (4) of this subsection, secondary transmissions to the public by a cable system of a primary transmission made by a broadcast station licensed by the Federal Communications Commission or by an appropriate governmental authority of Canada or Mexico and embodying a performance or display of a work shall be subject to compulsory licensing upon compliance with the requirements of subsection (d) where the carriage of the signals comprising the secondary transmission is permissible under the rules, regulations, or authorizations of the Federal Communications Commission.

(2) Notwithstanding the provisions of clause (1) of this subsection, the willful or repeated secondary transmission to the public by a cable system of a primary transmission made by a broadcast station licensed by the Federal Communications Commission or by an appropriate governmental authority of Canada or Mexico and embodying a performance or display of a work is actionable as an act of infringement under section 501, and is fully subject to the remedies provided by sections 502 through 506 and 509, in the following cases:

(A) where the carriage of the signals comprising the secondary transmission is not permissible under the rules, regulations, or authorizations of the Federal Communications Commission; or

(B) where the cable system has not recorded the notice specified by subsection (d) and deposited the statement of account and royalty fee required by subsection (d).

(3) Notwithstanding the provisions of clause (1) of this subsection and subject to the provisions of subsection (e) of this section, the secondary transmission to the public by a cable system of a primary transmission made by a broadcast station licensed by the Federal Communications Commission or by an appropriate governmental authority of Canada or Mexico and embodying a performance or display of a work is actionable as an act of infringement under section 501, and is fully subject to the remedies provided by sections 502 through 506 and sections 509 and 510, if the content of the particular program in which the performance or display is embodied, or any commercial advertising or station announcements transmitted by the primary transmitter during, or immediately before or after, the transmission of such program, is in any way willfully altered by the cable system through changes, deletions, or additions, except for the alteration, deletion, or substitution of commercial advertisements performed by those engaged in television commercial advertising market research: *Provided*, That the research company has obtained the prior consent of the advertiser who has purchased the original commercial advertisement, the television station broadcasting that commercial advertisement, and the cable system performing the secondary transmission: *And provided further*, That such commercial alteration, deletion, or substitution is not performed for the purpose of deriving income from the sale of that commercial time.

(4) Notwithstanding the provisions of clause (1) of this subsection, the secondary transmission to the public by a cable system of a primary transmission made by a broadcast station licensed by an appropriate governmental authority of Canada or

Mexico and embodying a performance or display of a work is actionable as an act of infringement under section 501, and is fully subject to the remedies provided by sections 502 through 506 and section 509, if (A) with respect to Canadian signals, the community of the cable system is located more than 150 miles from the United States-Canadian border and is also located south of the forty-second parallel of latitude, or (B) with respect to Mexican signals, the secondary transmission is made by a cable system which received the primary transmission by means other than direct interception of a free space radio wave emitted by such broadcast television station, unless prior to April 15, 1976, such cable system was actually carrying, or was specifically authorized to carry, the signal of such foreign station on the system pursuant to the rules, regulations, or authorizations of the Federal Communications Commission.

(d) COMPULSORY LICENSE FOR SECONDARY TRANSMISSIONS BY CABLE SYSTEMS.—

(1) For any secondary transmission to be subject to compulsory licensing under subsection (c), the cable system shall, at least one month before the date of the commencement of operations of the cable system or within one hundred and eighty days after the enactment of this Act, whichever is later, and thereafter within thirty days after each occasion on which the ownership or control or the signal carriage complement of the cable system changes, record in the Copyright Office a notice including a statement of the identity and address of the person who owns or operates the secondary transmission service or has power to exercise primary control over it, together with the name and location of the primary transmitter or primary transmitters whose signals are regularly carried by the cable system, and thereafter, from time to time, such further information as the Register of Copyrights, after consultation with the Copyright Royalty Tribunal (if and when the Tribunal has been constituted), shall prescribe by regulation to carry out the purpose of this clause.

(2) A cable system whose secondary transmissions have been subject to compulsory licensing under subsection (c) shall, on a semiannual basis, deposit with the Register of Copyrights, in accordance with requirements that the Register shall, after consultation with the Copyright Royalty Tribunal (if and when the Tribunal has been constituted), prescribe by regulation—

(A) a statement of account, covering the six months next preceding, specifying the number of channels on which the cable system made secondary transmissions to its subscribers, the names and locations of all primary transmitters whose transmissions were further transmitted by the cable system, the total number of subscribers, the gross amounts paid to the cable system for the basic service of providing secondary transmissions of primary broadcast transmitters, and such other data as the Register of Copyrights may, after consultation with the Copyright Royalty Tribunal (if and when the Tribunal has been constituted), from time to time prescribe by regulation. Such statement shall also include a special statement of account covering any nonnetwork television programming that was carried by the cable system in whole or in part beyond the local service area of the primary transmitter, under rules, regulations, or authorizations of the Federal Communications Commission permitting the substitution or addition of signals under certain circumstances, together with logs showing the times, dates, stations, and programs involved in such substituted or added carriage; and

(B) except in the case of a cable system whose royalty is specified in subclause (C) or (D), a total royalty fee for the period covered by the statement, computed on the basis of specified percentages of the gross receipts from subscribers to the cable service during said period for the basic service of providing secondary transmissions of primary broadcast transmitters, as follows:

(i) 0.675 of 1 per centum of such gross receipts for the privilege of further transmitting any nonnetwork programing of a primary transmitter in whole or in part beyond the local service area of such primary transmitter, such amount to be applied against the fee, if any, payable pursuant to paragraphs (ii) through (iv);

(ii) 0.675 of 1 per centum of such gross receipts for the first distant signal equivalent;

(iii) 0.425 of 1 per centum of such gross receipts for each of the second, third, and fourth distant signal equivalents;

(iv) 0.2 of 1 per centum of such gross receipts for the fifth distant signal equivalent and each additional distant signal equivalent thereafter; and

in computing the amounts payable under paragraph (ii) through (iv), above, any fraction of a distant signal equivalent shall be computed at its fractional value and, in the case of any cable system located partly within and partly without the local service area of a primary transmitter, gross receipts shall be limited to those gross receipts derived from subscribers located without the local service area of such primary transmitter; and

(C) if the actual gross receipts paid by subscribers to a cable system for the period covered by the statement for the basic service of providing secondary transmissions of primary broadcast transmitters total $80,000 or less, gross receipts of the cable system for the purpose of this subclause shall be computed by subtracting from such actual gross receipts the amount by which $80,000 exceeds such actual gross receipts, except that in no case shall a cable system's gross receipts be reduced to less than $3,000. The royalty fee payable under this subclause shall be 0.5 of 1 per centum, regardless of the number of distant signal equivalents, if any; and

(D) if the actual gross receipts paid by subscribers to a cable system for the period covered by the statement, for the basic service of providing secondary transmissions of primary broadcast transmitters, are more than $80,000 but less than $160,000, the royalty fee payable under this subclause shall be (i) 0.5 of 1 per centum of any gross receipts up to $80,000; and (ii) 1 per centum of any gross receipts in excess of $80,000 but less than $160,000, regardless of the number of distant signal equivalents, if any.

(3) The Register of Copyrights shall receive all fees deposited under this section and, after deducting the reasonable costs incurred by the Copyright Office under this section, shall deposit the balance in the Treasury of the United States, in such manner as the Secretary of the Treasury directs. All funds held by the

Secretary of the Treasury shall be invested in interest-bearing United States securities for later distribution with interest by the Copyright Royalty Tribunal as provided by this title. The Register shall submit to the Copyright Royalty Tribunal, on a semiannual basis, a compilation of all statements of account covering the relevant six-month period provided by clause (2) of this subsection.

(4) The royalty fees thus deposited shall, in accordance with the procedures provided by clause (5), be distributed to those among the following copyright owners who claim that their works were the subject of secondary transmissions by cable systems during the relevant semiannual period:

(A) any such owner whose work was included in a secondary transmission made by a cable system of a nonnetwork television program in whole or in part beyond the local service area of the primary transmitter; and

(B) any such owner whose work was included in a secondary transmission identified in a special statement of account deposited under clause (2)(A); and

(C) any such owner whose work was included in nonnetwork programing consisting exclusively of aural signals carried by a cable system in whole or in part beyond the local service area of the primary transmitter of such programs.

(5) The royalty fees thus deposited shall be distributed in accordance with the following procedures:

(A) During the month of July in each year, every person claiming to be entitled to compulsory license fees for secondary transmissions shall file a claim with the Copyright Royalty Tribunal, in accordance with requirements that the Tribunal shall prescribe by regulation. Notwithstanding any provisions of the antitrust laws, for purposes of this clause any claimants may agree among themselves as to the proportionate division of compulsory licensing fees among them, may lump their claims together and file them jointly or as a single claim, or may designate a common agent to receive payment on their behalf.

(B) After the first day of August of each year, the Copyright Royalty Tribunal shall determine whether there exists a controversy concerning the distribution of royalty fees. If the Tribunal determines that no such controversy exists, it shall, after deducting its reasonable administrative costs under this section, distribute such fees to the copyright owners entitled, or to their designated agents. If the Tribunal finds the existence of a controversy, it shall, pursuant to chapter 8 of this title, conduct a proceeding to determine the distribution of royalty fees.

(C) During the pendency of any proceeding under this subsection, the Copyright Royalty Tribunal shall withhold from distribution an amount sufficient to satisfy all claims with respect to which a controversy exists, but shall have discretion to proceed to distribute any amounts that are not in controversy.

(e) NONSIMULTANEOUS SECONDARY TRANSMISSIONS BY CABLE SYSTEMS.—

(1) Notwithstanding those provisions of the second paragraph of subsection (f) relating to nonsimultaneous secondary transmissions by a cable system, any such transmissions are actionable

as an act of infringement under section 501, and are fully subject to the remedies provided by sections 502 through 506 and sections 509 and 510, unless—

(A) the program on the videotape is transmitted no more than one time to the cable system's subscribers; and

(B) the copyrighted program, episode, or motion picture videotape, including the commercials contained within such program, episode, or picture, is transmitted without deletion or editing; and

(C) an owner or officer of the cable system (i) prevents the duplication of the videotape while in the possession of the system, (ii) prevents unauthorized duplication while in the possession of the facility making the videotape for the system if the system owns or controls the facility, or takes reasonable precautions to prevent such duplication if it does not own or control the facility, (iii) takes adequate precautions to prevent duplication while the tape is being transported, and (iv) subject to clause (2), erases or destroys, or causes the erasure or destruction of, the videotape; and

(D) within forty-five days after the end of each calendar quarter, an owner or officer of the cable system executes an affidavit attesting (i) to the steps and precautions taken to prevent duplication of the videotape, and (ii) subject to clause (2), to the erasure or destruction of all videotapes made or used during such quarter; and

(E) such owner or officer places or causes each such affidavit, and affidavits received pursuant to clause (2)(C), to be placed in a file, open to public inspection, at such system's main office in the community where the transmission is made or in the nearest community where such system maintains an office; and

(F) the nonsimultaneous transmission is one that the cable system would be authorized to transmit under the rules, regulations, and authorizations of the Federal Communications Commission in effect at the time of the nonsimultaneous transmission if the transmission had been made simultaneously, except that this subclause shall not apply to inadvertent or accidental transmissions.

(2) If a cable system transfers to any person a videotape of a program nonsimultaneously transmitted by it, such transfer is actionable as an act of infringement under section 501, and is fully subject to the remedies provided by sections 502 through 506 and 509, except that, pursuant to a written, nonprofit contract providing for the equitable sharing of the costs of such videotape and its transfer, a videotape nonsimultaneously transmitted by it, in accordance with clause (1), may be transferred by one cable system in Alaska to another system in Alaska, by one cable system in Hawaii permitted to make such nonsimultaneous transmissions to another such cable system in Hawaii, or by one cable system in Guam, the Northern Mariana Islands, or the Trust Territory of the Pacific Islands, to another cable system in any of those three territories, if—

(A) each such contract is available for public inspection in the offices of the cable systems involved, and a copy of such contract is filed, within thirty days after such contract is entered into, with the Copyright Office (which Office shall make each such contract available for public inspection); and

(B) the cable system to which the videotape is transferred

complies with clause (1)(A), (B), (C)(i), (iii), and (iv), and (D) through (F); and

(C) such system provides a copy of the affidavit required to be made in accordance with clause (1)(D) to each cable system making a previous nonsimultaneous transmission of the same videotape.

(3) This subsection shall not be construed to supersede the exclusivity protection provisions of any existing agreement, or any such agreement hereafter entered into, between a cable system and a television broadcast station in the area in which the cable system is located, or a network with which such station is affiliated.

(4) As used in this subsection, the term "videotape", and each of its variant forms, means the reproduction of the images and sounds of a program or programs broadcast by a television broadcast station licensed by the Federal Communications Commission, regardless of the nature of the material objects, such as tapes or films, in which the reproduction is embodied.

(f) DEFINITIONS.—As used in this section, the following terms and their variant forms mean the following:

A "primary transmission" is a transmission made to the public by the transmitting facility whose signals are being received and further transmitted by the secondary transmission service, regardless of where or when the performance or display was first transmitted.

A "secondary transmission" is the further transmitting of a primary transmission simultaneously with the primary transmission, or nonsimultaneously with the primary transmission if by a "cable system" not located in whole or in part within the boundary of the forty-eight contiguous States, Hawaii, or Puerto Rico: *Provided, however*, That a nonsimultaneous further transmission by a cable system located in Hawaii of a primary transmission shall be deemed to be a secondary transmission if the carriage of the television broadcast signal comprising such further transmission is permissible under the rules, regulations, or authorizations of the Federal Communications Commission.

A "cable system" is a facility, located in any State, Territory, Trust Territory, or Possession, that in whole or in part receives signals transmitted or programs broadcast by one or more television broadcast stations licensed by the Federal Communications Commission, and makes secondary transmissions of such signals or programs by wires, cables, or other communications channels to subscribing members of the public who pay for such service. For purposes of determining the royalty fee under subsection (d)(2), two or more cable systems in contiguous communities under common ownership or control or operating from one headend shall be considered as one system.

The "local service area of a primary transmitter", in the case of a television broadcast station, comprises the area in which such station is entitled to insist upon its signal being retransmitted by a cable system pursuant to the rules, regulations, and authorizations of the Federal Communications Commission in effect on April 15, 1976, or in the case of a television broadcast station licensed by an appropriate governmental authority of Canada or Mexico, the area in which it would be entitled to insist upon its signal being retransmitted if it were a television broadcast station subject to such rules, regulations, and authorizations. The "local service area of a primary transmitter", in the case of a radio broadcast station, comprises the primary service area of such station, pursuant to the rules and regulations of the Federal Communications Commission.

A "distant signal equivalent" is the value assigned to the secondary transmission of any nonnetwork television programing carried by a cable system in whole or in part beyond the local service area of the primary transmitter of such programing. It is computed by assigning a value of one to each independent station and a value of one-quarter to each network station and noncommercial educational station for the nonnetwork programing so carried pursuant to the rules, regulations, and authorizations of the Federal Communications Commission. The foregoing values for independent, network, and noncommercial educational stations are subject, however, to the following exceptions and limitations. Where the rules and regulations of the Federal Communications Commission require a cable system to omit the further transmission of a particular program and such rules and regulations also permit the substitution of another program embodying a performance or display of a work in place of the omitted transmission, or where such rules and regulations in effect on the date of enactment of this Act permit a cable system, at its election, to effect such deletion and substitution of a nonlive program or to carry additional programs not transmitted by primary transmitters within whose local service area the cable system is located, no value shall be assigned for the substituted or additional program; where the rules, regulations, or authorizations of the Federal Communications Commission in effect on the date of enactment of this Act permit a cable system, at its election, to omit the further transmission of a particular program and such rules, regulations, or authorizations also permit the substitution of another program embodying a performance or display of a work in place of the omitted transmission, the value assigned for the substituted or additional program shall be, in the case of a live program, the value of one full distant signal equivalent multiplied by a fraction that has as its numerator the number of days in the year in which such substitution occurs and as its denominator the number of days in the year. In the case of a station carried pursuant to the late-night or specialty programing rules of the Federal Communications Commission, or a station carried on a part-time basis where full-time carriage is not possible because the cable system lacks the activated channel capacity to retransmit on a full-time basis all signals which it is authorized to carry, the values for independent, network, and noncommercial educational stations set forth above, as the case may be, shall be multiplied by a fraction which is equal to the ratio of the broadcast hours of such station carried by the cable system to the total broadcast hours of the station.

A "network station" is a television broadcast station that is owned or operated by, or affiliated with, one or more of the television networks in the United States providing nationwide transmissons, and that transmits a substantial part of the programing supplied by such networks for a substantial part of that station's typical broadcast day.

An "independent station" is a commercial television broadcast station other than a network station.

A "noncommercial educational station" is a television station that is a noncommercial educational broadcast station as defined in section 397 of title 47.

HOUSE, SENATE, AND CONFERENCE REPORTS

[The three reports do not comment on matters pertaining to schools or libraries, so they have been omitted to save space.]

LAW

§ 112. Limitations on exclusive rights: Ephemeral recordings

(a) Notwithstanding the provisions of section 106, and except in the case of a motion picture or other audiovisual work, it is not an infringement of copyright for a transmitting organization entitled to transmit to the public a performance or display of a work, under a license or transfer of the copyright or under the limitations on exclusive rights in sound recordings specified by section 114(a), to make no more than one copy or phonorecord of a particular transmission program embodying the performance or display, if—

(1) the copy or phonorecord is retained and used solely by the transmitting organization that made it, and no further copies or phonorecords are reproduced from it; and

(2) the copy or phonorecord is used solely for the transmitting organization's own transmissions within its local service area, or for purposes of archival preservation or security; and

(3) unless preserved exclusively for archival purposes, the copy or phonorecord is destroyed within six months from the date the transmission program was first transmitted to the public.

(b) Notwithstanding the provisions of section 106, it is not an infringement of copyright for a governmental body or other nonprofit organization entitled to transmit a performance or display of a work, under section 110(2) or under the limitations on exclusive rights in sound recordings specified by section 114(a), to make no more than thirty copies or phonorecords of a particular transmission program embodying the performance or display, if—

(1) no further copies or phonorecords are reproduced from the copies or phonorecords made under this clause; and

(2) except for one copy or phonorecord that may be preserved exclusively for archival purposes, the copies or phonorecords are destroyed within seven years from the date the transmission program was first transmitted to the public.

(c) Notwithstanding the provisions of section 106, it is not an infringment of copyright for a governmental body or other nonprofit organization to make for distribution no more than one copy or phonorecord, for each transmitting organization specified in clause (2) of this subsection, of a particular transmission program embodying a performance of a nondramatic musical work of a religious nature, or of a sound recording of such a musical work, if—

(1) there is no direct or indirect charge for making or distributing any such copies or phonorecords; and

(2) none of such copies or phonorecords is used for any performance other than a single transmission to the public by a transmitting organization entitled to transmit to the public a performance of the work under a license or transfer of the copyright; and

(3) except for one copy or phonorecord that may be preserved exclusively for archival purposes, the copies or phonorecords are all destroyed within one year from the date the transmission program was first transmitted to the public.

(d) Notwithstanding the provisions of section 106, it is not an infringement of copyright for a governmental body or other nonprofit organization entitled to transmit a performance of a work under section 110(8) to make no more than ten copies or phonorecords embodying the performance, or to permit the use of any such copy or phonorecord by any governmental body or nonprofit organization entitled to transmit a performance of a work under section 110(8), if—

(1) any such copy or phonorecord is retained and used solely by the organization that made it, or by a governmental body or nonprofit organization entitled to transmit a performance of a work under section 110(8), and no further copies or phonorecords are reproduced from it; and

(2) any such copy or phonorecord is used solely for transmissions authorized under section 110(8), or for purposes of archival preservation or security; and

(3) the governmental body or nonprofit organization permitting any use of any such copy or phonorecord by any governmental body or nonprofit organization under this subsection does not make any charge for such use.

(e) The transmission program embodied in a copy or phonorecord made under this section is not subject to protection as a derivative work under this title except with the express consent of the owners of copyright in the preexisting works employed in the program.

HOUSE REPORT

SECTION 112. EPHEMERAL RECORDINGS

Section 112 of the bill concerns itself with a special problem that is not dealt with in the present statutes but is the subject of provisions in a number of foreign statutes and in the revisions of the Berne Convention since 1948. This is the problem of what are commonly called "ephemeral recordings": copies or phonorecords of a work made for purposes of later transmission by a broadcasting organization legally entitled to transmit the work. In other words, where a broadcaster has the privilege of performing or displaying a work either because he is licensed or because the performance or display is exempted under the statute, the question is whether he should be given the additional privilege of recording the performance or display to facilitate its transmission. The need for a limited exemption in these cases because of the practical exigencies of broadcasting has been generally recognized, but the scope of the exemption has been a controversial issue.

Recordings for licensed transmissions

Under subsection (a) of section 112, an organization that has acquired the right to transmit any work (other than a motion picture or other audiovisual work), or that is free to transmit a sound recording under section 114, may make a single copy or phonorecord of a particular program embodying the work, if the copy or phonorecord is used solely for the organization's own transmissions within its own area; after 6 months it must be destroyed or preserved solely for archival purposes.

Organizations covered.—The ephemeral recording privilege is given by subsection (a) to "a transmitting organization entitled to transmit to the public a performance or display of a work." Assuming that the transmission meets the other conditions of the provision, it makes no difference what type of public transmission the organization is making: commercial radio and television broadcasts, public radio and television broadcasts not exempted by section 110(2), pay-TV, closed circuit, background music, and so forth. However, to come within the scope of subsection (a), the organization must have the right to make the transmission "under a license or transfer of the copyright or under the limitations on exclusive rights in sound recordings specified by section 114(a)." Thus,* except in the case of copyrighted sound recordings (which have no exclusive performing rights under the bill),* the organization must be a transferee or licensee (including compulsory licensee) of performing rights in the work in order to make an ephemeral recording of it.

The words between the asterisks in the above sentence did not appear in the SENATE REPORT.

Some concern has been expressed by authors and publishers lest the term "organization" be construed to include a number of affiliated broadcasters who could exchange the recording without restrictions. The term is intended to cover a broadcasting network, or a local broadcaster or individual transmitter; but, under clauses (1) and (2) of the subsection, the ephemeral recording must be "retained and used solely by the transmitting organization that made it," and must be used solely for that organization's own transmissions within its own area. Thus, an ephemeral recording made by one transmitter, whether it be a network or local broadcaster, could not be made available for use by another transmitter. Likewise, this subsection does not apply to those nonsimultaneous transmissions by cable systems not located within the boundary of the forty-eight contiguous States that are granted a compulsory license under section 111.

Scope of the privilege.—Subsection (a) permits the transmitting organization to make "no more than one copy or phonorecord of a particular transmission program embodying the performance or display." A "transmission program" is defined in section 101 as a body of material produced for the sole purpose of transmission as a unit. Thus, under section 112(a), a transmitter could make only one copy or phonorecord of a particular "transmission program" containing a copyrighted work, but would not be limited as to the number of times the work itself could be duplicated as part of other "transmission programs."

Three specific limitations on the scope of the ephemeral recording privilege are set out in subsection (a), and unless all are met the making of an "ephemeral recording" becomes fully actionable as an infringement. The first requires that the copy or phonorecord be "retained and used solely by the transmitting organization that made it," and that "no further copies or phonorecords are reproduced from it." This means that a transmitting organization would have no privilege of exchanging ephemeral recordings with other transmitters or of allowing them to duplicate their own ephemeral recordings from the copy or phonorecord it has made. There is nothing in the provision to prevent a transmitting organization from having an ephemeral recording made by means of facilities other than its own, although it would not be permissible for a person or organization other than a transmitting organization to make a recording on its own initiative for possible sale or lease to a broadcaster. The ephemeral recording privilege would extend to copies or phonorecords made in advance for later broadcast, as well as recordings of a program that are made while it is being transmitted and are intended for deferred transmission or preservation.

Clause (2) of section 112(a) provides that, to be exempt from copyright, the copy or phonorecord must be "used solely for the transmitting organization's own transmissions within its local service area, or for purposes of archival preservation or security". The term "local service area" is defined in section 111(f).

SENATE REPORT

The following sentence in the SENATE REPORT was omitted in the HOUSE REPORT:

In the context of section 112 it means that, although a transmitter may use a ephemeral recording as many times as it wishes within the time limits specified in clause (3), its use must be confined to the organization's own transmissions within the radius that its signal "is expected to reach effectively under normal conditions."

HOUSE REPORT (Continued)

Clause (3) of section 112(a) provides that, unless preserved exclusively for archival purposes, the copy or phonorecord of a transmission program must be destroyed within six months from the date the transmission program was first transmitted to the public.

Recordings for instructional transmissions

Section 112(b) represents a response to the arguments of instructional broadcasters and other educational groups for special recording privileges, although it does not go as far as these groups requested. In general, it permits a nonprofit organization that is free to transmit a performance or display of a work, under section 110(2) or under the limitations on exclusive rights in sound recordings specified by section 114(a), to make not more than thirty copies or phonorecords and to use the ephemeral recordings for transmitting purposes for not more than seven years after the initial transmission.

Organizations covered.—The privilege of making ephemeral recordings under section 112(b) extends to a "governmental body or other nonprofit organization entitled to transmit a performance or display of a work under section 110(2) or under the limitations on exclusive rights in sound recordings specified by section 114(a)." Aside from phonorecords of copyrighted sound recordings, the ephemeral recordings made by an instructional broadcaster under subsection (b) must embody a performance or display that meets all of the qualifications for exemption under section 110(2). Copies or phonorecords made for educational broadcasts of a general cultural nature, or for transmission as part of an information storage and retrieval system, would not be exempted from copyright protection under section 112(b).

Motion pictures and other audiovisual works.—Since the performance exemption provided by section 110(2) applies only to nondramatic literary and musical works, there was no need to exclude motion pictures and other audiovisual works explicitly from the scope of section 112(b). Another point stressed by the producers of educational films in this connection, however, was that ephemeral recordings made by instructional broadcasters are in fact audiovisual works that often compete for exactly the same market. They argued that it is unfair to allow instructional broadcasters to reproduce multiple copies of films and tapes, and to exchange them with other broadcasters, without paying any copyright royalties, thereby directly injuring the market of producers of audiovisual works who now pay substantial fees to authors for the same uses. These arguments are persuasive and justify the placing of reasonable limits on the recording privilege.

Scope of the privilege.—Under subsection (b) an instructional broadcaster may make "no more than thirty copies or phonorecords of a particular transmission program embodying the performance or display." No further copies or phonorecords can be reproduced from those made under section 112(b), either by the nonprofit organization that made them or by anyone else.

On the other hand, if the nonprofit organization does nothing directly or indirectly to authorize, induce, or encourage others to duplicate additional copies or phonorecords of an ephemeral recording in excess of the limit of thirty, it would not be held responsible as participating in the infringement in such a case, and the unauthorized copies would not be counted against the organization's total of thirty.

The above paragraph did not appear in the SENATE REPORT.

Unlike ephemeral recordings made under subsection (a), exchanges of recordings among instructional broadcasters are permitted. An organization that has made copies or phonorecords under subsection (b) may use one of them for purposes of its own transmissions that are exempted by section 110(2), and it may also transfer the other 29 copies to other instructional broadcasters for use in the same way.

As in the case of ephemeral recordings made under section 112(a), a copy or phonorecord made for instructional broadcasting could be reused in any number of transmissions within the time limits specified in the provision. Because of the special problems of instructional broadcasters resulting from the scheduling of courses and the need to prerecord well in advance of transmission, the period of use has been extended to seven years from the date the transmission program was first transmitted to the public.

Religious broadcasts.

[Omitted to save space.]

Ephemeral recordings for transmissions to handicapped audiences

As a counterpart to its amendment of section 110(8), the Committee adopted a new provision, subsection (d) of section 112, to provide an ephemeral recording exemption in the case of transmissions to the blind and deaf. The new subsection would permit the making of one recording of a performance exempted under section 110(8), and its retention for an unlimited period. It would not permit the making of further reproductions or their exchange with other organizations.

The above paragraph did not appear in the SENATE REPORT.

Copyright status of ephemeral recordings

A program reproduced in an ephemeral recording made under section 112 in many cases will constitute a motion picture, a sound recording, or some other kind of derivative work, and will thus be potentially copyrightable under section 103. In section 112(e) it is provided that ephemeral recordings are not to be copyrightable as derivative works except with the consent of the owners of the copyrighted material employed in them.

LAW

§ 113. Scope of exclusive rights in pictorial, graphic, and sculptural works

(a) Subject to the provisions of subsections (b) and (c) of this section, the exclusive right to reproduce a copyrighted pictorial, graphic, or sculptural work in copies under section 106 includes the right to reproduce the work in or on any kind of article, whether useful or otherwise.

(b) This title does not afford, to the owner of copyright in a work that portrays a useful article as such, any greater or lesser rights with respect to the making, distribution, or display of the useful article so portrayed than those afforded to such works under the law, whether title 17 or the common law or statutes of a State, in effect on December 31, 1977, as held applicable and construed by a court in an action brought under this title.

(c) In the case of a work lawfully reproduced in useful articles that have been offered for sale or other distribution to the public, copyright does not include any right to prevent the making, distribution, or display of pictures or photographs of such articles in connection with advertisements or commentaries related to the distribution or display of such articles, or in connection with news reports.

HOUSE REPORT

SECTION 113. REPRODUCTION OF PICTORIAL, GRAPHIC, AND SCULPTURAL WORKS IN USEFUL ARTICLES

Section 113 deals with the extent of copyright protection in "works of applied art." The section takes as its starting point the Supreme Court's decision in *Mazer* v. *Stein*, 347 U.S. 201 (1954), and the first sentence of subsection (a) restates the basic principle established by that decision. The rule of *Mazer*, as affirmed by the bill, is that copyright in a pictorial, graphic, or sculptural work will not be affected if the work is employed as the design of a useful article, and will afford protection to the copyright owner against the unauthorized reproduction of his work in useful as well as nonuseful articles. The terms "pictorial, graphic, and sculptural works" and "useful article" are defined in section 101, and these definitions are discussed above in connection with section 102.

SENATE REPORT

In the SENATE REPORT, the last sentence reads:

The term "useful article" is defined in section 113(e) as "an article having an intrinsic utilitarian function that is not merely to portray the appearance of the article or to convey information."

Section 113(e) was omitted from the act prior to passage. The above definition of a useful article also appears in Sec. 101, on p. 66.

HOUSE REPORT (Continued)

The broad language of section 106(1) and of subsection (a) of section 113 raises questions as to the extent of copyright protection for a pictorial, graphic, or sculptural work that portrays, depicts, or represents an image of a useful article in such a way that the utilitarian nature of the article can be seen. To take the example usually cited, would copyright in a drawing or model of an automobile give the artist the exclusive right to make automobiles of the same design?

The 1961 Report of the Register of Copyrights stated, on the basis of judicial precedent, that "copyright in a pictorial, graphic, or sculptural work, portraying a useful article as such, does not extend to the manufacture of the useful article itself," and recommended specifically that "the distinctions drawn in this area by existing court decisions" not be altered by the statute. The Register's Supplementary Report, at page 48, cited a number of these decisions, and explained the insuperable difficulty of finding "any statutory formulation that would express the distinction satisfactorily." Section 113(b) reflects the Register's conclusion that "the real need is to make clear that there is no intention to change the present law with respect to the scope of protection in a work portraying a useful article as such."

Section 113(c) provides that it would not be an infringement of copyright, where a copyright work has been lawfully published as the design of useful articles, to make, distribute or display pictures of the articles in advertising, in feature stories about the articles, or in news reports.

In conformity with its deletion from the bill of Title II, relating to the protection of ornamental designs of useful articles, the Committee has deleted subsections (b), (c), and (d) of section 113 of S. 22 as adopted by the Senate, since they are no longer relevant.

SENATE REPORT

The report contains a lengthy discussion of copyright protection of ornamental designs which was omitted to save space. A brief note on the legislative history of copyright protection of ornamental designs appears on pp. 279-80.

LAW

§ 114. Scope of exclusive rights in sound recordings

(a) The exclusive rights of the owner of copyright in a sound recording are limited to the rights specified by clauses (1), (2), and (3) of section 106, and do not include any right of performance under section 106(4).

(b) The exclusive right of the owner of copyright in a sound recording under clause (1) of section 106 is limited to the right to duplicate

the sound recording in the form of phonorecords, or of copies of motion pictures and other audiovisual works, that directly or indirectly recapture the actual sounds fixed in the recording. The exclusive right of the owner of copyright in a sound recording under clause (2) of section 106 is limited to the right to prepare a derivative work in which the actual sounds fixed in the sound recording are rearranged, remixed, or otherwise altered in sequence or quality. The exclusive rights of the owner of copyright in a sound recording under clauses (1) and (2) of section 106 do not extend to the making or duplication of another sound recording that consists entirely of an independent fixation of other sounds, even though such sounds imitate or simulate those in the copyrighted sound recording. The exclusive rights of the owner of copyright in a sound recording under clauses (1), (2), and (3) of section 106 do not apply to sound recordings included in educational television and radio programs (as defined in section 397 of title 47) distributed or transmitted by or through public broadcasting entities (as defined by section 118(g)) : *Provided*, That copies or phonorecords of said programs are not commercially distributed by or through public broadcasting entities to the general public.

(c) This section does not limit or impair the exclusive right to perform publicly, by means of a phonorecord, any of the works specified by section 106(4).

(d) On January 3, 1978, the Register of Copyrights, after consulting with representatives of owners of copyrighted materials, representatives of the broadcasting, recording, motion picture, entertainment industries, and arts organizations, representatives of organized labor and performers of copyrighted materials, shall submit to the Congress a report setting forth recommendations as to whether this section should be amended to provide for performers and copyright owners of copyrighted material any performance rights in such material. The report should describe the status of such rights in foreign countries, the views of major interested parties, and specific legislative or other recommendations, if any.

The report by the Register of Copyrights required under Section 114(d) is identified on p. 155.

HOUSE REPORT

Section 114. Scope of Exclusive Rights in Sound Recordings

Subsection (a) of Section 114 specifies that the exclusive rights of the owner of copyright in a sound recording are limited to the rights to reproduce the sound recording in copies or phonorecords, to prepare derivative works based on the copyrighted sound recording, and to distribute copies or phonorecords of the sound recording to the public. Subsection (a) states explicitly that the owner's rights "do not include any right of performance under section 106(4)." The Committee considered at length the arguments in favor of estabilshing a limited performance right, in the form of a compulsory license, for copyrighted sound recordings, but concluded that the problem requires further study. It therefore added a new subsection (d) to the bill requiring the Register of Copyrights to submit to Congress, on January 3, 1978, "a report setting forth recommendations as to whether this section should be amended to provide for performers and copyright owners . . . any performance rights" in copyrighted sound recordings. Under the new subsection, the report "should describe the status of such rights in foreign countries, the views of major interested parties, and specific legislative or other recommendations, if any."

Subsection (b) of section 114 makes clear that statutory protection for sound recordings extends only to the particular sounds of which the recording consists, and would not prevent a separate recording of another performance in which those sounds are imitated. Thus, infringement takes place whenever all or any substantial portion of the actual sounds that go to make up a copyrighted sound recording are reproduced in phonorecords by repressing, transcribing, recapturing off the air, or any other method, or by reproducing them in the soundtrack or audio portion of a motion picture or other audiovisual work. Mere imitation of a recorded performance would not constitute a copyright infringement even where one performer deliberately sets out to simulate another's performance as exactly as possible.

Under section 114, the exclusive right of owner of copyright in a sound recording to prepare derivative works based on the copyrighted sound recording is recognized. However, in view of the expressed intention not to give exclusive rights against imitative or simulated performances and recordings, the Committee adopted an amendment to make clear the scope of rights under section 106(2) in this context. Section 114(b) provides that the "exclusive right of the owner of copyright in a sound recording under clause (2) of section 106 is limited to the right to prepare a derivative work in which the actual sounds fixed in the sound recording are rearranged, remixed, or otherwise altered in sequence or quality."

Another amendment deals with the use of copyrighted sound recordings "included in educational television and radio programs * * * distributed or transmitted by or through public broadcasting entities." This use of recordings is permissible without authorization from the owner of copyright in the sound recording, as long as "copies or phonorecords of said programs are not commercially distributed by or through public broadcasting entities to the general public."

During the 1975 hearings, the Register of Copyrights expressed some concern that an invaluable segment of this country's musical heritage—in the form of sound recordings—had become inaccesible to musicologists and to others for scholarly purposes. Several of the major recording companies have responded to the Register's concern by granting blanket licenses to the Library of Congress to permit it to make single copy duplications of sound recordings maintained in the Library's archives for research purposes. Moreover, steps are being taken to determine the feasibility of additional licensing arrangements as a means of satisfying the needs of key regional music libraries across the country. The Register has agreed to report to Congress if further legislative consideration should be undertaken.

Section 114(c) states explicitly that nothing in the provisions of section 114 should be construed to "limit or impair the exclusive right to perform publicly, by means of a phonorecord, any of the works specified by section 106(4)." This principle is already implicit in the bill, but it is restated to avoid the danger of confusion between rights in a sound recording and rights in the musical composition or other work embodied in the recording.

Section 114 in the two reports differs substantially; the text of the HOUSE REPORT appears above and the text of the SENATE REPORT follows:

SENATE REPORT

SECTION 114. SCOPE OF EXCLUSIVE RIGHTS IN SOUND RECORDINGS

Subsection (a) of Section 114 specifies that the exclusive rights of the owner of copyright in a sound recording are limited to the rights to reproduce, prepare derivative works, and distribute as stated in Section 106 and do not include any right of performance.

Subsection (b) provides that the rights do not extend to the making or duplication of another sound recording that is an independent fixation of other sounds, even though such sounds imitate or simulate those in the copyrighted recording. Subsection (c) states that nothing in the provisions of section 114 should be construed to "limit or impair the exclusive right to perform publicly, by means of a phonorecord, any of the works specified by section 106(4)." This principle is already implicit in the bill, but is restated to avoid the danger of confusion between rights in a sound recording and rights in the musical composition or other work embodied in the recording.

CONFERENCE REPORT

EXCLUSIVE RIGHTS IN SOUND RECORDINGS

Senate bill

The Senate bill, in section 114, limited the exclusive rights of the owner of copyright in a sound recording to those specified by clauses (1), (2), and (3) of section 106—that is, the rights to reproduce the work in phonorecords, to make derivative works, and to distribute phonorecords. It expressly denied the exclusive right of public performance under section 106(4) to sound recordings.

House bill

The House amendments to section 114 clarified the scope of the exclusive right to make derivative works in relation to sound recordings, and permitted the use of copyrighted sound recordings in the audio portions of educational radio and television programs under certain conditions. The House bill also required the Register of Copyrights to submit to Congress, on January 3, 1978, a report with recommendations as to whether copyright protection for sound recordings should be expanded to include performing rights.

Conference substitute

The conference substitute adopts the House amendments of section 114.

COPYRIGHT OFFICE

Section 114(d) requires the Register of Copyrights to file a report on performance rights in sound recordings. The report was issued as:

U.S. House of Representatives. Subcommittee on Courts, Civil Liberties, and the Administration of Justice. *Performance Rights in Sound Recordings*. Washington: The House of Representatives, 1978, 1162 pp. (Committee Print No. 15.)

LAW

§ 115. Scope of exclusive rights in nondramatic musical works: Compulsory license for making and distributing phonorecords

In the case of nondramatic musical works, the exclusive rights provided by clauses (1) and (3) of section 106, to make and to distribute phonorecords of such works, are subject to compulsory licensing under the conditions specified by this section.

(a) Availability and Scope of Compulsory License.—

(1) When phonorecords of a nondramatic musical work have been distributed to the public in the United States under the authority of the copyright owner, any other person may, by complying with the provisions of this section, obtain a compulsory license to make and distribute phonorecords of the work. A person may obtain a compulsory license only if his or her primary purpose in making phonorecords is to distribute them to the public for private use. A person may not obtain a compulsory license for use of the work in the making of phonorecords duplicating a sound recording fixed by another, unless: (i) such sound recording was fixed lawfully; and (ii) the making of the phonorecords was authorized by the owner of copyright in the sound recording or, if the sound recording was fixed before February 15, 1972, by any person who fixed the sound recording pursuant to an express license from the owner of the copyright in the musical work or pursuant to a valid compulsory license for use of such work in a sound recording.

(2) A compulsory license includes the privilege of making a musical arrangement of the work to the extent necessary to conform it to the style or manner of interpretation of the performance involved, but the arrangement shall not change the basic melody or fundamental character of the work, and shall not be subject to protection as a derivative work under this title, except with the express consent of the copyright owner.

(b) Notice of Intention To Obtain Compulsory License.—

(1) Any person who wishes to obtain a compulsory license under this section shall, before or within thirty days after making, and before distributing any phonorecords of the work, serve notice of intention to do so on the copyright owner. If the registration or other public records of the Copyright Office do not identify the copyright owner and include an address at which notice can be served, it shall be sufficient to file the notice of intention in the Copyright Office. The notice shall comply, in form, content, and manner of service, with requirements that the Register of Copyrights shall prescribe by regulation.

(2) Failure to serve or file the notice required by clause (1) forecloses the possibility of a compulsory license and, in the absence of a negotiated license, renders the making and distribution of phonorecords actionable as acts of infringement under section 501 and fully subject to the remedies provided by sections 502 through 506 and 509.

(c) Royalty Payable Under Compulsory License.—

(1) To be entitled to receive royalties under a compulsory license, the copyright owner must be identified in the registration or other public records of the Copyright Office. The owner is entitled to royalties for phonorecords made and distributed after being so identified, but is not entitled to recover for any phonorecords previously made and distributed.

(2) Except as provided by clause (1), the royalty under a compulsory license shall be payable for every phonorecord made and distributed in accordance with the license. For this purpose, a phonorecord is considered "distributed" if the person exercising the compulsory license has voluntarily and permanently parted with its possession. With respect to each work embodied in the phonorecord, the royalty shall be either two and three-fourths cents, or one-half of one cent per minute of playing time or fraction thereof, whichever amount is larger.

(3) Royalty payments shall be made on or before the twentieth day of each month and shall include all royalties for the month next preceding. Each monthly payment shall be made under oath and shall comply with requirements that the Register of Copyrights shall prescribe by regulation. The Register shall also prescribe regulations under which detailed cumulative annual statements of account, certified by a certified public accountant, shall be filed for every compulsory license under this section. The regulations covering both the monthly and the annual statements of account shall prescribe the form, content, and manner of certification with respect to the number of records made and the number of records distributed.

(4) If the copyright owner does not receive the monthly payment and the monthly and annual statements of account when due, the owner may give written notice to the licensee that, unless the default is remedied within thirty days from the date of the notice, the compulsory license will be automatically terminated. Such termination renders either the making or the distribution, or both, of all phonorecords for which the royalty has not been paid, actionable as acts of infringement under section 501 and fully subject to the remedies provided by sections 502 through 506 and 509.

HOUSE, SENATE, AND CONFERENCE REPORTS

[Section 115 applies to the producers and distributors of sound recordings. Since it has little application to libraries or educational institutions, the reports have been omitted to save space.]

See also Section 106 of the Transitional and Supplementary Provisions on p. 273.

LAW

§ 116. Scope of exclusive rights in nondramatic musical works: Public performances by means of coin-operated phonorecord players

(a) Limitation on Exclusive Right.—In the case of a nondramatic musical work embodied in a phonorecord, the exclusive right under clause (4) of section 106 to perform the work publicly by means of a coin-operated phonorecord player is limited as follows:

(1) The proprietor of the establishment in which the public performance takes place is not liable for infringement with respect to such public performance unless—

(A) such proprietor is the operator of the phonorecord player; or

(B) such proprietor refuses or fails, within one month after receipt by registered or certified mail of a request, at a time during which the certificate required by clause (1)(C) of subsection (b) is not affixed to the phonorecord player, by the copyright owner, to make full disclosure, by registered or certified mail, of the identity of the operator of the phonorecord player.

(2) The operator of the coin-operated phonorecord player may obtain a compulsory license to perform the work publicly on that phonorecord player by filing the application, affixing the certificate, and paying the royalties provided by subsection (b).

(b) RECORDATION OF COIN-OPERATED PHONORECORD PLAYER, AFFIXATION OF CERTIFICATE, AND ROYALTY PAYABLE UNDER COMPULSORY LICENSE.—

(1) Any operator who wishes to obtain a compulsory license for the public performance of works on a coin-operated phonorecord player shall fulfill the following requirements:

(A) Before or within one month after such performances are made available on a particular phonorecord player, and during the month of January in each succeeding year that such performances are made available on that particular phonorecord player, the operator shall file in the Copyright Office, in accordance with requirements that the Register of Copyrights, after consultation with the Copyright Royalty Tribunal (if and when the Tribunal has been constituted), shall prescribe by regulation, an application containing the name and address of the operator of the phonorecord player and the manufacturer and serial number or other explicit identification of the phonorecord player, and deposit with the Register of Copyrights a royalty fee for the current calendar year of $8 for that particular phonorecord player. If such performances are made available on a particular phonorecord player for the first time after July 1 of any year, the royalty fee to be deposited for the remainder of that year shall be $4.

(B) Within twenty days of receipt of an application and a royalty fee pursuant to subclause (A), the Register of Copyrights shall issue to the applicant a certificate for the phonorecord player.

(C) On or before March 1 of the year in which the certificate prescribed by subclause (B) of this clause is issued, or within ten days after the date of issue of the certificate, the operator shall affix to the particular phonorecord player, in a position where it can be readily examined by the public, the certificate, issued by the Register of Copyrights under subclause (B), of the latest application made by such operator under subclause (A) of this clause with respect to that phonorecord player.

(2) Failure to file the application, to affix the certificate, or to pay the royalty required by clause (1) of this subsection renders the public performance actionable as an act of infringement under section 501 and fully subject to the remedies provided by sections 502 through 506 and 509.

(c) DISTRIBUTION OF ROYALTIES.—

(1) The Register of Copyrights shall receive all fees deposited under this section and, after deducting the reasonable costs incurred by the Copyright Office under this section, shall deposit the balance in the Treasury of the United States, in such manner as the Secretary of the Treasury directs. All funds held by the Secretary of the Treasury shall be invested in interest-bearing

United States securities for later distribution with interest by the Copyright Royalty Tribunal as provided by this title. The Register shall submit to the Copyright Royalty Tribunal, on an annual basis, a detailed statement of account covering all fees received for the relevant period provided by subsection (b).

(2) During the month of January in each year, every person claiming to be entitled to compulsory license fees under this section for performances during the preceding twelve-month period shall file a claim with the Copyright Royalty Tribunal, in accordance with requirements that the Tribunal shall prescribe by regulation. Such claim shall include an agreement to accept as final, except as provided in section 810 of this title, the determination of the Copyright Royalty Tribunal in any controversy concerning the distribution of royalty fees deposited under subclause (A) of subsection (b)(1) of this section to which the claimant is a party. Notwithstanding any provisions of the antitrust laws, for purposes of this subsection any claimants may agree among themselves as to the proportionate division of compulsory licensing fees among them, may lump their claims together and file them jointly or as a single claim, or may designate a common agent to receive payment on their behalf.

(3) After the first day of October of each year, the Copyright Royalty Tribunal shall determine whether there exists a controversy concerning the distribution of royalty fees deposited under subclause (A) of subsection (b)(1). If the Tribunal determines that no such controversy exists, it shall, after deducting its reasonable administrative costs under this section, distribute such fees to the copyright owners entitled, or to their designated agents. If it finds that such a controversy exists, it shall, pursuant to chapter 8 of this title, conduct a proceeding to determine the distribution of royalty fees.

(4) The fees to be distributed shall be divided as follows:

(A) to every copyright owner not affiliated with a performing rights society, the pro rata share of the fees to be distributed to which such copyright owner proves entitlement.

(B) to the performing rights societies, the remainder of the fees to be distributed in such pro rata shares as they shall by agreement stipulate among themselves, or, if they fail to agree, the pro rata share to which such performing rights societies prove entitlement.

(C) during the pendency of any proceeding under this section, the Copyright Royalty Tribunal shall withhold from distribution an amount sufficient to satisfy all claims with respect to which a controversy exists, but shall have discretion to proceed to distribute any amounts that are not in controversy.

(5) The Copyright Royalty Tribunal shall promulgate regulations under which persons who can reasonably be expected to have claims may, during the year in which performances take place, without expense to or harassment of operators or proprietors of establishments in which phonorecord players are located, have such access to such establishments and to the phonorecord players located therein and such opportunity to obtain information with respect thereto as may be reasonably necessary to determine, by sampling procedures or otherwise, the proportion of contribution of the musical works of each such person to the earnings of the phonorecord players for which fees shall have been deposited.

Any person who alleges that he or she has been denied the access permitted under the regulations prescribed by the Copyright Royalty Tribunal may bring an action in the United States District Court for the District of Columbia for the cancellation of the compulsory license of the phonorecord player to which such access has been denied, and the court shall have the power to declare the compulsory license thereof invalid from the date of issue thereof.

(d) CRIMINAL PENALTIES.—Any person who knowingly makes a false representation of a material fact in an application filed under clause (1)(A) of subsection (b), or who knowingly alters a certificate issued under clause (1)(B) of subsection (b) or knowingly affixes such a certificate to a phonorecord player other than the one it covers, shall be fined not more than $2,500.

(e) DEFINITIONS.—As used in this section, the following terms and their variant forms mean the following:

(1) A "coin-operated phonorecord player" is a machine or device that—

(A) is employed solely for the performance of non-dramatic musical works by means of phonorecords upon being activated by insertion of coins, currency, tokens, or other monetary units or their equivalent;

(B) is located in an establishment making no direct or indirect charge for admission;

(C) is accompanied by a list of the titles of all the musical works available for performance on it, which list is affixed to the phonorecord player or posted in the establishment in a prominent position where it can be readily examined by the public; and

(D) affords a choice of works available for performance and permits the choice to be made by the patrons of the establishment in which it is located.

(2) An "operator" is any person who, alone or jointly with others:

(A) owns a coin-operated phonorecord player; or

(B) has the power to make a coin-operated phonorecord player available for placement in an establishment for purposes of public performance; or

(C) has the power to exercise primary control over the selection of the musical works made available for public performance on a coin-operated phonorecord player.

(3) A "performing rights society" is an association or corporation that licenses the public performance of nondramatic musical works on behalf of the copyright owners, such as the American Society of Composers, Authors and Publishers, Broadcast Music, Inc., and SESAC, Inc.

HOUSE AND SENATE REPORTS

[Omitted to save space.]

LAW

§ 117. Scope of exclusive rights: Use in conjunction with computers and similar information systems

Notwithstanding the provisions of sections 106 through 116 and 118, this title does not afford to the owner of copyright in a work any greater or lesser rights with respect to the use of the work in conjunction with automatic systems capable of storing, processing, retrieving, or transferring information, or in conjunction with any similar device, machine, or process, than those afforded to works under the law, whether title 17 or the common law or statutes of a State, in effect on December 31, 1977, as held applicable and construed by a court in an action brought under this title.

HOUSE REPORT

SECTION 117. COMPUTER USES

As the program for general revision of the copyright law has evolved, it has become increasingly apparent that in one major area the problems are not sufficiently developed for a definitive legislative solution. This is the area of computer uses of copyrighted works: the use of a work "in conjunction with automatic systems capable of storing, processing, retrieving, or transferring information." The Commission on New Technological Uses is, among other things, now engaged in making a thorough study of the emerging patterns in this field and it will, on the basis of its findings, recommend definitive copyright provisions to deal with the situation.

Since it would be premature to change existing law on computer uses at present, the purpose of section 117 is to preserve the status quo. It is intended neither to cut off any rights that may now exist, nor to create new rights that might be denied under the Act of 1909 or under common law principles currently applicable.

The provision deals only with the exclusive rights of a copyright owner with respect to computer uses, that is, the bundle of rights specified for other types of uses in section 106 and qualified in sections 107 through 116 and 118. With respect to the copyright-ability of computer programs, the ownership of copyrights in them, the term of protection, and the formal requirements of the remainder of the bill. the new statute would apply.

SENATE REPORT

The words "and 118" in the above paragraph do not appear in the SENATE REPORT.

HOUSE REPORT (Continued)

Under section 117, an action for infringement of a copyrighted work by means of a computer would necessarily be a federal action brought under the new title 17. The court, in deciding the scope of exclusive rights in the computer area, would first need to determine the applicable law, whether State statutory or common law or the Act of 1909. Having determined what law was applicable, its decision would depend upon its interpretation of what that law was on the point on the day before the effective date of the new statute.

CONTU FINAL REPORT

The National Commission on New Technological Uses of Copyrighted Works (CONTU) was established to study the impact of computers on copyright and to recommend changes in the law. The commission's final report recommends the following changes in Sec. 117:

B. Recommendations

COMPUTERS

Recommendations for Legislation

Software or Programs

The new copyright law should be amended 1) to make it explicit that computer programs, to the extent that they embody an author's original creation, are proper subject matter of copyright; 2) to apply to all computer uses of copyrighted programs by the deletion of the present Section 117; and 3) to assure that rightful possessors of copies of computer programs can use or adapt these copies for their use.

Commissioner Hersey's Dissent:
The Act of 1976 should be amended to make it explicit that copyright protection does not extend to a computer program in the form in which it is capable of being used to control computer operations.

Data Bases

The Act of 1976 should be amended to apply to all computer uses of copyrighted data bases and other copyrighted works fixed in computer-sensible media by the deletion of its present Section 117.

New Works

Works created by the use of computers should be afforded copyright protection if they are original works of authorship within the Act of 1976. Consequently no amendment is needed.

Recommendation for Regulations

The Register of Copyrights should adopt appropriate regulations regarding the affixation of notice to and the registration and deposit of works of authorship used in conjunction with computers.

LAW

§ 118. Scope of exclusive rights: Use of certain works in connection with noncommercial broadcasting

(a) The exclusive rights provided by section 106 shall, with respect to the works specified by subsection (b) and the activities specified by subsection (d), be subject to the conditions and limitations prescribed by this section.

(b) Not later than thirty days after the Copyright Royalty Tribunal has been constituted in accordance with section 802, the Chairman of the Tribunal shall cause notice to be published in the Federal Register of the initiation of proceedings for the purpose of determining reasonable terms and rates of royalty payments for the activities specified by subsection (d) with respect to published nondramatic musical works and published pictorial, graphic, and sculptural works during a period beginning as provided in clause (3) of this subsection and ending on December 31, 1982. Copyright owners and public broadcasting entities shall negotiate in good faith and cooperate fully with the Tribunal in an effort to reach reasonable and expeditious results. Notwithstanding any provision of the antitrust laws, any owners of copyright in works specified by this subsection and any public broadcasting entities, respectively, may negotiate and agree upon the terms and rates of royalty payments and the proportionate division of fees paid among various copyright owners, and may designate common agents to negotiate, agree to, pay, or receive payments.

(1) Any owner of copyright in a work specified in this subsection or any public broadcasting entity may, within one hundred and twenty days after publication of the notice specified in this subsection, submit to the Copyright Royalty Tribunal proposed licenses covering such activities with respect to such works. The Copyright Royalty Tribunal shall proceed on the basis of the proposals submitted to it as well as any other relevant information. The Copyright Royalty Tribunal shall permit any interested party to submit information relevant to such proceedings.

(2) License agreements voluntarily negotiated at any time between one or more copyright owners and one or more public broadcasting entities shall be given effect in lieu of any determination by the Tribunal: *Provided*, That copies of such agreements are filed in the Copyright Office within thirty days of execution in accordance with regulations that the Register of Copyrights shall prescribe.

(3) Within six months, but not earlier than one hundred and twenty days, from the date of publication of the notice specified in this subsection the Copyright Royalty Tribunal shall make a determination and publish in the Federal Register a schedule of rates and terms which, subject to clause (2) of this subsection, shall be binding on all owners of copyright in works specified by this subsection and public broadcasting entities, regardless of

whether or not such copyright owners and public broadcasting entities have submitted proposals to the Tribunal. In establishing such rates and terms the Copyright Royalty Tribunal may consider the rates for comparable circumstances under voluntary license agreements negotiated as provided in clause (2) of this subsection. The Copyright Royalty Tribunal shall also establish requirements by which copyright owners may receive reasonable notice of the use of their works under this section, and under which records of such use shall be kept by public broadcasting entities.

(4) With respect to the period beginning on the effective date of this title and ending on the date of publication of such rates and terms, this title shall not afford to owners of copyright or public broadcasting entities any greater or lesser rights with respect to the activities specified in subsection (d) as applied to works specified in this subsection than those afforded under the law in effect on December 31, 1977, as held applicable and construed by a court in an action brought under this title.

(c) The initial procedure specified in subsection (b) shall be repeated and concluded between June 30 and December 31, 1982, and at five-year intervals thereafter, in accordance with regulations that the Copyright Royalty Tribunal shall prescribe.

(d) Subject to the transitional provisions of subsection (b) (4), and to the terms of any voluntary license agreements that have been negotiated as provided by subsection (b) (2), a public broadcasting entity may, upon compliance with the provisions of this section, including the rates and terms established by the Copyright Royalty Tribunal under subsection (b) (3), engage in the following activities with respect to published nondramatic musical works and published pictorial, graphic, and sculptural works:

(1) performance or display of a work by or in the course of a transmission made by a noncommercial educational broadcast station referred to in subsection (g); and

(2) production of a transmission program, reproduction of copies or phonorecords of such a transmission program, and distribution of such copies or phonorecords, where such production, reproduction, or distribution is made by a nonprofit institution or organization solely for the purpose of transmissions specified in clause (1); and

(3) the making of reproductions by a governmental body or a nonprofit institution of a transmission program simultaneously with its transmission as specified in clause (1), and the performance or display of the contents of such program under the conditions specified by clause (1) of section 110, but only if the reproductions are used for performances or displays for a period of no more than seven days from the date of the transmission specified in clause (1), and are destroyed before or at the end of such period. No person supplying, in accordance with clause (2), a reproduction of a transmission program to governmental bodies or nonprofit institutions under this clause shall have any liability as a result of failure of such body or institution to destroy such reproduction: *Provided*, That it shall have notified such body or institution of the requirement for such destruction pursuant to this clause: *And provided further*, That if such body or institution itself fails to destroy such reproduction it shall be deemed to have infringed.

(e) Except as expressly provided in this subsection, this section shall have no applicability to works other than those specified in subsection (b).

(1) Owners of copyright in nondramatic literary works and public broadcasting entities may, during the course of voluntary negotiations, agree among themselves, respectively, as to the terms and rates of royalty payments without liability under the antitrust laws. Any such terms and rates of royalty payments shall be effective upon filing in the Copyright Office, in accordance with regulations that the Register of Copyrights shall prescribe.

(2) On January 3, 1980, the Register of Copyrights, after consulting with authors and other owners of copyright in nondramatic literary works and their representatives, and with public broadcasting entities and their representatives, shall submit to the Congress a report setting forth the extent to which voluntary licensing arrangements have been reached with respect to the use of nondramatic literary works by such broadcast stations. The report should also describe any problems that may have arisen, and present legislative or other recommendations, if warranted.

(f) Nothing in this section shall be construed to permit, beyond the limits of fair use as provided by section 107, the unauthorized dramatization of a nondramatic musical work, the production of a transmission program drawn to any substantial extent from a published compilation of pictorial, graphic, or sculptural works, or the unauthorized use of any portion of an audiovisual work.

(g) As used in this section, the term "public broadcasting entity" means a noncommercial educational broadcast station as defined in section 397 of title 47 and any nonprofit institution or organization engaged in the activities described in clause (2) of subsection (d).

The definition of "public broadcasting entity" appears under U.S. CODE OF FEDERAL REGULATIONS on page 174.

SENATE REPORT

This section of the bill was substantially revised as it passed between the two houses of Congress. The SENATE REPORT, which reflects earlier legislative efforts, appears first; it is followed by the HOUSE REPORT, which reflects the intent and language of the act.

SECTION 118. PUBLIC BROADCASTING

General Background

During the consideration in the Congress of the copyright revision legislation, public broadcasting proposed the addition to the bill of a section providing a compulsory license for the use of certain categories of copyrighted works by public broadcasting. Senator Charles McC Mathias, Jr. introduced such an amendment during the 93rd Congress to S. 1361, but the amendment was not actively considered with the understanding that the issue would be fully studied in the 94th Congress.

The Subcommittee on Patents, Trademarks, and Copyrights this year gave detailed consideration to the issues presented by the amendment of Senator Mathias. During the Subcommittee proceedings the Chairman of the Subcommittee requested the representatives of public broadcasting and of the copyright proprietors to explore the possibility of achieving agreements outside the copyright legislation, which would assure public broadcasting access to copyrighted materials upon the payment of reasonable royalties. Considerable progress was made during these discussions, and consequently the Subcommittee did not incorporate a public broadcasting compulsory license in S. 22. The Chairman and members of the Subcommittee issued a joint statement which noted that "tentative understandings have been achieved on a number of issues" and expresed the view of the Subcommittee that the isues still in dispute could be resolved "if the parties seek reasonable accommodations."

When the Committee on the Judiciary met on S. 22 on October 7, 1975, several issues still remained unresolved. These principally involve the amount of royalty payments and procedures for arbitration of disputes, the absence of central clearance bodies for certain categories of copyrighted works, and the necessity of an antitrust immunity provision to enable the implementation of a private agreement. Consequently the Committee by majority vote decided to incorporate in S. 22 a public broadcasting amendment proposed by Senator Mathias. While adopting this section, the Committee nevertheless still strongly urges the parties to continue negotiations to reach private agreements whereever possible. The Committee believes that this section should be appropriately modified to reflect such agreements as may be reached prior to enactment.

Policy Considerations

The proponents of the public broadcasting compulsory license contend that the creation of such a license is essential to assure public broadcasting broad access to copyrighted materials at reasonable royalties without protracted delays in obtaining permissions from copyright owners. Administrative costs for individual clearances would be larger than the royalties paid, and beyond the resources of public broadcasting. The compulsory license is intended to ease public broadcasting's transition from its previous "not for profit" exemption under the existing copyright law. As such, this provision does not constitute a subsidy of public broadcasting by the copyright proprietors since the amendment requires the payment of copyright royalties reflecting the fair value of the materials used. Furthermore, the compulsory license system extends only to nondramatic literary, musical and pictorial works, and would in no way affect the use of copyrighted material in dramatic works, which would still be freely negotiated. The limitation on the exclusive rights of copyright proprietors by the institution of compulsory licenses has been provided in several other sections of this legislation. The procedures for implementing the compulsory license parallel those provided in other sections of this legislation, but in the interests of establishing well-researched and reasonable rates, the amendment leaves the establishment of initial rates to the Copyright Royalty Tribunal.

The opponents of this section argue that it is unsound, unnecessary and unworkable. It is contended that the section constitutes a serious erosion of the exclusive rights of authors and copyright proprietors. The Register of Copyrights has objected to the "loss of control by authors over the use of their work in a major communications medium, and the dangers of State control and loss of freedom of expression implicit in the proposed system." The section is unnecessary because private agreements can adequately resolve the copyright problems of public broadcasting. The section will prove burdensome both to public broadcasting and to copyright proprietors. The Register of Copyrights has informed the Committee that "the failure to establish any statutory royalty makes the plan unworkable."

Works Subject to Compulsory License

Section 118(a) provides, as a limitation on the exclusive rights of copyright owners, that it is not an infringement of copyright for a public broadcasting entity to broadcast, subject to the conditions of this section, any nondramatic literary or musical work, pictorial, graphic, or sculptural work. Clearly excluded from the scope of the compulsory license are plays, operas, ballets and other stage presentations, motion pictures, television programs, documentary films, and audio-visual works. Subsection (e) of Section 118 further provides that the compulsory license shall not apply to unpublished nondramatic literary or musical works or to dramatization rights for nondramatic literary or musical works.

The compulsory license does include the reading or recital of poems, short stories, or portions of a book. Simple reading or recital of such works is not likely to interfere with the ability of authors to sell a work for film or television dramatization. But the license does not apply to the adaptation or dramatization of such works.

Procedures

The Committee in adopting a compulsory license for public broadcasting has endeavored to integrate the operation of this license with the procedures established in other sections of this legislation. To facilitate the incorporation of this compulsory license into the general structure of the bill, the section is set forth in rather general language. This section and other sections of this legislation provide adequate authorization for the Register of Copyrights to promulgate such rules and regulations as may be necessary to implement the policy objectives of this section.

The statutory compulsory license is only available to public broadcasting upon compliance with the requirements of this section and the regulations of the Copyright Office promulgated to implement the provisions of this section. Failure to observe these conditions renders all unauthorized uses as acts of infringement, fully subject to the remedies provided in Chapter 5.

In accordance with the regulations of the Register of Copyrights, a public broadcasting entity shall at periodic intervals file a notice with the Copyright Office containing such information necessary for the operation of this section as may be required by the Register of Copyrights. At such intervals as may be prescribed by the Register, the public broadcasting entity shall deposit with the Register of Copyrights a statement of account and the total royalty fees for the period covered by the statement. The statement of account shall be in such detail as may be required by the Register of Copyrights. It is the intent of this legislation that the statement of account and other relevant information filed with the Register of Copyrights shall be available for public study and inspection.

Royalty Fees

Subsection (c) provides that reasonable royalty fees "for public television and radio broadcasts by public broadcasting entities" shall be established by the Copyright Royalty Tribunal. Such fees may be calculated upon a per-use, per-program, prorated, or annual basis, as the Copyright Royalty Tribunal finds appropriate with respect to the type of the copyrighted work and the nature of broadcast use.

Since this section does not establish a statutory royalty schedule, it is contemplated that the Register of Copyrights shall upon the effective date of this section proceed to constitute a panel of the Tribunal to establish a royalty fee schedule. This legislation requires the payment of reasonable royalties by public broadcasting commencing with the effective date of the bill. The payment of such royalties, however, may be deferred in the absence of private license agreements, until a royalty schedule has been adopted by the Tribunal, and the Register of Copyrights has promulgated such regulations as may be necessary for the implementation of this section.

It is further provided that the royalty fee schedule may be changed or supplemented "from time to time" by the Copyright Royalty Tribunal may be substituted for the compulsory license provided in this section.

The Committee in adopting Section 118 anticipates that determinations as to the amount of the royalty to be paid for the use of works covered under this section will be decided by private license agreements or by the application of the rates provided in the fee schedule adopted by the Copyright Royalty Tribunal.

Subsection (d) provides that the royalty fees deposited with the Register of Copyrights shall be distributed according to the specified procedures. Each person claiming such fees must in July of each year file a claim with the Register of Copyrights. Notwithstanding any provisions of the antitrust laws, the claimants may agree among themselves as to the division and distribution of such fees. If no controversy exists as to the division of the fees, the Register of Copyrights, after deducting his reasonable administrative costs, shall distribute the fees to the copyright owners or their agents. If the Register of Copyrights finds the existence of a controversy, he shall proceed as is provided in Chapter 8 to constitute a panel of the Copyright Royalty Tribunal. The Register of Copyrights shall withhold from distribution an amount sufficient to satisfy all claims with respect to which a controversy exists, but shall have discretion to proceed to distribute any amounts that are not in controversy.

Definitions

Subsection (f) defines the terms "public broadcasting" and "public broadcasting entity." While these terms have been defined in comprehensive terms, the Committee in adopting this section intends that the compulsory licenses created by Section 118 are only operative for specific purposes. The compulsory license applies to public television and radio broadcasting of a "public broadcasting entity," and the recording of the broadcasts by or for a non-profit institution in their instructional activities within a limited time period from the date of the transmission. "Public broadcasting" includes such activities incdental to the transmssion of the broadcast as production and recording by or for use by public broadcasting and, distribution, sale or licensing solely to, and acquisition by, non-profit public broadcasting.

A public broadcasting entity is defined as a non-profit "licensee or permittee" of a noncommercial educational broadcast station as well as other nonprofit institutions such as, for example, independent non-profit production companies which have produced a program for distribution and broadcast by noncommercial educational broadcast stations. The compulsory license does not apply to commercial station broadcast of television or radio programs produced or distributed by public broadcasting entities.

HOUSE REPORT

General background

During its consideration of revision legislation in 1975, the Senate Judiciary Committee adopted an amendment offered by Senator Charles McC. Mathias. The amendment, now section 118 of the Senate bill, grants to public broadcasting a compulsory license for use of non-dramatic literary and musical works, as well as pictorial, graphic, and sculptural works, subject to payment of reasonable royalty fees to be set by the Copyright Royalty Tribunal established by that bill. The Mathias amendment requires that public broadcasters, at periodic intervals, file a notice with the Copyright Office containing information required by the Register of Copyrights and deposit a statement of account and the total royalty fees for the period covered by the statement. In July of each year all persons having a claim to such fees are to file their claims with the Register of Copyrights. If no controversy exists, the Register would distribute the royalties to the various copyright owners and their agents after deducting reasonable administrative costs; controversies are to be settled by the Tribunal.

On July 10, 1975, the House Subcommittee heard testimony on the Mathias amendment from representatives of public broadcasters, authors, publishers, and music performing rights societies. The public broadcasters pointed to Congressional concern for the development of their activities as evidenced by the Public Broadcasting Act. They urged that a compulsory license was essential to assure public broadcasting broad access to copyrighted materials at reasonable royalties and without administratively cumbersome and costly "clearance" problems that would impair the vitality of their operations. The opponents of the amendment argued that the nature of public broadcasting has changed significantly in the past decade, to the extent that it now competes with commercial broadcasting as a national entertainment and cultural medium. They asserted that the performing rights society arrangements under which copyrighted music is licensed for performance removed any problem in clearing music for broadcasting, and that voluntary agreements could adequately resolve the copyright problems feared by public broadcasters, at less expense and burden than the compulsory license, for synchronization and literary rights. The authors of literary works stressed that a compulsory licensing system would deny them the fundamental right to control the use of their works and protect their reputation in a major communications medium.

General policy considerations

The Committee is cognizant of the intent of Congress, in enacting the Public Broadcasting Act on November 7, 1967, that encouragement and support of noncommercial broadcasting is in the public interest. It is also aware that public broadcasting may encounter problems not confronted by commercial broadcasting enterprises, due to such factors as the special nature of programming, repeated use of programs, and, of course, limited financial resources. Thus, the Committee determined that the nature of public broadcasting does warrant special treatment in certain areas. However, the Committee did not feel that the broad compulsory license provided in the Senate bill is necessary to the continued successful operation of public broadcasting. In addition, the Committee believes that the system provided in the Senate bill for the deposit of royalty fees with the Copyright Office for distribution to claimants, and the resolution of disputes over such distribution by a statutory tribunal, can be replaced by payments directly between the parties, without the intervention of government machinery and its attendant administrative costs.

In general, the Committee amended the public broadcasting provisions of the Senate bill toward attainment of the objective clearly stated in the Report of the Senate Judiciary Committee, namely, that copyright owners and public broadcasters be encouraged to reach voluntary private agreements.

Procedures

Not later than thirty days following the publication by the President of the notice announcing the initial appointments to the Copyright Royalty Commission (specified in Chapter 8), the Chairman of the Commission is to publish notice in the Federal Register of the initiation of proceedings to determine "reasonable terms and rates" for certain uses of published nondramatic musical works and published pictorial, graphic and sculptural works, during a period ending on December 31, 1982.

Copyright owners and public broadcasting entities that do not reach voluntary agreement are bound by the terms and rates established by the Commission, which are to be published in the Federal Register within six months of the notice of initiation of proceedings. During the period between the effective date of the Act and the publication of the rates and terms, the Committee has preserved the status quo by providing, in section 118(b)(4), that the Act does not afford to copyright owners or public broadcasting entities any greater or lesser rights with respect to the relevant uses of nondramatic musical works and pictorial, graphic, and sculptural works than those afforded under the law in effect on December 31, 1977.

License agreements that have been voluntarily negotiated supersede, as between the parties to the agreement, the terms and rates established by the Commission, provided that copies of the agreements are properly filed with the Copyrigt Office within 30 days of execution. Under clause (2) of section 118(b), the agreements may be negotiated "at any time"—whether before, during, or after determinations by the Commission.

Under section 118(c), the procedures for the Commission's establishing such rates and terms are to be repeated in the last half of 1982 and every five years thereafter.

Establishment of reasonable terms and rates

In establishing reasonable terms and rates for public broadcasting use of the specified works, the Commission, under clause (b)(1) of section 118, is to consider proposals timely submitted to it, as well as "any other relevant information", including that put forward for its consideration "by any interested party."

The Committee does not intend that owners of copyrighted material be required to subsidize public broadcasting. It is intended that the Commission assure a fair return to copyright owners without unfairly burdening public broadcasters. Section 118(b)(3) provides that "the Commission may consider the rates for comparable circumstances under voluntary license agreements." The Commission is also expected to consider both the general public interest in encouraging the growth and development of public broadcasting, and the "promotion of science and the useful arts" through the ecouragement of musical and artistic creation.

The Committee anticipates that the "terms" established by the Commission shall include provisions as to acceptable methods of payment of royalties by public broadcasting entities to copyright owners. For example, where the whereabouts of the copyright owner may not be readily known, the terms should specify the nature of the obligation of the public broadcasting entity to locate the owner, or to set aside or otherwise assure payment of appropriate royalties, should he or she appear and make a claim. Section 118(b)(3) requires the Commission "to establish requirements by which copyright owners may receive reasonable notice of the use of their works." The Committee intends that these requirements shall not impose undue hardships on public broadcasting entities and, in the above illustration, shall provide for the specific termination of any period during which the public broadcasting entity is requred to set aside payments. It is expected that, in some cases, especially in the area of pictorial, graphic, and sculptural works, the whereabouts of the owners of copyright may not be known and they may never appear to claim payment of royalties.

The Commission is also to establish record keeping requirements for public broadcasting entities in order to facilitate the identification, calculation, allocation and payment of claims and royalties.

Works affected

Under sections 118(b) and (c) of the Committee's amendment, the establishment of rates and terms by the Copyright Royalty Commission pertains only to the use of published nondramatic musical works, and published pictorial, graphic, and sculptural works. As under the Senate bill, rights in plays, operas, ballet, and other stage presentations, motion pictures, and other audiovisual works are not affected.

Section 118(f) is intended to make clear that this section does not permit unauthorized use, beyond the limits of section 107, of individual frames from a filmstrip or any other portion of any audiovisual work. Additionally, the application of this section to pictorial, graphic, and sculptural works does not extend to the production of transmission programs drawn to any substantial extent from a compilation of such works.

The above section on "Works affected" appears in the "Correction of Errors in Printed House Report on S. 22" in the CONGRESSIONAL RECORD, Vol. 122, No. 143 (daily edition of September 21, 1976), pp. H-10727-10728.

The Committee also concluded that the performance of nondramatic literary works should not be subject to Commission determination. It was particularly concerned that a compulsory license for literary works would result in loss of control by authors over the use of their work in violation of basic principles of artistic and creative freedom. It is recognized that copyright not only provides compensation to authors, but also protection as to how and where their works are used. The Committee was assured by representatives of authors and publishers that licensing arrangements for readings from their books, poems, and other works on public broadcasting programs for reasonable compensation and under reasonable safeguards for authors' rights could be worked out in private negotiation. The Committee strongly urges the parties to work toward mutually acceptable licenses; to facilitate their negotiations and aid in the possible establishment of clearance mechanisms and rates, the Committee's amendment provides the parties, in section 118(e)(1), with an appropriately limited exemption from the anti-trust laws.

The Committee has also provided, in paragraph (2) of clause (e), that on January 3, 1980, the Register of Copyrights, after consultation with the interested parties, shall submit a report to Congress on the extent to which voluntary licensing arrangements have been reached with respect to public broadcast use of nondramatic literary works, and present legislative or other recommendations, if warranted.

The use of copyrighted sound recordings in educational television and radio programs distributed by or through public broadcasting entities is governed by section 114 and is discussed in connection with that section.

Activities affected

Section 118(d) specifies the activities which may be engaged in by public broadcasting entities under terms and rates established by the Commission. These include the performance or display of published nondramatic musical works, and of published pictorial graphic, and sculptural works, in the course of transmissions by noncommercial educational broadcast stations; and the production, reproduction, and distribution of transmission programs including such works by nonprofit organizations for the purpose of such transmissions. It is the intent of the Committee that "interconnection" activities serving as a technical adjunct to such transmissions, such as the use of satellites or microwave equipment, be included within the specified activities.

Paragraph (3) of clause (d) also includes the reproduction, simultaneously with transmission, of public broadcasting programs by governmental bodies or nonprofit institutions, and the performance or display of the contents of the reproduction under the conditions of section 110(1). However, the reproduction so made must be destroyed at the end of seven days from the transmission.

This limited provision for unauthorized simultaneous or off-the-air reproduction is limited to nondramatic musical works and pictorial graphic and sculptural works included in public broadcasting transmissions. It does not extend to other works included in the transmissions, or to the entire transmission program.

It is the intent of the Committee that schools be permitted to engage in off-the-air reproduction to the extent and under the conditions provided in 118(d)(3); however, in the event a public broadcasting station or producer makes the reproduction and distributes a copy to the school, the station or producer will not be held liable for the school's failure to destroy the reproduction, provided it has given notice of the requirement of destruction. In such a case the school itself, although it did not engage in the act of reproduction, is deemed an infringer fully subject to the remedies provided in Chapter 5 of the Act. The establishment of standards for adequate notice under this provision should be considered by the Commission.

Section 118(f) makes it clear that the rights of performance and other activities specified in subsection (d) do not extend to the unauthorized dramatization of a nondramatic musical work.

CONFERENCE REPORT

NONCOMMERCIAL BROADCASTING

Senate bill

Section 118 of the Senate bill granted to public broadcasting a compulsory license for the performance or display of nondramatic musical works, pictorial, graphic, and sculptural works, and nondramatic literary works, subject to the payment of reasonable royalty fees to be set by the Copyright Royalty Tribunal. The Senate bill required that public broadcasters, at periodic intervals, file a notice with the Copyright Office containing information required by the Register of Copyrights, and deposit a statement of account and the total royalty fees for the period covered by the statement. The Register was to receive claims to payment of royalty fees, and to distribute any amounts not in dispute; controversies were to be settled by the Tribunal, which was also charged with reviewing and, if appropriate, adjusting the royalty rates in 1980 and at ten year intervals thereafter. Sec. 113 of the Transitional and Supplementary provisions would start the machinery for establishment of the initial rates immediately upon enactment of the new law. Section 118(f) also contained a provision permitting nonprofit educational institutions to record educational television and radio programs off the air, for limited use in instructional activities during a week following the broadcast.

House bill

The House bill substantially changed the provisions of section 118, retaining a different form of compulsory licensing for the use in public broadcasting of nondramatic musical works and for pictorial, graphic, and sculptural works, but not subjecting the exclusive rights in nondramatic literary works to compulsory licensing. Under the House bill, within thirty days after appointment of the Royalty Commission, the chairman was to initiate proceedings to determine "reasonable terms and rates" under the section for a period running through 1982. Copyright owners and public broadcasting entities that did not reach voluntary agreement were to be by the terms and rates established by the Commission.

In establishing those rates and terms, the Commission was to consider, among other relevant information, proposals put forward to it within specified time limits. The House bill deleted Sec. 113 of the Transitional and Supplementary Provisions of the Act, but provided in section 118(b)(4) that, during the period between the effective date of the Act and publication of the initial rates and terms, the status quo as to liability under the present law would be preserved. Payment of royalties under section 118 were to be handled among the parties without government intervention. The royalty review cycle would begin in 1982 and continue at five-year intervals thereafter. Section 118(d)(3) retained the provision permitting off-the-air taping of public broadcasts by educational institutions, but with amendments clarifying and tightening the provision.

Although nondramatic literary works were not included in the compulsory licensing scheme of section 118, subsection (e) provided an exemption from the antitrust laws with respect to voluntary negotiations aimed at licensing agreements for the public broadcasting of such works. The subsection also required the Register of Copyrights, on January 3, 1980, to report upon the extent to which such voluntary agreements had been achieved, the problems that had arisen, and any recommendations for legislation that might be appropriate.

Conference substitute

The conference substitute adopts the House amendments.

U.S. CODE OF FEDERAL REGULATIONS

Section 118(g) of the Copyright Act refers to the definition of "public broadcasting entity" in the U.S. Code of Federal Regulations, Title 47, Section 397. That definition follows:

> The term "public broadcasting entity" means the Corporation, any licensee or permittee of a noncommercial educational broadcast station, or any nonprofit institution engaged primarily in the production, acquisition, distribution, or dissemination of educational television or radio programs.

Source: *U.S. Code of Federal Regulations*, Title 47, Sec. 397(11). (Washington: Office of the Federal Register, 1979).

LAW

Chapter 2.—COPYRIGHT OWNERSHIP AND TRANSFER

§ 201. Ownership of copyright

(a) Initial Ownership.—Copyright in a work protected under this title vests initially in the author or authors of the work. The authors of a joint work are coowners of copyright in the work.

(b) Works Made for Hire.—In the case of a work made for hire, the employer or other person for whom the work was prepared is considered the author for purposes of this title, and, unless the parties have expressly agreed otherwise in a written instrument signed by them, owns all of the rights comprised in the copyright.

(c) Contributions to Collective Works.—Copyright in each separate contribution to a collective work is distinct from copyright in the collective work as a whole, and vests initially in the author of the contribution. In the absence of an express transfer of the copyright or of any rights under it, the owner of copyright in the collective work is presumed to have acquired only the privilege of reproducing and distributing the contribution as part of that particular collective work, any revision of that collective work, and any later collective work in the same series.

(d) Transfer of Ownership.—

(1) The ownership of a copyright may be transferred in whole or in part by any means of conveyance or by operation of law, and may be bequeathed by will or pass as personal property by the applicable laws of intestate succession.

(2) Any of the exclusive rights comprised in a copyright, including any subdivision of any of the rights specified by section 106, may be transferred as provided by clause (1) and owned separately. The owner of any particular exclusive right is entitled, to the extent of that right, to all of the protection and remedies accorded to the copyright owner by this title.

(e) Involuntary Transfer.—When an individual author's ownership of a copyright, or of any of the exclusive rights under a copyright, has not previously been transferred voluntarily by that individual author, no action by any governmental body or other official or organization purporting to seize, expropriate, transfer, or exercise rights of ownership with respect to the copyright, or any of the exclusive rights under a copyright, shall be given effect under this title.

HOUSE REPORT

SECTION 201. OWNERSHIP OF COPYRIGHT

Initial ownership

Two basic and well-established principles of copyright law are restated in section 201(a): that the source of copyright ownership is the author of the work, and that, in the case of a "joint work," the coauthors of the work are likewise coowners of the copyright. Under the definition of section 101, a work is "joint" if the authors collaborated with each other, or if each of the authors prepared his or her contribution with the knowledge and intention that it would be merged with the contributions of other authors as "inseparable or interdependent parts of a unitary whole." The touchstone here is the intention, at the time the writing is done, that the parts be absorbed or combined into an integrated unit, although the parts themselves may be either "inseparable" (as the case of a novel or painting) or "interdependent" (as in the case of a motion picture, opera, or the words and music of a song). The definition of "joint work" is to be contrasted with the definition of "collective work," also in section 101, in which the elements of merger and unity are lacking; there the key elements are assemblage or gathering of "separate and independent works * * * into a collective whole."

The definition of "joint works" has prompted some concern lest it be construed as converting the authors of previously written works, such as plays, novels, and music, into coauthors of a motion picture in which their work is incorporated. It is true that a motion picture would normally be a joint rather than a collective work with respect to those authors who actually work on the film, although their usual status as employees for hire would keep the question of coownership from coming up. On the other hand, although a novelist, playwright, or songwriter may write a work with the hope or expectation that it will be used in a motion picture, this is clearly a case of separate or independent authorship rather than one where the basic intention behind the writing of the work was for motion picture use. In this case, the motion picture is a derivative work within the definition of that term, and section 103 makes plain that copyright in a derivative work is independent of, and does not enlarge the scope of rights in, any pre-existing material incorporated in it. There is thus no need to spell this conclusion out in the definition of "joint work."

There is also no need for a specific statutory provision concerning the rights and duties of the coowners of a work; court-made law on this point is left undisturbed. Under the bill, as under the present law, coowners of a copyright would be treated generally as tenants in common, with each coowner having an independent right to use or license the use of a work, subject to a duty of accounting to the other coowners for any profits.

Works made for hire

Section 201(b) of the bill adopts one of the basic principles of the present law: that in the case of works made for hire the employer is considered the author of the work, and is regarded as the initial owner of copyright unless there has been an agreement otherwise. The subsection also requires that any agreement under which the employee is to own rights be in writing and signed by the parties.

The work-made-for-hire provisions of this bill represent a carefully balanced compromise, and as such they do not incorporate the amendments proposed by screenwriters and composers for motion pictures. Their proposal was for the recognition of something similar to the "shop right" doctrine of patent law: with some exceptions, the employer would acquire the right to use the employee's work to the extent needed for purposes of his regular business, but the employee would retain all other rights as long as he or she refrained from the authorizing of competing uses. However, while this change might theoretically improve the bargaining position of screenwriters and others as a group, the practical benefits that individual authors would receive are highly conjectural. The pesumption that initial ownership rights vest in the employer for hire is well established in American copyright law, and to exchange that for the uncertainties of the shop right doctrine would not only be of dubious value to employers and employees alike, but might also reopen a number of other issues.

The status of works prepared on special order or commission was a major issue in the development of the definition of "works made for hire" in section 101, which has undergone extensive revision during the legislative process. The basic problem is how to draw a statutory line between those works written on special order or commission that should be considered as "works made for hire," and those that should not. The definition now provided by the bill represents a compromise which, in effect, spells out those specific categories of commissioned works that can be considered "works made for hire" under certain circumstances.

Of these, one of the most important categories is that of "instructional texts." This term is given its own definition in the bill: "a literary, pictorial, or graphic work prepared for publication with the purpose of use in systematic instructional activities." The concept is intended to include what might be loosely called "textbook material," whether or not in book form or prepared in the form of text matter. The basic characteristic of "instructional texts" is the purpose of their preparation for "use in systematic instructional activities," and they are to be distinguished from works prepared for use by a general readership.

SENATE REPORT

The following paragraph was omitted in the HOUSE REPORT.

Another specific category under the definition of "works made for hire" is a "a photographic or other portrait of one or more persons." Works of this sort are frequently commissioned and should be considered "works made for hire" if, as in the other specified categories, both of the parties sign a written agreement to this effect.

HOUSE REPORT (Continued)

Contributions to collective works

Subsection (c) of section 201 deals with the troublesome problem of ownership of copyright in contributions to collective works, and the relationship between copyright ownership in a contribution and in the collective work in which it appears. The first sentence establishes the basic principle that copyright in the individual contribution and copyright in the collective work as a whole are separate and distinct, and that the author of the contribution is, as in every other case, the first owner of copyright in it. Under the definitions in section 101, a "collective work" is a species of "compilation" and, by its nature, must involve the selection, assembly, and arrangement of "a number of contributions." Examples of "collective works" would ordinarily include periodical issues, anthologies, symposia, and collections of the discrete writings of the same authors, but not cases, such as a composition consisting of words and music, a work published with illustrations or front matter, or three one-act plays, where relatively few separate elements have been brought together. Unlike the contents of other types of "compilations," each of the contributions incorporated in a "collective work" must itself constitute a "separate and independent" work, therefore ruling out compilations of information or other uncopyrightable material and works published with editorial revisions or annotations. Moreover, as noted above, there is a basic distinction between a "joint work," where the separate elements merge into a unified whole, and a "collective work," where they remain unintegrated and disparate.

The bill does nothing to change the rights of the owner of copyright in a collective work under the present law. These exclusive rights extend to the elements of compilation and editing that went into the collective work as a whole, as well as the contributions that were written for hire by employees of the owner of the collective work, and those copyrighted contributions that have been transferred in writing to the owner by their authors. However, one of the most significant aims of the bill is to clarify and improve the present confused and frequently unfair legal situation with respect to rights in contributions.

The second sentence of section 201(c), in conjunction with the provisions of section 404 dealing with copyright notice, will preserve the author's copyright in a contribution even if the contribution does not bear a separate notice in the author's name, and without requiring any unqualified transfer of rights to the owner of the collective work. This is coupled with a presumption that, unless there has been an express transfer of more, the owner of the collective work acquires "only the privilege of reproducing and distributing the contribution as part of that particular collective work, any revision of that collective work, and any later collective work in the same series."

The basic presumption of section 201(c) is fully consistent with present law and practice, and represents a fair balancing of equities. At the same time, the last clause of the subsection, under which the privilege of republishing the contribution under certain limited circumstances would be presumed, is an essential counterpart of the basic presumption. Under the language of this clause a publishing company could reprint a contribution from one issue in a later issue of its magazine, and could reprint an article from a 1980 edition of an encyclopedia in a 1990 revision of it; the publisher could not revise the contribution itself or include it in a new anthology or an entirely different magazine or other collective work.

Transfer of ownership

The principle of unlimited alienability of copyright is stated in clause (1) of section 201(d). Under that provision the ownership of a copyright, or of any part of it, may be transferred by any means of conveyance or by operation of law, and is to be treated as personal property upon the death of the owner. The term "transfer of copyright ownership" is defined in section 101 to cover any "conveyance, alienation, or hypothecation," including assignments, mortgages, and exclusive licenses, but not including nonexclusive licenses. Representatives of motion picture producers have argued that foreclosures of copyright mortgages should not be left to varying State laws, and that the statute should establish a Federal foreclosure system. However, the benefits of such a system would be of very limited application, and would not justify the complicated statutory and procedural requirements that would have to be established.

Clause (2) of subsection (d) contains the first explicit statutory recognition of the principle of divisibility of copyright in our law. This provision, which has long been sought by authors and their representatives, and which has attracted wide support from other groups, means that any of the exclusive rights that go to make up a copyright, including those enumerated in section 106 and any subdivision of them, can be transferred and owned separately. The definition of "transfer of copyright ownership" in section 101 makes clear that the principle of divisibility applies whether or not the transfer is "limited in time or place of effect," and another definition in the same section provides that the term "copyright owner," with respect to any one exclusive right, refers to the owner of that particular right. The last sentence of section 201(d)(2) adds that the owner, with respect to the particular exclusive right he or she owns, is entitled "to all of the protection and remedies accorded to the copyright owner by this title." It is thus clear, for example, that a local broadcasting station holding an exclusive license to transmit a particular work within a particular geographic area and for a particular period of time, could sue, in its own name as copyright owner, someone who infringed that particular exclusive right.

Subsection (e) provides that when an individual author's ownership of a copyright, or of any of the exclusive rights under a copyright, have not previously been voluntarily transferred, no action by any governmental body or other official or organization purporting to seize, expropriate, transfer, or exercise rights of ownership with respect to the copyright, or any of the exclusive rights under a copyright, shall be given effect under this title.

The purpose of this subsection is to reaffirm the basic principle that the United States copyright of an individual author shall be secured to that author, and cannot be taken away by any involuntary transfer. It is the intent of the subsection that the author be entitled, despite any purported expropriation or involuntary transfer, to continue exercising all rights under the United States statute, and that the governmental body or organization may not enforce or exercise any rights under this title in that situation.

It may sometimes be difficult to ascertain whether a transfer of copyright is voluntary or is coerced by covert pressure. But subsection (e) would protect foreign authors against laws and decrees purporting to divest them of their rights under the United States copyright statute, and would protect authors within the foreign country who choose to resist such covert pressures.

Traditional legal actions that may involve transfer of ownership, such as bankruptcy proceedings and mortgage foreclosures, are not within the scope of this subsection; the authors in such cases have voluntarily consented to these legal processes by their overt actions—for example, by filing in bankruptcy or by hypothecating a copyright.

LAW

§ 202. Ownership of copyright as distinct from ownership of material object

Ownership of a copyright, or of any of the exclusive rights under a copyright, is distinct from ownership of any material object in which the work is embodied. Transfer of ownership of any material object, including the copy or phonorecord in which the work is first fixed, does not of itself convey any rights in the copyrighted work embodied in the object; nor, in the absence of an agreement, does transfer of ownership of a copyright or of any exclusive rights under a copyright convey property rights in any material object.

HOUSE REPORT

SECTION 202. DISTINCTION BETWEEN OWNERSHIP OF COPYRIGHT AND MATERIAL OBJECT

The principle restated in section 202 is a fundamental and important one: that copyright ownership and ownership of a material object in which the copyrighted work is embodied are entirely separate things. Thus, transfer of a material object does not of itself carry any rights under the copyright, and this includes transfer of the copy or phonorecord—the original manuscript, the photographic negative, the unique painting or statue, the master tape recording, etc.—in which the work was first fixed. Conversely, transfer of a copyright does not necessarily require the conveyance of any material object.

As a result of the interaction of this section and the provisions of section 204(a) and 301, the bill would change a common law doctrine exemplified by the decision in *Pushman v. New York Graphic Society, Inc.*, 287 N.Y. 302, 39 N.E. 2d 249 (1942). Under that doctrine, authors or artists are generally presumed to transfer common law literary property rights when they sell their manuscript or work of art, unless those rights are specifically reserved. This presumption would be reversed under the bill, since a specific written conveyance of rights would be required in order for a sale of any material object to carry with it a transfer of copyright.

LAW

§ 203. Termination of transfers and licenses granted by the author

(a) Conditions for Termination.—In the case of any work other than a work made for hire, the exclusive or nonexclusive grant of a transfer or license of copyright or of any right under a copyright, executed by the author on or after January 1, 1978, otherwise than by will, is subject to termination under the following conditions:

(1) In the case of a grant executed by one author, termination of the grant may be effected by that author or, if the author is dead, by the person or persons who, under clause (2) of this subsection, own and are entitled to exercise a total of more than one-half of that author's termination interest. In the case of a grant executed by two or more authors of a joint work, termination of the grant may be effected by a majority of the authors who executed it; if any of such authors is dead, the termination interest of any such author may be exercised as a unit by the person or persons who, under clause (2) of this subsection, own and are entitled to exercise a total of more than one-half of that author's interest.

(2) Where an author is dead, his or her termination interest is owned, and may be exercised, by his widow or her widower and his or her children or grandchildren as follows:

(A) the widow or widower owns the author's entire termination interest unless there are any surviving children or grandchildren of the author, in which case the widow or widower owns one-half of the author's interest;

(B) the author's surviving children, and the surviving children of any dead child of the author, own the author's entire termination interest unless there is a widow or widower, in which case the ownership of one-half of the author's interest is divided among them;

(C) the rights of the author's children and grandchildren are in all cases divided among them and exercised on a per stirpes basis according to the number of such author's children represented; the share of the children of a dead child in a termination interest can be exercised only by the action of a majority of them.

(3) Termination of the grant may be effected at any time during a period of five years beginning at the end of thirty-five years from the date of execution of the grant; or, if the grant covers the right of publication of the work, the period begins at the end of thirty-five years from the date of publication of the work under the grant or at the end of forty years from the date of execution of the grant, whichever term ends earlier.

(4) The termination shall be effected by serving an advance notice in writing, signed by the number and proportion of owners of termination interests required under clauses (1) and (2) of this subsection, or by their duly authorized agents, upon the grantee or the grantee's successor in title.

(A) The notice shall state the effective date of the termination, which shall fall within the five-year period specified by clause (3) of this subsection, and the notice shall be served not less than two or more than ten years before that date. A copy of the notice shall be recorded in the Copyright Office before the effective date of termination, as a condition to its taking effect.

(B) The notice shall comply, in form, content, and manner of service, with requirements that the Register of Copyrights shall prescribe by regulation.

(5) Termination of the grant may be effected notwithstanding any agreement to the contrary, including an agreement to make a will or to make any future grant.

(b) EFFECT OF TERMINATION.—Upon the effective date of termination, all rights under this title that were covered by the terminated grants revert to the author, authors, and other persons owning termination interests under clauses (1) and (2) of subsection (a), including those owners who did not join in signing the notice of termination under clause (4) of subsection (a), but with the following limitations:

(1) A derivative work prepared under authority of the grant before its termination may continue to be utilized under the terms of the grant after its termination, but this privilege does not extend to the preparation after the termination of other derivative works based upon the copyrighted work covered by the terminated grant.

(2) The future rights that will revert upon termination of the grant become vested on the date the notice of termination has been served as provided by clause (4) of subsection (a). The rights vest in the author, authors, and other persons named in, and in the proportionate shares provided by, clauses (1) and (2) of subsection (a).

(3) Subject to the provisions of clause (4) of this subsection, a further grant, or agreement to make a further grant, of any right covered by a terminated grant is valid only if it is signed by the same number and proportion of the owners, in whom the right has vested under clause (2) of this subsection, as are required to terminate the grant under clauses (1) and (2) of subsection (a). Such further grant or agreement is effective with respect to all of the persons in whom the right it covers has vested under clause (2) of this subsection, including those who did not join in signing it. If any person dies after rights under a terminated grant have vested in him or her, that person's legal representatives, legatees, or heirs at law represent him or her for purposes of this clause.

(4) A further grant, or agreement to make a further grant, of any right covered by a terminated grant is valid only if it is made after the effective date of the termination. As an exception, however, an agreement for such a further grant may be made between the persons provided by clause (3) of this subsection and the original grantee or such grantee's successor in title, after the notice of termination has been served as provided by clause (4) of subsection (a).

(5) Termination of a grant under this section affects only those rights covered by the grants that arise under this title, and in no way affects rights arising under any other Federal, State, or foreign laws.

(6) Unless and until termination is effected under this section, the grant, if it does not provide otherwise, continues in effect for the term of copyright provided by this title.

HOUSE REPORT

SECTION 203. TERMINATION OF TRANSFERS AND LICENSES

The problem in general

The provisions of section 203 are based on the premise that the reversionary provisions of the present section on copyright renewal (17 U.S.C. sec. 24) should be eliminated, and that the proposed law should substitute for them a provision safeguarding authors against unremunerative transfers. A provision of this sort is needed because of the unequal bargaining position of authors, resulting in part from the impossibility of determining a work's value until it has been exploited. Section 203 reflects a practical compromise that will further the objectives of the copyright law while recognizing the problems and legitimate needs of all interests involved.

Scope of the provision

Instead of being automatic, as is theoretically the case under the present renewal provision, the termination of a transfer or license under section 203 would require the serving of an advance notice within specified time limits and under specified conditions. However, although affirmative action is needed to effect a termination, the right to take this action cannot be waived in advance or contracted away. Under section 203(a) the right of termination would apply only to transfers and licenses executed after the effective date of the new statute, and would have no retroactive effect.

The right of termination would be confined to inter vivos transfers or licenses executed by the author, and would not apply to transfers by the author's successors in interest or to the author's own bequests. The scope of the right would extend not only to any "transfer of copyright ownership," as defined in section 101, but also to nonexclusive licenses. The right of termination would not apply to "works made for hire," which is one of the principal reasons the definition of that term assumed importance in the development of the bill.

Who can terminate a grant

Two issues emerged from the disputes over section 203 as to the persons empowered to terminate a grant: (1) the specific classes of beneficiaries in the case of joint works; and (2) whether anything less than unanimous consent of all those entitled to terminate should be required to make a termination effective. The bill to some extent reflects a compromise on these points, including a recognition of the dangers of one or more beneficiaries being induced to "hold out" and of unknown children or grandchildren being discovered later. The provision can be summarized as follows:

1. In the case of a work of joint authorship, where the grant was signed by two or more of the authors, majority action by those who signed the grant, or by their interests, would be required to terminate it.

2. There are three different situations in which the shares of joint authors, or of a dead author's widow or widower, children, and grandchildren, must be divided under the statute: (1) The right to effect a termination; (2) the ownership of the terminated rights; and (3) the right to make further grants of reverted rights. The respective shares of the authors, and of a dead

author's widow or widower, children, and grandchildren, would be divided in exactly the same way in each of these situations. The terms "widow," "widower," and "children" are defined in section 101 in an effort to avoid problems and uncertainties that have arisen under the present renewal section.

3. The principle of per stirpes representation would also be applied in exactly the same way in all three situations. Take for example, a case where a dead author left a widow, two living children, and three grandchildren by a third child who is dead. The widow will own half of the reverted interests, the two children will each own 16⅔ percent, and the three grandchildren will each own a share of roughly 5½ percent. But who can exercise the right of termination? Obviously, since she owns 50 percent, the widow is an essential party, but suppose neither of the two surviving children is willing to join her in the termination; is it enough that she gets one of the children of the dead child to join, or can the dead child's interest be exercised only by the action of a majority of his children? Consistent with the per stirpes principle, the interest of a dead child can be exercised only as a unit by majority action of his surviving children. Thus, even though the widow and one grandchild would own 55½ percent of the reverted copyright, they would have to be joined by another child or grandchild in order to effect a termination or a further transfer of reverted rights. This principle also applies where, for example, two joint authors executed a grant and one of them is dead; in order to effect a termination, the living author must be joined by a per stirpes majority of the dead author's beneficiaries. The notice of termination may be signed by the specified owners of termination interests or by "their duly authorized agents," which would include the legally appointed guardians or committees of persons incompetent to sign because of age or mental disability.

When a grant can be terminated

Section 203 draws a distinction between the date when a termination becomes effective and the earlier date when the advance notice of termination is served. With respect to the ultimate effective date, section 203(a)(3) provides, as a general rule, that a grant may be terminated during the 5 years following the expiration of a period of 35 years from the execution of the grant. As an exception to this basic 35-year rule, the bill also provides that "if the grant covers the right of publication of the work, the period begins at the end of 35 years from the date of publication of the work under the grant or at the end of 40 years from the date of execution of the grant, whichever term ends earlier." This alternative method of computation is intended to cover cases where years elapse between the signing of a publication contract and the eventual publication of the work.

The effective date of termination, which must be stated in the advance notice, is required to fall within the 5 years following the end of the applicable 35- or 40-year period, but the advance notice itself must be served earlier. Under section 203(a)(4)(A), the notice must be served "not less than two or more than ten years" before the effective date stated in it.

As an example of how these time-limit requirements would operate in practice, we suggest two typical contract situations:

Case 1: Contract for theatrical production signed on September 2, 1987. Termination of grant can be made to take effect between September 2, 2022 (35 years from execution) and September 1, 2027 (end of 5 year termination period). Assuming that the author decides to terminate on September 1, 2022 (the earliest possible date) the advance notice must be filed between September 1, 2012 and September 1, 2020.

Case 2: Contract for book publication executed on April 10, 1980; book finally published on August 23, 1987. Since contract covers the right of publication, the 5-year termination period would begin on April 10, 2020 (40 years from execution) rather than April 10, 2015 (35 years from execution) or August 23, 2022 (35 years from publication). Assuming that the author decides to make the termination effective on January 1, 2024, the advance notice would have to be served between January 1, 2014, and January 1, 2022.

Effect of termination

Section 203(b) makes clear that, unless effectively terminated within the applicable 5-year period, all rights covered by an existing grant will continue unchanged, and that rights under other Federal, State, or foreign laws are unaffected. However, assuming that a copyright transfer or license is terminated under section 203, who are bound by the termination and how are they affected?

Under the bill, termination means that ownership of the rights covered by the terminated grant reverts to everyone who owns termination interests on the date the notice of termination was served, whether they joined in signing the notice or not. In other words, if a person could have signed the notice, that person is bound by the action of the majority who did; the termination of the grant will be effective as to that person, and a proportionate share of the reverted rights automatically vests in that person. Ownership is divided proportionately on the same per stirpes basis as that provided for the right to effect termination under section 203(a) and, since the reverted rights vest on the date notice is served, the heirs of a dead beneficiary would inherit his or her share.

Under clause (3) of subsection (b), majority action is required to make a further grant of reverted rights. A problem here, of course, is that years may have passed between the time the reverted rights vested and the time the new owners want to make a further transfer; people may have died and children may have been born in the interim. To deal with this problem, the bill looks back to the date of vesting; out of the group in whom rights vested on that date, it requires the further transfer or license to be signed by "the same number and proportion of the owners" (though not necessarily the same individuals) as were then required to terminate the grant under subsection (a). If some of those in whom the rights originally vested have died, their "legal representatives, legatees, or heirs at law" may represent them for this purpose and, as in the case of the termination itself, any one of the minority who does not join in the further grant is nevertheless bound by it.

An important limitation on the rights of a copyright owner under a terminated grant is specified in section 203(b)(1). This clause provides that, notwithstanding a termination, a derivative work prepared earlier may "continue to be utilized" under the conditions of the terminated grant; the clause adds, however, that this privilege is not broad enough to permit the preparation of other derivative works. In other words, a film made from a play could continue to be licensed for performance after the motion picture contract had been terminated but any remake rights covered by the contract would be cut off. For this purpose, a motion picture would be considered as a "derivative work" with respect to every "preexisting work" incorporated in it, whether the preexisting work was created independently or was prepared expressly for the motion picture.

Section 203 would not prevent the parties to a transfer or license from voluntarily agreeing at any time to terminate an existing grant and negotiating a new one, thereby causing another 35-year period to start running. However, the bill seeks to avoid the situation that has arisen under the present renewal provision, in which third parties have bought up contingent future interests as a form of speculation. Section 203(b)(4) would make a further grant of rights that revert under a terminated grant valid "only if it is made after the effective date of the termination." An exception, in the nature of a right of "first refusal," would permit the original grantee or a successor of such grantee to negotiate a new agreement with the persons effecting the termination at any time after the notice of termination has been served.

Nothing contained in this section or elsewhere in this legislation is intended to extend the duration of any license, transfer or assignment made for a period of less than thirty-five years. If, for example, an agreement provides an earlier termination date or lesser duration, or if it allows the author the right of cancelling or terminating the agreement under certain circumstances, the duration is governed by the agreement.

The preceding sentence did not appear in the SENATE REPORT.

Likewise, nothing in this section or legislation is intended to change the existing state of the law of contracts concerning the circumstances in which an author may cancel or terminate a license, transfer, or assignment.

Section 203(b)(6) provides that, unless and until termination is effected under this section, the grant, "if it does not provide otherwise," continues for the term of copyright. This section means that, if the agreement does not contain provisions specifying its term or duration, and the author has not terminated the agreement under this section, the agreement continues for the term of the copyright, subject to any right of termination under circumstances which may be specified therein. If, however, an agreement does contain provisions governing its duration—for example, a term of fifty years—and the author has not exercised his or her right of termination under the statute, the agreement will continue according to its terms—in this example, for only fifty years.

The two preceding sentences did not appear in the SENATE REPORT.

The quoted language is not to be construed as requiring agreements to reserve the right of termination.

LAW

§ 204. Execution of transfers of copyright ownership

(a) A transfer of copyright ownership, other than by operation of law, is not valid unless an instrument of conveyance, or a note or memorandum of the transfer, is in writing and signed by the owner of the rights conveyed or such owner's duly authorized agent.

(b) A certificate of acknowledgement is not required for the validity of a transfer, but is prima facie evidence of the execution of the transfer if—

(1) in the case of a transfer executed in the United States, the certificate is issued by a person authorized to administer oaths within the United States; or

(2) in the case of a transfer executed in a foreign country, the certificate is issued by a diplomatic or consular officer of the United States, or by a person authorized to administer oaths whose authority is proved by a certificate of such an officer.

HOUSE REPORT

The commentary on Sections 204 and 205 appears after Section 205 of the LAW.

LAW

§ 205. Recordation of transfers and other documents

(a) Conditions for Recordation.—Any transfer of copyright ownership or other document pertaining to a copyright may be recorded in the Copyright Office if the document filed for recordation bears the actual signature of the person who executed it, or if it is accompanied by a sworn or official certification that it is a true copy of the original, signed document.

(b) Certificate of Recordation.—The Register of Copyrights shall, upon receipt of a document as provided by subsection (a) and of the fee provided by section 708, record the document and return it with a certificate of recordation.

(c) Recordation as Constructive Notice.—Recordation of a document in the Copyright Office gives all persons constructive notice of the facts stated in the recorded document, but only if—

(1) the document, or material attached to it, specifically identifies the work to which it pertains so that, after the document is indexed by the Register of Copyrights, it would be revealed by a reasonable search under the title or registration number of the work; and

(2) registration has been made for the work.

(d) Recordation as Prerequisite to Infringement Suit.—No person claiming by virtue of a transfer to be the owner of copyright or of any exclusive right under a copyright is entitled to institute an infringement action under this title until the instrument of transfer under which such person claims has been recorded in the Copyright Office, but suit may be instituted after such recordation on a cause of action that arose before recordation.

(e) Priority Between Conflicting Transfers.—As between two conflicting transfers, the one executed first prevails if it is recorded, in the manner required to give constructive notice under subsection (c), within one month after its execution in the United States or within two months after its execution outside the United States, or

at any time before recordation in such manner of the later transfer. Otherwise the later transfer prevails if recorded first in such manner, and if taken in good faith, for valuable consideration or on the basis of a binding promise to pay royalties, and without notice of the earlier transfer.

(f) Priority Between Conflicting Transfer of Ownership and Nonexclusive License.—A nonexclusive license, whether recorded or not, prevails over a conflicting transfer of copyright ownership if the license is evidenced by a written instrument signed by the owner of the rights licensed or such owner's duly authorized agent, and if—

(1) the license was taken before execution of the transfer; or

(2) the license was taken in good faith before recordation of the transfer and without notice of it.

HOUSE REPORT

Sections 204, 205. Execution and Recordation of Transfers

Section 204 is a somewhat broadened and liberalized counterpart of sections 28 and 29 of the present statute. Under subsection (a), a transfer of copyright ownership (other than one brought about by operation of law) is valid only if there exists an instrument of conveyance, or alternatively a "note or memorandum of the transfer," which is in writing and signed by the copyright owner "or such owner's duly authorized agent." Subsection (b) makes clear that a notarial or consular acknowledgment is not essential to the validity of any transfer, whether executed in the United States or abroad. However, the subsection would liberalize the conditions under which certificates of acknowledgment of documents executed abroad are to be accorded prima facie weight, and would give the same weight to domestic acknowledgments under appropriate circumstances.

The recording and priority provisions of section 205 are intended to clear up a number of uncertainties arising from sections 30 and 31 of the present law and to make them more effective and practical in operation. Any "document pertaining to a copyright" may be recorded under subsection (a) if it "bears that actual signature of the person who executed it," or if it is appropriately certified as a true copy. However, subsection (c) makes clear that the recorded document will give constructive notice of its contents only if two conditions are met: (1) the document or attached material specifically identifies the work to which it pertains so that a reasonable search under the title or registration number would reveal it, and (2) registration has been made for the work. Moreover, even though the Register of Copyrights may be compelled to accept for recordation documents that on their face appear self-serving or colorable, the Register should take care that their nature is not concealed from the public in the Copyright Office's indexing and search reports.

The provisions of subsection (d), requiring recordation of transfers as a prerequisite to the institution of an infringement suit, represent a desirable change in the law. The one- and three-month grace periods provided in subsection (e) are a reasonable compromise between those who want a longer hiatus and those who argue that any grace period makes it impossible for a bona fide transferee to rely on the record at any particular time.

Under subsection (f) of section 205, a nonexclusive license in writing and signed, whether recorded or not, would be valid against a later transfer, and would also prevail as against a prior unrecorded transfer if taken in good faith and without notice. Objections were raised by motion picture producers, particularly to the provision allowing unrecorded nonexclusive licenses to prevail over subsequent transfers, on the ground that a nonexclusive license can have drastic effects on the value of a copyright. On the other hand, the impracticalities and burdens that would accompany any requirement of recordation of nonexclusive licenses outweigh the limited advantages of a statutory recordation system for them.

DURATION OF COPYRIGHT

LAW

Chapter 3.—DURATION OF COPYRIGHT

§ 301. Preemption with respect to other laws

(a) On and after January 1, 1978, all legal or equitable rights that are equivalent to any of the exclusive rights within the general scope of copyright as specified by section 106 in works of authorship that are fixed in a tangible medium of expression and come within the subject matter of copyright as specified by sections 102 and 103, whether created before or after that date and whether published or unpublished, are governed exclusively by this title. Thereafter, no person is entitled to any such right or equivalent right in any such work under the common law or statutes of any State.

(b) Nothing in this title annuls or limits any rights or remedies under the common law or statutes of any State with respect to—

(1) subject matter that does not come within the subject matter of copyright as specified by sections 102 and 103, including works of authorship not fixed in any tangible medium of expression; or

(2) any cause of action arising from undertakings commenced before January 1, 1978; or

(3) activities violating legal or equitable rights that are not equivalent to any of the exclusive rights within the general scope of copyright as specified by section 106.

(c) With respect to sound recordings fixed before February 15, 1972, any rights or remedies under the common law or statutes of any State shall not be annulled or limited by this title until February 15, 2047. The preemptive provisions of subsection (a) shall apply to any such rights and remedies pertaining to any cause of action arising from undertakings commenced on and after February 15, 2047. Notwithstanding the provisions of section 303, no sound recording fixed before February 15, 1972, shall be subject to copyright under this title before, on, or after February 15, 2047.

(d) Nothing in this title annuls or limits any rights or remedies under any other Federal statute.

HOUSE REPORT

SECTION 301. FEDERAL PREEMPTION OF RIGHTS EQUIVALENT TO COPYRIGHT

Single Federal system

Section 301, one of the bedrock provisions of the bill, would accomplish a fundamental and significant change in the present law. Instead of a dual system of "common law copyright" for unpublished works and statutory copyright for published works, which has been the system in effect in the United States since the first copyright statute in 1790, the bill adopts a single system of Federal statutory copyright from creation. Under section 301 a work would obtain statutory protection as soon as it is "created" or, as that term is defined in section 101, when it is "fixed in a copy or phonorecord for the first time." Common law copyright protection for works coming within the scope of the statute would be abrogated, and the concept of publication would lose its all-embracing importance as a dividing line between common law and statutory protection and between both of these forms of legal protection and the public domain.

By substituting a single Federal system for the present anachronistic, uncertain, impractical, and highly complicated dual system, the bill would greatly improve the operation of the copyright law and would be much more effective in carrying out the basic constitutional aims of uniformity and the promotion of writing and scholarship. The main arguments in favor of a single Federal system can be summarized as follows:

1. One of the fundamental purposes behind the copyright clause of the Constitution, as shown in Madison's comments in The Federalist, was to promote national uniformity and to avoid the practical difficulties of determining and enforcing an author's rights under the differing laws and in the separate courts of the various States. Today, when the methods for dissemination of an author's work are incomparably broader and faster than they were in 1789, national uniformity in copyright protection is even more essential than it was then to carry out the constitutional intent.

2. "Publication," perhaps the most important single concept under the present law, also represents its most serious defect. Although at one time, when works were disseminated almost exclusively through printed copies, "publication" could serve as a practical dividing line between common law and statutory protection, this is no longer true. With the development of the 20th-century communications revolution, the concept of publication has become increasingly artificial and obscure. To cope with the legal consequences of an established concept that has lost much of its meaning and justification, the courts have given "publication" a number of diverse interpretations, some of them radically different. Not unexpectedly, the results in individual cases have become unpredictable and often unfair. A single Federal system would help to clear up this chaotic situation.

3. Enactment of section 301 would also implement the "limited times" provision of the Constitution, which has become distorted under the traditional concept of "publication." Common law protection in "unpublished" works is now perpetual, no matter how widely they may be disseminated by means other than "publication"; the bill would place a time limit on the duration of exclusive rights in them. The provision would also aid scholarship and the dissemination of historical materials by making unpublished, undisseminated manuscripts available for publication after a reasonable period.

4. Adoption of a uniform national copyright system would greatly improve international dealings in copyrighted material. No other country has anything like our present dual system. In an

era when copyrighted works can be disseminated instantaneously to every country on the globe, the need for effective international copyright relations, and the concomitant need for national uniformity, assume ever greater importance.

Under section 301, the statute would apply to all works created after its effective date, whether or not they are ever published or disseminated. With respect to works created before the effective date of the statute and still under common law protection, section 303 of the statute would provide protection from that date on, and would guarantee a minimum period of statutory copyright.

Preemption of State law

The intention of section 301 is to preempt and abolish any rights under the common law or statutes of a State that are equivalent to copyright and that extend to works coming within the scope of the Federal copyright law. The declaration of this principle in section 301 is intended to be stated in the clearest and most unequivocal language possible, so as to foreclose any conceivable misinterpretation of its unqualified intention that Congress shall act preemptively, and to avoid the development of any vague borderline areas between State and Federal protection.

SENATE REPORT

The following sentence was omitted from the HOUSE REPORT.

The language in this section of the bill and its analysis in this report have been modified from that contained in S. 1361 and Senate Report 93-983 so as to more exactly define the intent of Congress.

HOUSE REPORT (Continued)

Under section 301(a) all "legal or equitable rights that are equivalent to any of the exclusive rights within the general scope of copyright as specified by section 106 are governed exclusively by the Federal copyright statute if the works involved are "works of authorship that are fixed in a tangible medium of expression and come within the subject matter of copyright as specified by sections 102 and 103."

SENATE REPORT (Continued)

The following was omitted from the last sentence.

. . . are governed exclusively by the Federal copyright statute if the work involved is of a kind covered by the statute.

HOUSE REPORT (Continued)

All corresponding State laws, whether common law or statutory, are preempted and abrogated. Regardless of when the work was created and whether it is published or unpublished, disseminated or undisseminated, in the public domain or copyrighted under the Federal statute, the States cannot offer it protection equivalent to copyright. Section 1338 of title 28, United States Code, also makes clear that any action involving rights under the Federal copyright law would come within the exclusive jurisdiction of the Federal courts. The preemptive effect of section 301 is limited to State laws; as stated expressly in subsection (d) of section 301, there is no intention to deal with the question of whether Congress can or should offer the equivalent of copyright protection under some constitutional provision other than the patent-copyright clause of article 1, section 8.

As long as a work fits within one of the general subject matter categories of sections 102 and 103, the bill prevents the States from protecting it even if it fails to achieve Federal statutory copyright because it is too minimal or lacking in originality to qualify, or because it has fallen into the public domain. On the other hand, section 301(b) explicitly preserves common law copyright protection for one important class of works: works that have not been "fixed in any tangible medium of expression." Examples would include choreography that has never been filmed or notated, an extemporaneous speech, "original works of authorship" communicated solely through conversations or live broadcasts, and a dramatic sketch or musical composition improvised or developed from memory and without being recorded or written down. As mentioned above in connection with section 102, unfixed works are not included in the specified "subject matter of copyright." They are therefore not affected by the preemption of section 301, and would continue to be subject to protection under State statute or common law until fixed in tangible form.

SENATE REPORT (Continued)

The following sentence was omitted in the HOUSE REPORT.

Because of the significance of this principle, the committee amended section 301(b) of the 1965 bill to make it explicit.

HOUSE REPORT (Continued)

The preemption of rights under State law is complete with respect to any work coming within the scope of the bill, even though the scope of exclusive rights given the work under the bill is narrower than the scope of common law rights in the work might have been.

Representatives of printers, while not opposed to the principle of section 301, expressed concern about its potential impact on protection of preliminary advertising copy and layouts prepared by printers. They argued that this material is frequently "pirated" by competitors, and that it would be a substantial burden if, in order to obtain full protection, the printer would have to make registrations and bear the expense and bother of suing in Federal rather than State courts. On the other hand, these practical problems are essentially procedural rather than substantive, and the proposal for a special exemption to preserve common law rights equivalent to copyright in unpublished advertising material cannot be justified. Moreover, subsection (b), discussed below, will preserve other legal grounds on which the printers can protect themselves against "pirates" under State laws.

In a general way subsection (b) of section 301 represents the obverse of subsection (a). It sets out, in broad terms and without necessarily being exhaustive, some of the principal areas of protection that preemption would not prevent the States from protecting. Its purpose is to make clear, consistent with the 1964 Supreme Court decisions in *Sears, Roebuck & Co.* v. *Stiffel Co.*, 376 U.S. 225, and *Compco Corp.* v. *Day-Brite Lighting, Inc.*, 376 U.S. 234, that preemption does not extend to causes of action, or subject matter outside the scope of the revised Federal copyright statute.

The numbered clauses of subsection (b) list three general areas left unaffected by the preemption: (1) subject matter that does not come within the subject matter of copyright; (2) causes of action arising under State law before the effective date of the statute; and (3) violations of rights that are not equivalent to any of the exclusive rights under copyright.

The examples in clause (3), while not exhaustive, are intended to illustrate rights and remedies that are different in nature from the rights comprised in a copyright and that may continue to be protected under State common law or statute. The evolving common law rights of "privacy," "publicity," and trade secrets, and the general laws of defamation and fraud, would remain unaffected as long as the causes of action contain elements, such as an invasion of personal rights or a breach of trust or confidentiality, that are different in kind from copyright infringement. Nothing in the bill derogates from the rights of parties to contract with each other and to sue for breaches of contract; however, to the extent that the unfair competition concept known as "interference with contract relations" is merely the equivalent of copyright protection, it would be preempted.

The last example listed in clause (3)—"deceptive trade practices such as passing off and false representation"—represents an effort to distinguish between those causes of action known as "unfair competition" that the copyright statute is not intended to preempt and those that it is. Section 301 is not intended to preempt common law protection in cases involving activities such as false labeling, fraudulent representation, and passing off even where the subject matter involved comes within the scope of the copyright statute.

"Misappropriation" is not necessarily synonymous with copyright infringement, and thus a cause of action labeled as "misappropriation" is not preempted if it is in fact based neither on a right within the general scope of copyright as specified by section 106 nor on a right equivalent thereto. For example, state law should have the flexibility to afford a remedy (under traditional principles of equity) against a consistent pattern of unauthorized appropriation by a competitor of the facts (i.e., not the literary expression) constituting "hot" news, whether in the traditional mold of *International News Service* v. *Associated Press*, 248 U.S. 215 (1918), or in the newer form of data updates from scientific, business, or financial data bases. Likewise, a person having no trust or other relationship with the proprietor of a computerized data base should not be immunized from sanctions against electronically or cryptographically breaching the proprietor's security arrangements and accessing the proprietor's data. The unauthorized data access which should be remediable might also be achieved by the intentional interception of data transmissions by wire, microwave or laser transmissions, or by the common unintentional means of "crossed" telephone lines occasioned by errors in switching.

The proprietor of data displayed on the cathode ray tube of a computer terminal should be afforded protection against unauthorized printouts by third parties (with or without improper access), even if the data are not copyrightable. For example, the data may not be copyrighted because they are not fixed in a tangible medium of expression (i.e., the data are not displayed for a period or not more than transitory duration).

Nothing contained in section 301 precludes the owner of a material embodiment of a copy or a phonorecord from enforcing a claim of conversion against one who takes possession of the copy or phonorecord without consent.

The following text did not appear in the SENATE REPORT.

A unique and difficult problem is presented with respect to the status of sound recordings fixed before February 12, 1972, the effective date of the amendment bringing recordings fixed after that date under Federal copyright protection. In its testimony during the 1975 hearings, the Department of Justice pointed out that, under section 301 as then written:

> This language could be read as abrogating the anti-piracy laws now existing in 29 states relating to pre-February 15, 1972, sound recordings on the grounds that these statutes proscribe activities violating rights equivalent to * * * the exclusive rights within the general scope of copyright. * * *" Certainly such a result cannot have been intended for it would likely effect the immediate resurgence of piracy of pre-February 15, 1972, sound recordings.

The Department recommended that section 301(b) be amended to exclude sound recordings fixed prior to February 15, 1972 from the effect of the preemption.

The Senate adopted this suggestion when it passed S. 22. The result of the Senate amendment would be to leave pre-1972 sound recordings as entitled to perpetual protection under State law, while post-1972 recordings would eventually fall into the public domain as provided in the bill.

The Committee recognizes that, under recent court decisions, pre-1972 recordings are protected by State statute or common law, and that should not all be thrown into the public domain instantly upon the coming into effect of the new law. However, it cannot agree that they should in effect be accorded perpetual protection, as under the Senate amendment, and it has therefore revised clause (4) to establish a future date for the pre-emption to take effect. The date chosen is February 15, 2047, which is 75 years from the effective date of the statute extending Federal protection to recordings.

SENATE REPORT (Continued)

The following paragraph in the SENATE REPORT was omitted in the HOUSE REPORT.

At the present time, 32 states prohibit record piracy by statute, and four more do so under common law. The Congress and many states have determined that record pirates unfairly appropriate the property, efforts and capital of the legitimate music industry. There is no justification for exposing pre-1972 recordings to expropriation by record pirates.

HOUSE REPORT (Continued)

Subsection (c) makes clear that nothing contained in Title 17 annuls or limits any rights or remedies under any other Federal statute.

CONFERENCE REPORT

SCOPE OF FEDERAL PREEMPTION

Senate bill

In establishing a single Federal system of copyright, section 301 of the Senate bill preempts all equivalent rights under State law in copyrightable works that have been fixed in tangible form. In stating the obverse of this proposition, section 301(b)(3) preserved rights under State law with respect to activities violating rights that are not equivalent to any of the exclusive rights within the general scope of copyright, "including rights against misappropriation not equivalent to any of such exclusive rights, breaches of contract, breaches of trust, . . . [etc.]." The Senate bill specifically excepted from the preemption "sound recordings fixed prior to February 15, 1972."

House bill

The House bill deleted the clause of section 301(b)(3) enumerating illustrative examples of causes of action, such as certain types of misappropriation, not preempted under section 301. It revised the provision dealing with sound recordings fixed before February 15, 1972 to make the Federal preemption of rights in such works effective on February 15, 2047.

Conference substitute

The conference substitute adopts the House amendment of section 301.

LAW

§ 302. Duration of copyright: Works created on or after January 1, 1978

(a) In General.—Copyright in a work created on or after January 1, 1978, subsists from its creation and, except as provided by the following subsections, endures for a term consisting of the life of the author and fifty years after the author's death.

(b) Joint Works.—In the case of a joint work prepared by two or more authors who did not work for hire, the copyright endures for a term consisting of the life of the last surviving author and fifty years after such last surviving author's death.

(c) Anonymous Works, Pseudonymous Works, and Works Made for Hire.—In the case of an anonymous work, a pseudonymous work, or a work made for hire, the copyright endures for a term of seventy-five years from the year of its first publication, or a term of one hundred years from the year of its creation, whichever expires first. If, before the end of such term, the identity of one or more of the authors of an anonymous or pseudonymous work is revealed in the records of a registration made for that work under subsections (a) or (d) of section 408, or in the records provided by this subsection, the copyright in the work endures for the term specified by subsection (a) or (b), based on the life of the author or authors whose identity has been revealed. Any person having an interest in the copyright in an anonymous or pseudonymous work may at any time record, in records to be maintained by the Copyright Office for that purpose, a statement identifying one or more authors of the work; the statement shall also identify the person filing it, the nature of that person's interest, the source of the information recorded, and the particular work affected, and shall comply in form and content with requirements that the Register of Copyrights shall prescribe by regulation.

(d) RECORDS RELATING TO DEATH OF AUTHORS.—Any person having an interest in a copyright may at any time record in the Copyright Office a statement of the date of death of the author of the copyrighted work, or a statement that the author is still living on a particular date. The statement shall identify the person filing it, the nature of that person's interest, and the source of the information recorded, and shall comply in form and content with requirements that the Register of Copyrights shall prescribe by regulation. The Register shall maintain current records of information relating to the death of authors of copyrighted works, based on such recorded statements and, to the extent the Register considers practicable, on data contained in any of the records of the Copyright Office or in other reference sources.

(e) PRESUMPTION AS TO AUTHOR'S DEATH.—After a period of seventy-five years from the year of first publication of a work, or a period of one hundred years from the year of its creation, whichever expires first, any person who obtains from the Copyright Office a certified report that the records provided by subsection (d) disclose nothing to indicate that the author of the work is living, or died less than fifty years before, is entitled to the benefit of a presumption that the author has been dead for at least fifty years. Reliance in good faith upon this presumption shall be a complete defense to any action for infringement under this title.

HOUSE REPORT

SECTION 302. DURATION OF COPYRIGHT IN WORKS CREATED AFTER EFFECTIVE DATE

In general

The debate over how long a copyright should last is as old as the oldest copyright statute and will doubtless continue as long as there is a copyright law. With certain exceptions, there appears to be strong support for the principle, as embodied in the bill, of a copyright term consisting of the life of the author and 50 years after his death. In particular, the authors and their representatives stressed that the adoption of a life-plus-50 term was by far their most important legislative goal in copyright law revision. The Register of Copyrights now regards a life-plus-50 term as the foundation of the entire bill.

Under the present law statutory copyright protection begins on the date of publication (or on the date of registration in unpublished form) and continues for 28 years from that date; it may be renewed for a second 28 years, making a total potential term of 56 years in all cases.[1] The principal elements of this system—a definite number of years, computed from either publication or registration, with a renewal feature—have been a part of the U.S. copyright law since the first statute in 1790. The arguments for changing this system to one based on the life of the author can be summarized as follows:

1. The present 56-year term is not long enough to insure an author and his dependents the fair economic benefits from his works. Life expectancy has increased substantially, and more and more authors are seeing their works fall into the public domain during their lifetimes, forcing later works to compete with their own early works in which copyright has expired.

2. The tremendous growth in communications media has substantially lengthened the commercial life of a great many works. A short term is particularly discriminatory against serious works of music, literature, and art, whose value may not be recognized until after many years.

3. Although limitations on the term of copyright are obviously necessary, too short a term harms the author without giving any substantial benefit to the public. The public frequently pays the same for works in the public domain as it does for copyrighted works, and the only result is a commercial windfall to certain users at the author's expense. In some cases the lack of copyright protection actually restrains dissemination of the work, since publishers and other users cannot risk investing in the work unless assured of exclusive rights.

4. A system based on the life of the author would go a long way toward clearing up the confusion and uncertainty involved in the vague concept of "publication," and would provide a much simpler, clearer method for computing the term. The death of the author is a definite, determinable event, and it would be the only date that a potential user would have to worry about. All of a particular author's works, including successive revisions of them, would fall into the public domain at the same time, thus avoiding the present problems of determining a multitude of publication dates and of distinguishing "old" and "new" matter in later editions. The bill answers the problems of determining when relatively obscure authors died, by establishing a registry of death dates and a system of presumptions.

5. One of the worst features of the present copyright law is the provision for renewal of copyright. A substantial burden and expense, this unclear and highly technical requirement results in incalculable amounts of unproductive work. In a number of cases it is the cause of inadvertent and unjust loss of copyright. Under a life-plus-50 system the renewal device would be inappropriate and unnecessary.

[1] Under Public Laws 87–668, 89–142, 90–141, 90–416, 91–147, 91–555, 92–170, 92–566, and 93–573, copyrights that were subsisting in their renewal term on September 19, 1962, and that were scheduled to expire before Dec. 31, 1976, have been extended to that later date, in anticipation that general revision legislation extending their terms still further will be enacted by then.

6. Under the preemption provisions of section 301 and the single Federal system they would establish, authors will be giving up perpetual, unlimited exclusive common law rights in their unpublished works, including works that have been widely disseminated by means other than publication. A statutory term of life-plus-50 years is no more than a fair recompense for the loss of these perpetual rights.

7. A very large majority of the world's countries have adopted a copyright term of the life of the author and 50 years after the author's death. Since American authors are frequently protected longer in foreign countries than in the United States, the disparity in the duration of copyright has provoked consider able resentment and some proposals for retaliatory legislation. Copyrighted works move across national borders faster and more easily than virtually any other economic commodity, and with the techniques now in common use this movement has in many cases become instantaneous and effortless. The need to conform the duration of U.S. copyright to that prevalent throughout the rest of the world is increasingly pressing in order to provide certainty and simplicity in international business dealings. Even more important, a change in the basis of our copyright term would place the United States in the forefront of the international copyright community. Without this change, the possibility of future United States adherence to the Berne Copyright Union would evaporate, but with it would come a great and immediate improvement in our copyright relations. All of these benefits would accrue directly to American and foreign authors alike.

The need for a longer total term of copyright has been conclusively demonstrated. It is true that a major reason for the striking statistical increase in life expectancy since 1909 is the reduction in infant mortality, but this does not mean that the increase can be discounted. Although not nearly as great as the total increase in life expectancy, there has been a marked increase in longevity, and with medical discoveries and health programs for the elderly this trend shows every indication of continuing. If life expectancy in 1909, which was in the neighborhood of 56 years, offered a rough guide to the length of copyright protection, then life expectancy in the 1970's which is well over 70 years, should offer a similar guide; the Register's 1961 Report included statistics indicating that something between 70 and 76 years was then the average equivalent of life-plus-50 years. A copyright should extend beyond the author's lifetime, and judged by this standard the present term of 56 years is too short.

The arguments as to the benefits of uniformity with foreign laws, and the advantages of international comity that would result from adoption of a life-plus-50 term, are also highly significant. The system has worked well in other countries, and on the whole it would appear to make computation of terms considerably simpler and easier. The registry of death dates and the system of presumptions established in section 302 would solve most of the problems in determining when an individual author died.

SENATE REPORT

The first 16 words of the SENATE REPORT were omitted in the following paragraph.

Aside from the Philippines, whose copyright statute was patterned after the United States Act of 1909. . . .

HOUSE REPORT (Continued)

No country in the world has provisions on the duration of copyright like ours. Virtually every other copyright law in the world bases the term of protection for works by natural persons on the life of the author, and a substantial majority of these accord protection for 50 years after the author's death. This term is required for adherence to the Berne Convention. It is worth noting that the 1965 revision of the copyright law of the Federal Republic of Germany adopted a term of life plus 70 years.

A point that has concerned some educational groups arose from the possibility that, since a large majority (now about 85 percent) of all copyrighted works are not renewed, a life-plus-50 year term would tie up a substantial body of material that is probably of no commercial interest but that would be more readily available for scholarly use if free of copyright restrictions. A statistical study of renewal registrations made by the Copyright Office in 1966 supports the generalization that most material which is considered to be of continuing or potential commercial value is renewed. Of the remainder, a certain proportion is of practically no value to anyone, but there are a large number of unrenewed works that have scholarly value to historians, archivists, and specialists in a variety of fields. This consideration lay behind the proposals for retaining the renewal device or for limiting the term for unpublished or unregistered works.

It is true that today's ephemera represent tomorrow's social history, and that works of scholarly value, which are now falling into the public domain after 28 years, would be protected much longer under the bill. Balanced against this are the burdens and expenses of renewals, the near impossibility of distinguishing between types of works in fixing a statutory term, and the extremely strong case in favor of a life-plus-50 system. Moreover, it is important to realize that the bill would not restrain scholars from using any work as source material or from making "fair use" of it; the restrictions would extend only to the unauthorized reproduction or distribution of copies of the work, its public performance, or some other use that would actually infringe the copyright owner's exclusive rights. The advantages of a basic term of copyright enduring for the life of the author and for 50 years after the author's death outweigh any possible disadvantages.

Basic copyright term

Under subsection (a) of section 302, a work "created" on or after the effective date of the revised statute would be protected by statutory copyright "from its creation" and, with exceptions to be noted below, "endures for a term consisting of the life of the author and 50 years after the author's death."

Under this provision, as a general rule, the life-plus-50 term would apply equally to unpublished works, to works published during the author's lifetime, and to works published posthumously.

The definition of "created" in section 101, which will be discussed in more detail in connection with section 302(c) below, makes clear that "creation" for this purpose means the first time the work is fixed in a copy or phonorecord; up to that point the work is not "created," and is subject to common law protection, even though it may exist in someone's mind and may have been communicated to others in unfixed form.

Joint works

Since by definition a "joint work" has two or more authors, a statute basing the term of copyright on the life of the author must provide a special method of computing the term of "joint works." Under the system in effect in many foreign countries, the term of copyright is measured from the death of the last survivor of a group of joint authors, no matter how many there are. The bill adopts this system as the simplest and fairest of the alternatives for dealing with the problem.

Anonymous works, pseudonymous works, and works made for hire

Computing the term from the author's death also requires special provisions to deal with cases where the authorship is not revealed or where the "author" is not an individual. Section 302(c) therefore provides a special term for anonymous works, pseudonymous works, and works made for hire: 75 years from publication or 100 years from creation, whichever is shorter. The definitions in section 101 make the status of anonymous and pseudonymous works depend on what is revealed on the copies or phonorecords of a work; a work is "anonymous" if "no natural person is identified as author," and is "pseudonymous" if "the author is identified under a fictitious name."

Section 302(c) provides that the 75- and 100-year terms for an anonymous or pseudonymous work can be converted to the ordinary life-plus-50 term if "the identity of one or more authors * * * is revealed" in special records maintained for this purpose in the Copyright Office. The term in such cases would be "based on the life of the author or authors whose identity has been revealed." Instead of forcing a user to search through countless Copyright Office records to determine if an author's identity has been revealed, the bill sets up a special registry for the purpose, with requirements concerning the filing of identifying statements that parallel those of the following subsection (d) with respect to statements of the date of an author's death.

The alternative terms established in section 302(c)—75 years from publication or 100 years from creation, whichever expires first—are necessary to set a time limit on protection of unpublished material. For example, copyright in a work created in 1978 and published in 1988 would expire in 2063 (75 years from publication). A question arises as to when the copyright should expire if the work is never published. Both the Constitution and the underlying purposes of the bill require the establishment of an alternative term for unpublished work and the only practicable basis for this alternative is "creation." Under the bill a work created in 1980 but not published until after 2005 (or never published) would fall into the public domain in 2080 (100 years after creation).

The definition in section 101 provides that "creation" takes place when a work "is fixed in a copy or phonorecord for the first time." Although the concept of "creation" is inherently lacking in precision, its adoption in the bill would, for example, enable a scholar to use an unpublished manuscript written anonymously, pseudonymously, or for hire, if he determines on the basis of internal or external evidence that the manuscript is at least 100 years old. In the case of works written over a period of time or in successive revised versions, the definition provides that the portion of the work "that has been fixed at any particular time constitutes the work as of that time," and that, "where the work has been prepared in different versions, each version constitutes a separate work." Thus, a scholar or other user, in attempting to determine whether a particular work is in the public domain, needs to look no further than the particular version he wishes to use.

Although "publication" would no longer play the central role assigned to it under the present law, the concept would still have substantial significance under provisions throughout the bill, including those on Federal preemption and duration. Under the definition in section 101, a work is "published" if one or more copies or phonorecords embodying it are distributed to the public—that is, generally to persons under no explicit or implicit restrictions with respect to disclosure of its contents—without regard to the manner in which the copies or phonorecords changed hands. The definition clears up the question of whether the sale of phonorecords constitutes publication, and it also makes plain that any form or dissemination in which a material object does not change hands—performances or displays on television, for example—is not a publication no matter how many people are exposed to the work. On the other hand, the definition also makes clear that, when copies or phonorecords are offered to a group of wholesalers, broadcasters, motion pictures, theaters, etc., publication takes place if the purpose is "further distribution, public performance, or public display."

Although the periods of 75 or 100 years for anonymous and pseudonymous works and works made for hire seem to be longer than the equivalent term provided by foreign laws and the Berne Conventions, this difference is more apparent than real. In general, the terms in these special cases approximate, on the average, the term of the life of the author plus 50 years established for other works. The 100-year maximum term for unpublished works, although much more limited than the perpetual term now available under common law in the United States and under statute in some foreign countries, is sufficient to guard against unjustified invasions of privacy and to fulfill our obligations under the Universal Copyright Convention.

Records and presumption as to author's death

Subsections (d) and (e) of section 302 together furnish an answer to the practical problems of how to discover the death dates of obscure or unknown authors. Subsection (d) provides a procedure for recording statements that an author died, or that he was still living, on a particular date, and also requires the Register of Copyrights to maintain obituary records on a current basis. Under subsection (e) anyone who, after a specified period, obtains certification from the Copyright Office that its records show nothing to indicate that the author is living or died less than 50 years before, is entitled to rely upon a presumption that the author has been dead for more than 50 years. The period specified in subsection (e)—75 years from publication or 100 years from creation—is purposely uniform with the special term provided in subsection (c).

LAW

§ 303. Duration of copyright: Works created but not published or copyrighted before January 1, 1978

Copyright in a work created before January 1, 1978, but not theretofore in the public domain or copyrighted, subsists from January 1, 1978, and endures for the term provided by section 302. In no case, however, shall the term of copyright in such a work expire before December 31, 2002; and, if the work is published on or before December 31, 2002, the term of copyright shall not expire before December 31, 2027.

HOUSE REPORT

SECTION 303. PREEXISTING WORKS UNDER COMMON LAW PROTECTION

Theoretically, at least, the legal impact of section 303 would be far reaching. Under it, every "original work of authorship" fixed in tangible form that is in existence would be given statutory copyright protection as long as the work is not in the public domain in this country. The vast majority of these works consist of private material that no one is interested in protecting or infringing, but section 303 would still have practical effects for a prodigious body of material already in existence.

Looked at another way, however, section 303 would have a genuinely restrictive effect. Its basic purpose is to substitute statutory for common law copyright for everything now protected at common law, and to substitute reasonable time limits for the perpetual protection now available. In general, the substituted time limits are those applicable to works created after the effective date of the law; for example, an unpublished work written in 1945 whose author dies in 1980 would be protected under the statute from the effective date through 2030 (50 years after the author's death).

A special problem under this provision is what to do with works whose ordinary statutory terms will have expired or will be nearing expiration on the effective date. The committee believes that a provision taking away subsisting common law rights and substituting statutory rights for a reasonable period is fully in harmony with the constitutional requirements of due process, but it is necessary to fix a "reasonable period" for this purpose. Section 303 provides that under no circumstances would copyright protection expire before December 31, 2002, and also attempts to encourage publication by providing 25 years more protection (through 2027) if the work were published before the end of 2002.

LAW

§ 304. Duration of copyright: Subsisting copyrights

(a) COPYRIGHTS IN THEIR FIRST TERM ON JANUARY 1, 1978.—Any copyright, the first term of which is subsisting on January 1, 1978, shall endure for twenty-eight years from the date it was originally secured: *Provided*, That in the case of any posthumous work or of any periodical, cyclopedic, or other composite work upon which the copyright was originally secured by the proprietor thereof, or of any work copyrighted by a corporate body (otherwise than as assignee or licensee of the individual author) or by an employer for whom such work is made for hire, the proprietor of such copyright shall be entitled to a renewal and extension of the copyright in such work for the further term of forty-seven years when application for such renewal and extension shall have been made to the Copyright Office and duly registered therein within one year prior to the expiration of the original term of copyright: *And provided further*, That in the case of any other copyrighted work, including a contribution by an individual author to a periodical or to a cyclopedic or other composite work, the author of such work, if still living, or the widow, widower, or children of the author, if the author be not living, or if such author, widow, widower, or children be not living, then the author's executors, or in the absence of a will, his or her next of kin shall be entitled to a renewal and extension of the copyright in such work for a further term of forty-seven years when application for such renewal and extension shall have been made to the Copyright Office and duly registered therein within one year prior to the expiration of the original term of copyright: *And provided further*, That in default of the registration of such application for renewal and extension, the copyright in any work shall terminate at the expiration of twenty-eight years from the date copyright was originally secured.

(b) Copyrights in Their Renewal Term or Registered for Renewal Before January 1, 1978.—The duration of any copyright, the renewal term of which is subsisting at any time between December 31, 1976, and December 31, 1977, inclusive, or for which renewal registration is made between December 31, 1976, and December 31, 1977, inclusive, is extended to endure for a term of seventy-five years from the date copyright was originally secured.

(c) Termination of Transfers and Licenses Covering Extended Renewal Term.—In the case of any copyright subsisting in either its first or renewal term on January 1, 1978, other than a copyright in a work made for hire, the exclusive or nonexclusive grant of a transfer or license of the renewal copyright or any right under it, executed before January 1, 1978, by any of the persons designated by the second proviso of subsection (a) of this section, otherwise than by will, is subject to termination under the following conditions:

(1) In the case of a grant executed by a person or persons other than the author, termination of the grant may be effected by the surviving person or persons who executed it. In the case of a grant executed by one or more of the authors of the work, termination of the grant may be effected, to the extent of a particular author's share in the ownership of the renewal copyright, by the author who executed it or, if such author is dead, by the person or persons who, under clause (2) of this subsection, own and are entitled to exercise a total of more than one-half of that author's termination interest.

(2) Where an author is dead, his or her termination interest is owned, and may be exercised, by his widow or her widower and his or her children or grandchildren as follows:

(A) the widow or widower owns the author's entire termination interest unless there are any surviving children or grandchildren of the author, in which case the widow or widower owns one-half of the author's interest;

(B) the author's surviving children, and the surviving children of any dead child of the author, own the author's entire termination interest unless there is a widow or widower, in which case the ownership of one-half of the author's interest is divided among them;

(C) the rights of the author's children and grandchildren are in all cases divided among them and exercised on a per stirpes basis according to the number of such author's children represented; the share of the children of a dead child in a termination interest can be exercised only by the action of a majority of them.

(3) Termination of the grant may be effected at any time during a period of five years beginning at the end of fifty-six years from the date copyright was originally secured, or beginning on January 1, 1978, whichever is later.

(4) The termination shall be effected by serving an advance notice in writing upon the grantee or the grantee's successor in title. In the case of a grant executed by a person or persons other than the author, the notice shall be signed by all of those entitled to terminate the grant under clause (1) of this subsection, or by their duly authorized agents. In the case of a grant executed by one or more of the authors of the work, the notice as to any one author's share shall be signed by that author or his or her duly authorized agent or, if that author is dead, by the number and proportion of the owners of his or her termination interest required under clauses (1) and (2) of this subsection, or by their duly authorized agents.

(A) The notice shall state the effective date of the termination, which shall fall within the five-year period specified by clause (3) of this subsection, and the notice shall be served not less than two or more than ten years before that date. A copy of the notice shall be recorded in the Copyright Office before the effective date of termination, as a condition to its taking effect.

(B) The notice shall comply, in form, content, and manner of service, with requirements that the Register of Copyrights shall prescribe by regulation.

(5) Termination of the grant may be effected notwithstanding any agreement to the contrary, including an agreement to make a will or to make any future grant.

(6) In the case of a grant executed by a person or persons other than the author, all rights under this title that were covered by the terminated grant revert, upon the effective date of termination, to all of those entitled to terminate the grant under clause (1) of this subsection. In the case of a grant executed by one or more of the authors of the work, all of a particular author's rights under this title that were covered by the terminated grant revert, upon the effective date of termination, to that author or, if that author is dead, to the persons owning his or her termination interest under clause (2) of this subsection, including those owners who did not join in signing the notice of termination under clause (4) of this subsection. In all cases the reversion of rights is subject to the following limitations:

(A) A derivative work prepared under authority of the grant before its termination may continue to be utilized under the terms of the grant after its termination, but this privilege does not extend to the preparation after the termination of other derivative works based upon the copyrighted work covered by the terminated grant.

(B) The future rights that will revert upon termination of the grant become vested on the date the notice of termination has been served as provided by clause (4) of this subsection.

(C) Where the author's rights revert to two or more persons under clause (2) of this subsection, they shall vest in those persons in the proportionate shares provided by that clause. In such a case, and subject to the provisions of subclause (D) of this clause, a further grant, or agreement to make a further grant, of a particular author's share with respect to any right covered by a terminated grant is valid only if it is signed by the same number and proportion of the owners, in whom the right has vested under this clause, as are required to terminate the grant under clause (2) of this subsection. Such further grant or agreement is effective with respect to all of the persons in whom the right it covers has vested under this subclause, including those who did not join in signing it. If any person dies after rights under a terminated grant have vested in him or her, that person's legal representatives, legatees, or heirs at law represent him or her for purposes of this subclause.

(D) A further grant, or agreement to make a further grant, of any right covered by a terminated grant is valid only if it is made after the effective date of the termination. As an exception, however, an agreement for such a further grant may be made between the author or any of the persons provided by the first sentence of clause (6) of this subsection, or between the persons provided by subclause (C) of this clause, and the original grantee or such grantee's successor in title, after the notice of termination has been served as provided by clause (4) of this subsection.

(E) Termination of a grant under this subsection affects only those rights covered by the grant that arise under this title, and in no way affects rights arising under any other Federal, State, or foreign laws.

(F) Unless and until termination is effected under this subsection, the grant, if it does not provide otherwise, continues in effect for the remainder of the extended renewal term.

SENATE REPORT

In the following paragraph, only the text between the asterisks appeared in the HOUS REPORT.

SECTION 304. DURATION OF SUBSISTING COPYRIGHTS

It has been estimated that when the new law goes into effect there will be at least 6.6 million copyrights already subsisting: approximately 6 million still in their first term and 600,000 that have been renewed.* The arguments in favor of lengthening the duration of copyright apply to subsisting as well as future copyrights, and that the bill's basic approach of increasing the present 56-year term to 75 years in the case of copyrights subsisting in both their first and their renewal terms* is the simplest and fairest solution of the problem.

HOUSE REPORT

Copyrights in their first term

Subsection (a) of section 304 reenacts and preserves the renewal provision, now in section 24 of the statute, for all of the works presently in their first 28-year term. A great many of the present expectancies in these cases are the subject of existing contracts, and it would be unfair and immensely confusing to cut off or alter these interests. Renewal registration will be required during the 28th year of the copyright but the length of the renewal term will be increased from 28 to 47 years.

Although the bill preserves the language of the present renewal provision without any change in substance, the Committee intends that the reference to a "posthumous work" in this section has the meaning given to it in *Bartok* v. *Boosey & Hawkes, Inc.*, 523 F. 2d 941 (2d Cir. 1975)—one as to which no copyright assignment or other contract for exploitation of the work has occurred during an author's lifetime, rather than one which is simply first published after the author's death.

The preceding paragraph did not appear in the SENATE REPORT.

Copyrights in their renewal term

Renewed copyrights that are subsisting in their second term at any time during the period between December 31, 1976, and December 31, 1977, inclusive, would be extended under section 304(b) to run for a total of 75 years. This provision would add another 19 years to the duration of any renewed copyright whose second term started during the 28 years immediately preceding the effective date of the act (January 1, 1978). In addition, it would extend by varying lesser amounts the duration of nenewal copyrights already extended under Public Laws 87-668, 89-142, 90-141, 90-416, 91-417, 91-555, 92-170, 92-566, and 93–573, all of which would otherwise expire on December 31, 1976. The subsection would also extend the duration of renewal copyrights whose second 28-year term is scheduled to expire during 1977. In none of these cases, however, would the total terms of copyright for the work be longer than 75 years.

SENATE REPORT

The following paragraph was omitted in the HOUSE REPORT.

The reference to a "posthumous work" in this section means one as to which no assignment has occurred during the author's lifetime, rather than one which is simply first published after the author's death.

HOUSE REPORT (Continued)

Subsection (b) also covers the special situation of a subsisting first-term copyright that becomes eligible for renewal registration during the year before the act comes into effect. If a renewal registration is not made before the effective date, the case is governed by the provisions of section 304(a). If a renewal registration is made during the year before the new law takes effect, however, the copyright would be treated as if it were already subsisting in its second term and would be extended to the full period of 75 years without the need for further renewal.

Termination of grants covering extended term

An issue underlying the 19-year extension of renewal terms under both subsections (a) and (b) of section 304 is whether, in a case where their rights have already been transferred, the author or the dependents of the author should be given a chance to benefit from the extended term. The arguments for granting rights of termination are even more persuasive under section 304 than they are under section 203; the extended term represents a completely new property right, and there are strong reasons for giving the author, who is the fundamental beneficiary of copyright under the Constitution, an opportunity to share in it.

Subsection (c) of section 304 is a close but not exact counterpart of section 203. In the case of either a first-term or renewal copyright already subsisting when the new statute becomes effective, any grant of rights covering the renewal copyright in the work, executed before the effective date, may be terminated under conditions and limitations similar to those provided in section 203. Except for transfers and licenses covering renewal copyrights already extended under Public Laws 87–668, 89–142, 90–141, 90–416, 91–147, 91–555, 92–170, 92–566, and 93–573, which would become subject to termination immediately upon the coming into effect of the revised law, the 5-year period during which termination could be made effective would start 56 years after copyright was originally secured.

The bill distinguishes between the persons who can terminate a grant under section 203 and those entitled to terminate a grant covering an extended term under section 304. Instead of being limited to transfers and licenses executed by the author, the right of termination under section 304(c) also extends to grants executed by those beneficiaries of the author who can claim renewal under the present law: his or her widow or widower, children, executors, or next of kin.

There is good reason for this difference. Under section 203, an author's widow or widower and children are given rights of termination if the author is dead, but these rights apply only to grants by the author, and any effort by a widow, widower, or child to transfer contingent future interests under a termination would be ineffective. In contrast, under the present renewal provisions, any statutory beneficiary of the author can make a valid transfer or license of future renewal rights, which is completely binding if the author is dead and the person who executed the grant turns out to be the proper renewal claimant. Because of this, a great many contingent transfers of future renewal rights have been obtained from widows, widowers, children, and next of kin, and a substantial number of these will be binding. After the present 28-year renewal period has ended, a statutory beneficiary who has signed a disadvantageous grant of this sort should have the opportunity to reclaim the extended term.

As explained above in connection with section 203, the bill adopts the principle that, where a transfer or license by the author is involved, termination may be effected by a per stirpes majority of those entitled to terminate, and this principle also applies to the ownership of rights under a termination and to the making of further grants of reverted rights. In general, this principle has also been adopted with respect to the termination of rights under an extended renewal copyright in section 304, but with several differences made necessary by the differences between the legal status of transfers and licenses made after the effective date of the new law (governed by section 203) and that of grants of renewal rights made earlier and governed by section 304(c). The following are the most important distinctions between the termination rights under the two sections:

1. Joint authorship.—Under section 304, a grant of renewal rights executed by joint authors during the first term of copyright would be effective only as to those who were living at the time of renewal; where any of them are dead, their statutory beneficiaries are entitled to claim the renewal independently as a new estate. It would therefore be inappropriate to impose a requirement of majority action with respect to transfers executed by two or more joint authors.

2. Grants not executed by author.—Section 304(c) adopts the majority principle underlying the amendments of section 203 with respect to the termination rights of a dead author's widow or widower and children. There is much less reason, as a matter of policy, to apply this principle in the case of transfers and licenses of renewal rights executed under the present law by the author's widow, widower, children, executors, or next of kin, and the practical arguments against doing so are conclusive. It is not clear how the shares of a class of renewal beneficiaries are to be divided under the existing law, and greater difficulties would be presented if any attempt were made to apply the majority principle to further beneficiaries in cases where one or more of the renewal beneficiaries are dead. Therefore, where the grant was executed by a person or persons other than the author, termination can be effected only by the unanimous action of the survivors of those who executed it.

3. Further grants.—The reason against adopting a principle of majority action with respect to the right to terminate grants by joint authors and grants not executed by the author apply equally with respect to the right to make further grants under section 304(c). The requirement for majority action in clause (6)(C) is therefore confined to cases where the rights under a grant by the author have reverted to his or her widow or widower, or children, or both. Where the extended term reverts to joint authors or to a class of renewal beneficiaries who have joined in executing a grant, their rights would be governed by the general rules of tenancy in common; each coowner would have an independent right to sell his share, or to use or license the work subject to an accounting.

Nothing contained in this section or elsewhere in this legislation is intended to extend the duration of any license, transfer, or assignment made for a period of less than fifty-six years.*If, for example, an agreement provides an earlier termination date or lesser duration, or if it allows the author the right of cancelling or terminating the agreement under certain circumstances, the duration is governed by the agreement.*Likewise, nothing in this section or legislation is intended to change the existing state of the law of contracts concerning the circumstances in which an author may terminate a license, transfer or assignment.

In the preceding paragraph, the text between the asterisks did not appear in the SENATE REPORT.

Section 304(c)(6)(E) provides that, unless and until termination is effected under this section, the grant, "if it does not provide otherwise," continues for the term of copyright.* This section means that, if the agreement does not contain provisions specifying its term or duration, and the author has not terminated the agreement under this section, the agreement continues for the term of the copyright, subject to any right of termination under circumstances which may be specified therein. If, however, an agreement does contain provisions governing its duration—for example, a term of sixty years—and the author has not exercised his or her right of termination under the statute, the agreement will continue according to its terms—in this example, for only sixty years.* The quoted language is not to be construed as requiring agreements to reserve the right of termination.

In the preceding paragraph, the text between the asterisks did not appear in the SENATE REPORT.

COPYRIGHT OFFICE

Section 304(c)(4)(B) of the LAW specifies that the termination of transfers and licenses must comply with requirements prescribed by the Register of Copyrights. This requirement is found in Section 201.10 of the Copyright Office Regulations; the regulation and several pages of explanation are found in the Federal Register, Vol. 42, No. 177 (September 13, 1977), pp. 45916-45921.

See also the Transitional and Supplementary Provisions, Section 107, on p. 273.

LAW

§ 305. Duration of copyright: Terminal date

All terms of copyright provided by sections 302 through 304 run to the end of the calendar year in which they would otherwise expire.

HOUSE REPORT

SECTION 305. YEAR END EXPIRATION OF TERMS

Under section 305, which has its counterpart in the laws of most foreign countries, the term of copyright protection for a work extends through December 31 of the year in which the term would otherwise have expired. This will make the duration of copyright much easier to compute, since it will be enough to determine the year, rather than the exact date, of the event from which the term is based.

Sction 305 applies only to "terms of copyright provided by sections 302 through 304," which are the sections dealing with duration of copyright. It therefore has no effect on the other time periods specified in the bill; and, since they do not involve "terms of copyright," the periods provided in section 304(c) with respect to termination of grants are not affected by section 305.

The terminal date section would change the duration of subsisting copyrights under section 304 by extending the total terms of protection under subsections (a) and (b) to the end of the 75th year from the date copyright was secured. A copyright subsisting in its first term on the effective date of the act would run through December 31 of the 28th year and would then expire unless renewed. Since all copyright terms under the bill expire on December 31, and since section 304 (a) requires that renewal be made "within one year prior to the expiration of the original term of copyright," the period for renewal registration in all cases will run from December 31 through December 31.

A special situation arises with respect to subsisting copyrights whose first 28-year term expires during the first year after the act comes into effect. As already explained in connection with section 304 (b), if a renewal registration for a copyright of this sort is made before the effective date, the total term is extended to 75 years without the need for a further renewal registration. But, if renewal has not yet been made when the act becomes effective, the period for renewal registration may in some cases be extended. If, as the bill provides, the act becomes effective on January 1, 1978, a copyright that was originally secured on September 1, 1950, could have been renewed by virtue of the present statute between September 1, 1977, and December 31, 1977; if not, it can still be renewed under section 304(a) of the new act between January 1, 1978, and December 31, 1978.

COPYRIGHT NOTICE, DEPOSIT, AND REGISTRATION

LAW

Chapter 4.—COPYRIGHT NOTICE, DEPOSIT, AND REGISTRATION

§ 401. Notice of copyright: Visually perceptible copies

(a) General Requirement.—Whenever a work protected under this title is published in the United States or elsewhere by authority of the copyright owner, a notice of copyright as provided by this section shall be placed on all publicly distributed copies from which the work can be visually perceived, either directly or with the aid of a machine or device.

(b) Form of Notice.—The notice appearing on the copies shall consist of the following three elements:

(1) the symbol © (the letter C in a circle), or the word "Copyright", or the abbreviation "Copr."; and

(2) the year of first publication of the work; in the case of compilations or derivative works incorporating previously published material, the year date of first publication of the compilation or derivative work is sufficient. The year date may be omitted where a pictorial, graphic, or sculptural work, with accompanying text matter, if any, is reproduced in or on greeting cards, postcards, stationery, jewelry, dolls, toys, or any useful articles; and

(3) the name of the owner of copyright in the work, or an abbreviation by which the name can be recognized, or a generally known alternative designation of the owner.

(c) Position of Notice.—The notice shall be affixed to the copies in such manner and location as to give reasonable notice of the claim of copyright. The Register of Copyrights shall prescribe by regulation, as examples, specific methods of affixation and positions of the notice on various types of works that will satisfy this requirement, but these specifications shall not be considered exhaustive.

HOUSE REPORT

SECTION 401. NOTICE ON VISUALLY-PERCEPTIBLE COPIES

A requirement that the public be given formal notice of every work in which copyright is claimed was a part of the first U.S. copyright statute enacted in 1790, and since 1802 our copyright laws have always provided that the published copies of copyrighted works must bear a specified notice as a condition of protection. Under the present law the copyright notice serves four principal functions:

(1) It has the effect of placing in the public domain a substantial body of published material that no one is interested in copyrighting;

(2) It informs the public as to whether a particular work is copyrighted;

(3) It identifies the copyright owner; and

(4) It shows the date of publication.

Ranged against these values of a notice requirement are its burdens and unfairness to copyright owners. One of the strongest arguments for revision of the present statute has been the need to avoid the arbitrary and unjust forfeitures now resulting from unintentional or relatively unimportant omissions or errors in the copyright notice. It has been contended that the disadvantages of the notice requirement outweigh its values and that it should therefore be eliminated or substantially liberalized.

The fundamental principle underlying the notice provisions of the bill is that the copyright notice has real values which should be preserved, and that this should be done by inducing use of notice without causing outright forfeiture for errors or omissions. Subject to certain safeguards for innocent infringers, protection would not be lost by the complete omission of copyright notice from large numbers of copies or from a whole edition, if registration for the work is made before or within 5 years after publication. Errors in the name or date in the notice could be corrected without forfeiture of copyright.

Sections 401 and 402 set out the basic notice requirements of the bill, the former dealing with "copies from which the work can be visually perceived," and the latter covering "phonorecords" of a "sound recording." The notice requirements established by these parallel provisions apply only when copies or phonorecords of the work are "publicly distributed." No copyright notice would be required in connection with the public display of a copy by any means, including projectors, television, or cathode ray tubes connected with information storage and retrieval systems, or in connection with the public performance of a work by means of copies or phonorecords, whether in the presence of an audience or through television, radio, computer transmission, or any other process.

It should be noted that, under the definition of "publication" in section 101, there would no longer be any basis for holding, as a few court decisions have done in the past, that the public display of a work of art under some conditions (e.g., without restriction against its reproduction) would constitute publication of the work. And, as indicated above, the public display of a work of art would not require that a copyright notice be placed on the copy displayed.

Subsections (a) of both section 401 and section 402 require that a notice be used whenever the work "is published in the United States or elsewhere by authority of the copyright owner." The phrase "or elsewhere," which does not appear in the present law, makes the notice requirements applicable to copies or phonorecords distributed to the public anywhere in the world, regardless of where and when the work was first published. The values of notice are fully applicable to foreign editions of works copyrighted in the United States, especially with the increased flow of intellectual materials across national boundaries, and the gains in the use of notice on editions published abroad under the Universal Copyright Convention should not be wiped out. The consequences of omissions or mistakes with respect to the notice are far less serious under the bill than under the present law, and section 405(a) makes doubly clear that a copyright owner may guard himself against errors or omissions by others if he makes use of the prescribed notice an express condition of his publishing licenses.

Subsection (b) of section 401, which sets out the form of notice to appear on visually-perceptible copies, retains the basic elements of the notice under the present law: the word "Copyright", the abbreviation "Copr.", or the symbol "©"; the year of first publication; and the name of the copyright owner. The year of publication, which is still significant in computing the term and determining the status of a work, is required for all categories of copyrightable works. Clause (2) of subsection (b) makes clear that, in the case of a derivative work or compilation, it is not necessary to list the dates of publication of all preexisting material incorporated in the work;* however, as noted below in connection with section 409, the application for registration covering a compilation or derivative work must identify "any preexisting work or works that it is based on or incorporates."* Clause (3) establishes that a recognizable abbreviation or a generally known alternative designation may be used instead of the full name of the copyright owner.

In the preceding paragraph, the text between the asterisks did not appear in the SENATE REPORT.

By providing simply that the notice "shall be affixed to the copies in such manner and location as to give reasonable notice of the claim of copyright," subsection (c) follows the flexible approach of the Universal Copyright Convention. The further provision empowering the Register of Copyrights to set forth in regulations a list of examples of "specific methods of affixation and positions of the notice on various types of works that will satisfy this requirement" will offer substantial guidance and avoid a good deal of uncertainty. A notice placed or affixed in accordance with the regulations would clearly meet the requirements but, since the Register's specifications are not to "be considered exhaustive," a notice placed or affixed in some other way might also comply with the law if it were found to "give reasonable notice" of the copyright claim.

COPYRIGHT OFFICE

Section 401(c) of the LAW directs the Register of Copyrights to issue regulations on the methods of affixation and the position of copyright notices. These regulations had not been issued at the time the manuscript left the editor's hands. The Proposed Rulemaking for this regulation may be found in the FEDERAL REGISTER, Vol. 42, No. 247 (December 23, 1977), pp. 64374-64378. The copy in the FEDERAL REGISTER contains five errors; a corrected copy of the Proposed Rulemaking (Announcement ML-182) is available from the Copyright Office, Library of Congress, Washington, DC 20559.

See also the Transitional and Supplementary Provisions, Section 108, on p. 274.

LAW

§ 402. Notice of copyright: Phonorecords of sound recordings

(a) General Requirement.—Whenever a sound recording protected under this title is published in the United States or elsewhere by authority of the copyright owner, a notice of copyright as provided by this section shall be placed on all publicly distributed phonorecords of the sound recording.

(b) Form of Notice.—The notice appearing on the phonorecords shall consist of the following three elements:

(1) the symbol ℗ (the letter P in a circle); and

(2) the year of first publication of the sound recording; and

(3) the name of the owner of copyright in the sound recording, or an abbreviation by which the name can be recognized, or a generally known alternative designation of the owner; if the producer of the sound recording is named on the phonorecord labels or containers, and if no other name appears in conjunction with the notice, the producer's name shall be considered a part of the notice.

(c) Position of Notice.—The notice shall be placed on the surface of the phonorecord, or on the phonorecord label or container, in such manner and location as to give reasonable notice of the claim of copyright.

HOUSE REPORT

Section 402. Notice on Phonorecords of Sound Recordings

A special notice requirement, applicable only to the subject matter of sound recordings, is established by section 402. Since the bill protects sound recordings as separate works, independent of protection for any literary or musical works embodied in them, there would be a likelihood of confusion if the same notice requirements applied to sound recordings and to the works they incorporate. Like the present law, therefore, section 402 thus sets forth requirements for a notice to appear on the "phonorecords" of "sound recordings" that are different from the notice requirements established by section 401 for the "copies" of all other types of copyrightable works. Since "phonorecords" are not "copies," there is no need to place a section 401 notice on "phonorecords" to protect the literary or musical works embodied in the records.

In general, the form of the notice specified by section 402(b) consists of the symbol "℗"; the year of first publication of the sound recording; and the name of the copyright owner or an admissible variant. Where the record producer's name appears on the record label, album, sleeve, jacket, or other container, it will be considered a part of the notice if no other name appears in conjunction with it. Under subsection (c), the notice for a copyrighted sound recording may be affixed to the surface, label, or container of the phonorecord "in such manner and location as to give reasonable notice of the claim of copyright."

There are at least three reasons for prescribing use of the symbol "℗" rather than "©" in the notice to appear on phonorecords of sound recordings. Aside from the need to avoid confusion between claims to copyright in the sound recording and in the musical or literary work embodied in it, there is also a necessity for distinguishing between copyright claims in the sound recording and in the printed text or art work appearing on the record label, album cover, liner notes, et cetera. The symbol "℗" has also been adopted as the international symbol for the protection of sound recordings by the "Phonograms Convention" (the Convention for the Protection of Producers of Phonograms Against Unauthorized Duplication of Their Phonograms, done at Geneva October 29, 1971), to which the United States is a party.

SENATE REPORT

The last sentence differs substantially between the two reports. The closing sentence in the SENATE REPORT reads:

The United States ratified the convention on November 9, 1973.

LAW

§ 403. Notice of copyright: Publications incorporating United States Government works

Whenever a work is published in copies or phonorecords consisting preponderantly of one or more works of the United States Government, the notice of copyright provided by sections 401 or 402 shall also include a statement identifying, either affirmatively or negatively, those portions of the copies or phonorecords embodying any work or works protected under this title.

HOUSE REPORT

SECTION 403. NOTICE FOR PUBLICATIONS INCORPORATING UNITED STATES WORKS

Section 403 is aimed at a publishing practice that, while technically justified under the present law, has been the object of considerable criticism. In cases where a Government work is published or republished commercially, it has frequently been the practice to add some "new matter" in the form of an introduction, editing, illustrations, etc., and to include a general copyright notice in the name of the commercial publisher. This in no way suggests to the public that the bulk of the work is uncopyrightable and therefore free for use.

To make the notice meaningful rather than misleading, section 403 requires that, when the copies or phonorecords consist "preponderantly of one or more works of the United States Government," the copyright notice (if any) identify those parts of the work in which copyright is claimed. A failure to meet this requirement would be treated as an omission of the notice, subject to the provisions of section 405.

LAW

§ 404. Notice of copyright: Contributions to collective works

(a) A separate contribution to a collective work may bear its own notice of copyright, as provided by sections 401 through 403. However, a single notice applicable to the collective work as a whole is sufficient to satisfy the requirements of sections 401 through 403 with respect to the separate contributions it contains (not including advertisements inserted on behalf of persons other than the owner of copyright in the collective work), regardless of the ownership of copyright in the contributions and whether or not they have been previously published.

(b) Where the person named in a single notice applicable to a collective work as a whole is not the owner of copyright in a separate contribution that does not bear its own notice, the case is governed by the provisions of section 406(a).

HOUSE REPORT

SECTION 404. NOTICE FOR CONTRIBUTIONS TO COLLECTIVE WORKS

In conjunction with the provisions of section 201(c), section 404 deals with a troublesome problem under the present law: the notice requirements applicable to contributions published in periodicals and other collective works. The basic approach of the section is threefold:

(1) To permit but not require a separate contribution to bear its own notice;

(2) To make a single notice, covering the collective work as a whole, sufficient to satisfy the notice requirement for the separate contributions it contains, even if they have been previously published or their ownership is different; and

(3) To protect the interests of an innocent infringer of copyright in a contribution that does not bear its own notice, who has dealt in good faith with the person named in the notice covering the collective work as a whole.

As a general rule, under this section, the rights in an individual contribution to a collective work would not be affected by the lack of a separate copyright notice, as long as the collective work as a whole bears a notice. One exception to this rule would apply to "advertisements inserted on behalf of persons other than the owner of copyright in the collective work." Collective works, notably newspapers and magazines, are major advertising media, and it is common for the same advertisement to be published in a number of different periodicals. The general copyright notice in a particular issue would not ordinarily protect the advertisements inserted in it, and relatively little advertising matter today is published with a separate copyright notice. The exception in section 404(a), under which separate notices would be required for most advertisements published in collective works, would impose no undue burdens on copyright owners and is justified by the special circumstances.

Under section 404(b) a separate contribution that does not bear its own notice, and that is published in a collective work with a general notice containing the name of someone other than the copyright owner of the contribution, is treated as if it has been published with the wrong name in the notice. The case is governed by section 406(a), which means that an innocent infringer who in good faith took a license from the person named in the general notice would be shielded from liability to some extent.

LAW

§ 405. Notice of copyright: Omission of notice

(a) EFFECT OF OMISSION ON COPYRIGHT.—The omission of the copyright notice prescribed by sections 401 through 403 from copies or phonorecords publicly distributed by authority of the copyright owner does not invalidate the copyright in a work if—

(1) the notice has been omitted from no more than a relatively small number of copies or phonorecords distributed to the public; or

(2) registration for the work has been made before or is made within five years after the publication without notice, and a reasonable effort is made to add notice to all copies or phonorecords that are distributed to the public in the United States after the omission has been discovered; or

(3) the notice has been omitted in violation of an express requirement in writing that, as a condition of the copyright owner's authorization of the public distribution of copies or phonorecords, they bear the prescribed notice.

(b) EFFECT OF OMISSION ON INNOCENT INFRINGERS.—Any person who innocently infringes a copyright, in reliance upon an authorized copy or phonorecord from which the copyright notice has been omitted, incurs no liability for actual or statutory damages under section 504 for any infringing acts committed before receiving actual notice that registration for the work has been made under section 408, if such person proves that he or she was misled by the omission of notice. In a suit for infringement in such a case the court may allow or disallow recovery of any of the infringer's profits attributable to the infringement, and may enjoin the continuation of the infringing undertaking or may require, as a condition or permitting the continuation of the infringing undertaking, that the infringer pay the copyright owner a reasonable license fee in an amount and on terms fixed by the court.

(c) REMOVAL OF NOTICE.—Protection under this title is not affected by the removal, destruction, or obliteration of the notice, without the authorization of the copyright owner, from any publicly distributed copies or phonorecords.

HOUSE REPORT

SECTION 405. OMISSION OF COPYRIGHT NOTICE

Effect of omission on copyright protection

The provisions of section 405(a) make clear that the notice requirements of section 401, 402, and 403 are not absolute and that, unlike the law now in effect, the outright omission of a copyright notice does not automatically forfeit protection and throw the work into the public domain. This not only represents a major change in the theoretical framework of American copyright law, but it also seems certain to have immediate practical consequences in a great many individual cases. Under the proposed law a work published without any copyright notice will still be subject to statutory protection for at least 5 years, whether the omission was partial or total, unintentional or deliberate.

Under the general scheme of the bill, statutory copyright protection is secured automatically when a work is created, and is not lost when the work is published, even if the copyright notice is omitted entirely. Subsection (a) of section 405 provides that omission of notice, whether intentional or unintentional, does not invalidate the copright if either of two conditions is met:

(1) if "no more than a relatively small number" of copies or phonorecords have been publicly distributed without notice; or

(2) if registration for the work has already been made, or is made within 5 years after the publication without notice, and a reasonable effort is made to add notice to copies or phonorecords publicly distributed in the United States after the omission is discovered.

Thus, if notice is omitted from more than a "relatively small number" of copies or phonorecords, copyright is not lost immediately, but the work will go into the public domain if no effort is made to correct the error or if the work is not registered within 5 years.

Section 405(a) takes a middle-ground approach in an effort to encourage use of a copyright notice without causing unfair and unjustifiable forfeitures on technical grounds. Clause (1) provides that, as long as the omission is from "no more than a relatively small number of copies or phonorecords," there is no effect upon the copyright owner's rights except in the case of an innocent infringement covered by section 405(b); there is no need for registration or for efforts to correct the error if this clause is applicable. The phrase "relatively small number" is intended to be less restrictive than the phrase "a paritcular copy or copies" now in section 21 of the present law.

Under clause (2) of subsection (a), the first condition for curing an omission from a larger number of copies is that registration be made before the end of 5 years from the defective publication. This registration may have been made before the omission took place or before the work had been published in any form and, since the reasons for the omission have no bearing on the validity of copyright, there would be no need for the application to refer to them. Some time limit for registration is essential and the 5-year period is reasonable and consistent with the period provided in section 410(c).

The second condition established by clause (2) is that the copyright owner make a "reasonable effort," after discovering the error, to add the notice to copies or phonorecords distributed thereafter. This condition is specifically limited to copies or phonorecords publicly distributed in the United States, since it would be burdensome and impractical to require an American copyright owner to police the activities of foreign licensees in this situation.

The basic notice requirements set forth in sections 401(a) and 402(a) are limited to cases where a work is published "by authority of the copyright owner" and, in prescribing the effect of omission of notice, section 405(a) refers only to omission "from copies or phonorecords publicly distributed by authority of the copyright owner." The intention behind this language is that, where the copyright owner authorized publication of the work, the notice requirements would not be met if copies or phonorecords are publicly distributed without a notice, even if he expected a notice to be used. However, if the copyright owner authorized publication only on the express condition that all copies or phonorecords bear a prescribed notice, the provisions of section 401 or 402 and of section 405 would not apply since the publication itself would not be authorized. This principle is stated directly in section 405(a)(3).

Effect of omission on innocent infringers

In addition to the possibility that copyright protection will be forfeited under section 405(a)(2) if the notice is omitted, a second major inducement to use of the notice is found in subsection (b) of section 405. That provision, which limits the rights of a copyright owner against innocent infringers under certain circumstances, would be applicable whether the notice has been omitted from a large number or from a "relatively small number" of copies. The general postulates underlying the provision are that a person acting in good faith and with no reason to think otherwise should ordinarily be able to assume that a work is in the public domain if there is no notice on an authorized copy or phonorecord and that, if he relies on this assumption, he should be shielded from unreasonable liability.

Under section 405(b) an innocent infringer who acts "in reliance upon an authorized copy or phonorecord from which the copyright notice has been omitted", and who proves that he was misled by the omission, is shielded from liability for actual or statutory damages with respect to "any infringing acts committed before receiving actual notice" of registration. Thus, where the infringement is completed before actual notice has been served—as would be the usual case with respect to relatively minor infringements by teachers, librarians, journalists, and the like—liability, if any, would be limited to the profits the infringer realized from the act of infringement. On the other hand, where the infringing enterprise is one running over a period of time, the copyright owner would be able to seek an injunction against continuation of the infringement, and to obtain full monetary recovery for all infringing acts committed after he had served notice of registration. Persons who undertake major enterprises of this sort should check the Copyright Office registration records before starting, even where copies have been published without notice.

The purpose of the second sentence of subsection (b) is to give the courts broad discretion to balance the equities within the framework of section 405. Where an infringer made profits from infringing acts committed innocently before receiving notice from the copyright owner, the court may allow or withhold their recovery in light of the circumstances. The court may enjoin an infringement or may permit its continuation on condition that the copyright owner be paid a reasonable license fee.

Removal of notice by others

Subsection (c) of section 405 involves the situation arising when, following an authorized publication with notice, someone further down the chain of commerce removes, destroys, or obliterates the notice. The courts dealing with this problem under the present law, especially in connection with copyright notices on the selvage of textile fabrics, have generally upheld the validity of a notice that was securely attached to the copies when they left the control of the copyright owner, even though removal of the notice at some later stage was likely. This conclusion is incorporated in subsection (c).

LAW

§ 406. Notice of copyright: Error in name or date

(a) Error in Name.—Where the person named in the copyright notice on copies or phonorecords publicly distributed by authority of the copyright owner is not the owner of copyright, the validity and ownership of the copyright are not affected. In such a case, however, any person who innocently begins an undertaking that infringes the copyright has a complete defense to any action for such infringement if such person proves that he or she was misled by the notice and began the undertaking in good faith under a purported transfer or license from the person named therein, unless before the undertaking was begun—

(1) registration for the work had been made in the name of the owner of copyright; or

(2) a document executed by the person named in the notice and showing the ownership of the copyright had been recorded.

The person named in the notice is liable to account to the copyright owner for all receipts from transfers or licenses purportedly made under the copyright by the person named in the notice.

(b) Error in Date.—When the year date in the notice on copies or phonorecords distributed by authority of the copyright owner is earlier than the year in which publication first occurred, any period computed from the year of first publication under section 302 is to be computed from the year in the notice. Where the year date is more than one year later than the year in which publication first occurred, the work is considered to have been published without any notice and is governed by the provisions of section 405.

(c) Omission of Name or Date.—Where copies or phonorecords publicly distributed by authority of the copyright owner contain no name or no date that could reasonably be considered a part of the notice, the work is considered to have been published without any notice and is governed by the provisions of section 405.

HOUSE REPORT

Section 406. Error With Respect to Name or Date in Notice

In addition to cases where notice has been omitted entirely, it is common under the present law for a copyright notice to be fatally defective because the name or date has been omitted or wrongly stated. Section 406 is intended to avoid technical forfeitures in these cases, while at the same time inducing use of the correct name and date and protecting users who rely on erroneous information.

Error in name

Section 406(a) begins with a statement that the use of the wrong name in the notice will not affect the validity or ownership of the copyright, and then deals with situations where someone acting innocently and in good faith infringes a copyright by relying on a purported transfer or license from the person erroneously named in the notice. In such a case the innocent infringer is given a complete defense unless a search of the Copyright Office records would have shown that the owner was someone other than the person named in the notice. Use of the wrong name in the notice is no defense if, at the time infringement was begun, registration had been made in the name of the true owner, or if "a document executed by the person named in the notice and showing the ownership of the copyright had been recorded."

The situation dealt with in section 406(a) presupposes a contractual relation between the copyright owner and the person named in the notice. The copies or phonorecords bearing the defective notice have been "distributed by authority of the copyright owner" and, unless the publication can be considered unauthorized because of breach of an express condition in the contract or other reasons, the owner must be presumed to have acquiesced in the use of the wrong name. If the person named in the notice grants a license for use of the work in good faith or under a misapprehension, that person should not be liable as a copyright infringer, but the last sentence of section 406(a) would make the person named in the notice liable to account to the copyright owner for "all receipts, from transfers or licenses purportedly made under the copyright" by that person.

SENATE REPORT

The last sentence in the above paragraph reads:

The last sentence of section 406(a) would make him liable to account to the copyright owner for all of his gross receipts, subject to deduction of any costs he can justify.

HOUSE REPORT (Continued)

Error in date

The familiar problems of antedated and postdated notices are dealt with in subsection (b) of section 406. In the case of an antedated notice, where the year in the notice is earlier than the year of first publication, the bill adopts the established judicial principle that any statutory term measured from the year of publication will be computed from the year given in the notice. This provision would apply not only to the copyright terms of anonymous works, pseudonymous works, and works made for hire under section 302(c), but also to the presumptive periods set forth in section 302(e).

As for postdated notices, subsection (b) provides that, where the year in the notice is more than one year later than the year of first publication the case is treated as if the notice had been omitted and is governed by section 405. Notices postdated by one year are quite common on works published near the end of a year, and it would be unnecessarily strict to equate cases of that sort with works published without notice of any sort.

Omission of name or date

Section 406(c) provides that, if the copies or phonorecords "contain no name or no date that could reasonably be considered a part of the notice," the result is the same as if the notice had been omitted entirely, and section 405 controls. Unlike the present law, the bill contains no provision requiring the elements of the copyright notice to "accompany" each other, and under section 406(c) a name or date that could reasonably be read with the other elements may satisfy the requirements even if somewhat separated from them. Direct contiguity or juxtaposition of the elements is no longer necessary; but if the elements are too widely separated for their relation to be apparent, or if uncertainty is created by the presence of other names or dates, the case would have to be treated as if the name or date, and hence the notice itself had been omitted altogether.

LAW

§ 407. Deposit of copies or phonorecords for Library of Congress

(a) Except as provided by subsection (c), and subject to the provisions of subsection (e), the owner of copyright or of the exclusive right of publication in a work published with notice of copyright in the United States shall deposit, within three months after the date of such publication—

(1) two complete copies of the best edition; or

(2) if the work is a sound recording, two complete phonorecords of the best edition, together with any printed or other visually perceptible material published with such phonorecords.

Neither the deposit requirements of this subsection nor the acquisition provisions of subsection (e) are conditions of copyright protection.

(b) The required copies or phonorecords shall be deposited in the Copyright Office for the use or disposition of the Library of Congress. The Register of Copyrights shall, when requested by the depositor and upon payment of the fee prescribed by section 708, issue a receipt for the deposit.

(c) The Register of Copyrights may by regulation exempt any categories of material from the deposit requirements of this section, or require deposit of only one copy or phonorecord with respect to any categories. Such regulations shall provide either for complete exemption from the deposit requirements of this section, or for alternative forms of deposit aimed at providing a satisfactory archival record of a work without imposing practical or financial hardships on the depositor, where the individual author is the owner of copyright in a pictorial, graphic, or sculptural work and (i) less than five copies of the work have been published, or (ii) the work has been published in a limited edition consisting of numbered copies, the monetary value of which would make the mandatory deposit of two copies of the best edition of the work burdensome, unfair, or unreasonable.

(d) At any time after publication of a work as provided by subsection (a), the Register of Copyrights may make written demand for the required deposit on any of the persons obligated to make the deposit under subsection (a). Unless deposit is made within three months after the demand is received, the person or persons on whom the demand was made are liable—

(1) to a fine of not more than $250 for each work; and

(2) to pay into a specially designated fund in the Library of Congress the total retail price of the copies or phonorecords

demanded, or, if no retail price has been fixed, the reasonable cost of the Library of Congress of acquiring them; and

(3) to pay a fine of $2,500, in addition to any fine or liability imposed under clauses (1) and (2), if such person willfully or repeatedly fails or refuses to comply with such a demand.

(e) With respect to transmission programs that have been fixed and transmitted to the public in the United States but have not been published, the Register of Copyrights shall, after consulting with the Librarian of Congress and other interested organizations and officials, establish regulations governing the acquisition, through deposit or otherwise, of copies or phonorecords of such programs for the collections of the Library of Congress.

(1) The Librarian of Congress shall be permitted, under the standards and conditions set forth in such regulations, to make a fixation of a transmission program directly from a transmission to the public, and to reproduce one copy or phonorecord from such fixation for archival purposes.

(2) Such regulations shall also provide standards and procedures by which the Register of Copyrights may make written demand, upon the owner of the right of transmission in the United States, for the deposit of a copy or phonorecord of a specific transmission program. Such deposit may, at the option of the owner of the right of transmission in the United States, be accomplished by gift, by loan for purposes of reproduction, or by sale at a price not to exceed the cost of reproducing and supplying the copy or phonorecord. The regulations established under this clause shall provide reasonable periods of not less than three months for compliance with a demand, and shall allow for extensions of such periods and adjustments in the scope of the demand or the methods for fulfilling it, as reasonably warranted by the circumstances. Willful failure or refusal to comply with the conditions prescribed by such regulations shall subject the owner of the right of transmission in the United States to liability for an amount, not to exceed the cost of reproducing and supplying the copy or phonorecord in question, to be paid into a specially designated fund in the Library of Congress.

(3) Nothing in this subsection shall be construed to require the making or retention, for purposes of deposit, of any copy or phonorecord of an unpublished transmission program, the transmission of which occurs before the receipt of a specific written demand as provided by clause (2).

(4) No activity undertaken in compliance with regulations prescribed under clauses (1) or (2) of this subsection shall result in liability if intended solely to assist in the acquisition of copies or phonorecords under this subsection.

HOUSE REPORT

SECTION 407. DEPOSIT FOR THE LIBRARY OF CONGRESS

The provisions of sections 407 through 411 of the bill mark another departure from the present law. Under the 1909 statute, deposit of copies for the collections of the Library of Congress and deposit of copies for purposes of copyright registration have been treated as the same thing. The bill's basic approach is to regard deposit and registration as separate though closely related: deposit of copies or phonorecords for the Library of Congress is mandatory, but exceptions can be made for material the Library neither needs nor wants; copyright registration is not generally mandatory, but is a condition of certain remedies for copyright infringement. Deposit for the Library of Congress can be, and in the bulk of cases undoubtedly will be, combined with copyright registration.

The basic requirement of the deposit provision, section 407, is that within 3 months after a work has been published with notice of copyright in the United States, the "owner of copyright or of the exclusive right of publication" must deposit two copies or phonorecords of the work in the Copyright Office. The Register of Copyrights is authorized to exempt any category of material from the deposit requirements. Where the category is not exempted and deposit is not made, the Register may demand it; failure to comply would be penalized by a fine.

Under the present law deposits for the Library of Congress must be combined with copyright registration, and failure to comply with a formal demand for deposit and registration results in complete loss of copyright. Under section 407 of the bill, the deposit requirements can be satisfied without ever making registration, and subsection (a) makes clear that deposit "is not a condition of copyright protection." A realistic fine, coupled with the increased inducements for voluntary registration and deposit under other sections of the bill, seems likely to produce a more effective deposit system than the present one. The bill's approach will also avoid the danger that, under a divisible copyright, one copyright owner's rights could be destroyed by another owner's failure to deposit.

Although the basic deposit requirements are limited to works "published with notice of copyright in the United States," they would become applicable as soon as a work first published abroad is published in this country through the distribution of copies or phonorecords that are either imported or are part of an American edition. With respect to all types of works other than sound recordings, the basic obligation is to deposit "two complete copies of the best edition"; the term best edition," as defined in section 101, makes clear that the Library of Congress is entitled to receive copies of phonorecords from the edition it believes best suits its needs regardless of the quantiy or quality of other U.S. editions that may also have been published before the time of deposit. Once the deposit requirements for a particular work have been satisfied under section 407, however, the Library cannot claim deposit of future editions unless they represent newly copyrightable works under section 103.

The deposit requirement for sound recordings includes "two complete phonorecords of the best edition" and any other visually-perceptible material published with the phonorecords. The reference here is to the text or pictorial matter appearing on record sleeves and album covers or embodied in separate leaflets or booklets included in a sleeve, album, or other container. The required deposit in the case of a sound recording would extend to the entire "package" and not just to the disk, tape, or other phonorecord included as part of it.

Deposits under section 407, although made in the Copyright Office, are "for the use or disposition of the Library of Congress." Thus, the fundamental criteria governing regulations issued under section 407 (c), which allows exemptions from the deposit requirements for certain categories of works, would be the needs and wants of the Library.

The purpose of this provision is to make the deposit requirements as flexible as possible, so that there will be no obligation to make deposits where it serves no purpose, so that only one copy or phonorecord may be deposited where two are not needed, and so that reasonable adjustments can be made to meet practical needs in special cases. The regulations, in establishing special categories for these purposes, would necessarily balance the value of the copies or phonorecords to the collections of the Library of Congress against the burdens and costs to the copyright owner of providing them.

The following paragraph did not appear in the SENATE REPORT:

The Committee adopted an amendment to subsection (c) of section 407, aimed at meeting the concerns expressed by representatives of various artists' groups concerning the deposit of expensive art works and graphics published in limited editions. Under the present law, optional deposit of photographs is permitted for various classes of works, but not for fine prints, and this has resulted in many artists choosing to forfeit copyright protection rather than bear the expense of depositing "two copies of the best edition." To avoid this unfair result, the last sentence of subsection (c) would require the Register to issue regulations under which such works would either be exempted entirely from the mandatory deposit or would be subject to an appropriate alternative form of deposit.

If, within three months after the Register of Copyright has made a formal demand for deposit in accordance with section 407(d), the person on whom the demand was made has not complied, that person becomes liable to a fine up to $250 for each work, plus the "total retail price of the copies or phonorecords demanded." If no retail price has been fixed, clause (2) of subection (d) establishes the additional amount as "the reasonable cost to the Library of Congress of acquiring them." Thus, where the copies or phonorecords are not available for sale through normal trade channels—as would be true of many motion picture films, video tapes, and computer tapes, for example—the item of cost to be included in the fine would be equal to the basic expense of duplicating the copies or phonorecords plus a reasonable amount representing what it would have cost the Library to obtain them under its normal acquisitions procedures, if they had been available.

The next two paragraphs did not appear in the SENATE REPORT.

There have been cases under the present law in which the mandatory deposit provisions have been deliberately and repeatedly ignored, presumably on the assumption that the Library is unlikely to enforce them. In addition to the penalties provided in the current bill, the last clause of subsection (d) would add a fine of $2,500 for willful or repeated failure or refusal to deposit upon demand.

The Committee also amended section 407 by adding a new subsection (e), with conforming amendments of sections 407(a) and 408 (b). These amendments are intended to provide a basis for the Library of Congress to acquire, as a part of the copyright deposit system, copies or recordings of non-syndicated radio and television programs, without imposing any hardships on broadcasters. Under subsection

(e) the Library is authorized to tape programs off the air in all cases and may "demand" that the broadcaster supply the Library with a copy or phonorecord of a particular program. However, this "demand" authority is extremely limited: (1) The broadcaster is not required to retain any recording of a program after it has been transmitted unless a demand has already been received; (2) the demand would cover only a particular program; "blanket" demands would not be permitted; (3) the broadcaster would have the option of supplying the demand by gift, by loan for purposes of reproduciton, or by sale at cost; and (4) the penalty for willful failure or refusal to comply with a demand is limited to the cost of reproducing and supplying the copy or phonorecord in question.

CONFERENCE REPORT

DEPOSIT OF RADIO AND TELEVISION PROGRAMS

Senate bill

The Senate bill contained no provisions for the deposit of unpublished transmission programs, or for the preservation of published and unpublished programs in a Federal archive.

House bill

The House bill amended section 407 to provide a basis for the Library of Congress to acquire, as a part of the copyright deposit system, copies or recordings of nonsyndicated radio and television programs. Under section 407(e) the Library would be authorized to tape programs off the air in all cases, and could under certain conditions obtain a copy or phonorecord from the copyright owner by gift, by loan for purposes of reproduction, or by purchase at cost. A correlative provision in Sec. 113 of the bill's Transitional and Supplementary Provisions established an American Television and Radio Archive in the Library of Congress to provide a repository for the preservation of radio and television programs.

Conference substitute

The conference substitute adopts the House amendments.

COPYRIGHT OFFICE

Section 407(c) permits the Register of Copyrights to exempt certain categories of works from the deposit requirements. These exemptions are found in Sections 202.19 through 202.21 of the Copyright Office Regulations. They also appeared, with comments, in the FEDERAL REGISTER, Vol. 43, No. 182 (September 19, 1978), pp. 41975-41984. They have not been included here because of their length.

POSTAL REGULATIONS

Copyright Office Circular R30, "Special Library Postage Rate for Books Mailed to the Copyright Office," issued in January, 1978, advises:

"The Postal Service has confirmed that books mailed to the Copyright Office by publishers and distributors, including books accompanied by copyright applications, can be mailed at the fourth-class library rate. (When books and applications are mailed together, additional first-class postage must be paid for the applications . . .)."

. . . if these books are mailed by an individual to the Library of Congress, they are not eligible for mailing at the library rate."

. . . .

Books mailed to the Copyright Office by a library also may be sent by the library rate.

See also the Transitional and Supplementary Provisions, Section 110, p. 274.

LAW

§ 408. Copyright registration in general

(a) Registration Permissive.—At any time during the subsistence of copyright in any published or unpublished work, the owner of copyright or of any exclusive right in the work may obtain registration of the copyright claim by delivering to the Copyright Office the deposit specified by this section, together with the application and fee specified by sections 409 and 708. Subject to the provisions of section 405(a), such registration is not a condition of copyright protection.

(b) Deposit for Copyright Registration.—Except as provided by subsection (c), the material deposited for registration shall include—

(1) in the case of an unpublished work, one complete copy or phonorecord;

(2) in the case of a published work, two complete copies or phonorecords of the best edition;

(3) in the case of a work first published outside the United States, one complete copy or phonorecord as so published;

(4) in the case of a contribution to a collective work, one complete copy or phonorecord of the best edition of the collective work.

Copies or phonorecords deposited for the Library of Congress under section 407 may be used to satisfy the deposit provisions of this section, if they are accompanied by the prescribed application and fee, and by any additional identifying material that the Register may, by regulation, require. The Register shall also prescribe regulations establishing requirements under which copies or phonorecords acquired for the Library of Congress under subsection (e) of section 407, otherwise than by deposit, may be used to satisfy the deposit provisions of this section.

(c) Administrative Classification and Optional Deposit.—

(1) The Register of Copyrights is authorized to specify by regulation the administrative classes into which works are to be placed for purposes of deposit and registration, and the nature of the copies or phonorecords to be deposited in the various classes specified. The regulations may require or permit, for particular classes, the deposit of identifying material instead of copies or phonorecords, the deposit of only one copy or phonorecord where two would normally be required, or a single registration for a group of related works. This administrative classification of works has no significance with respect to the subject matter of copyright or the exclusive rights provided by this title.

(2) Without prejudice to the general authority provided under clause (1), the Register of Copyrights shall establish regulations specifically permitting a single registration for a group of works by the same individual author, all first published as contributions to periodicals, including newspapers, within a twelve-month

period, on the basis of a single deposit. application, and registration fee, under all of the following conditions—

(A) if each of the works as first published bore a separate copyright notice, and the name of the owner of copyright in the work, or an abbreviation by which the name can be recognized, or a generally known alternative designation of the owner was the same in each notice; and

(B) if the deposit consists of one copy of the entire issue of the periodical, or of the entire section in the case of a newspaper, in which each contribution was first published; and

(C) if the application identifies each work separately, including the periodical containing it and its date of first publication.

(3) As an alternative to separate renewal registrations under subsection (a) of section 304, a single renewal registration may be made for a group of works by the same individual author, all first published as contributions to periodicals, including newspapers, upon the filing of a single application and fee, under all of the following conditions:

(A) the renewal claimant or claimants, and the basis of claim or claims under section 304(a), is the same for each of the works; and

(B) the works were all copyrighted upon their first publication, either through separate copyright notice and registration or by virtue of a general copyright notice in the periodical issue as a whole; and

(C) the renewal application and fee are received not more than twenty-eight or less than twenty-seven years after the thirty-first day of December of the calendar year in which all of the works were first published; and

(D) the renewal application identifies each work separately, including the periodical containing it and its date of first publication.

(d) CORRECTIONS AND AMPLIFICATIONS.—The Register may also establish, by regulation, formal procedures for the filing of an application for supplementary registration, to correct an error in a copyright registration or to amplify the information given in a registration. Such application shall be accompanied by the fee provided by section 708, and shall clearly identify the registration to be corrected or amplified. The information contained in a supplementary registration augments but does not supersede that contained in the earlier registration.

(e) PUBLISHED EDITION OF PREVIOUSLY REGISTERED WORK.—Registration for the first published edition of a work previously registered in unpublished form may be made even though the work as published is substantially the same as the unpublished version.

HOUSE REPORT

SECTION 408. COPYRIGHT REGISTRATION IN GENERAL

Permissive registration

Under section 408(a), registration of a claim to copyright in any work, whether published or unpublished, can be made voluntarily by "the owner of copyright or of any exclusive right in the work" at any time during the copyright term. The claim may be registered in the

Copyright Office by depositing the copies, phonorecords, or other material specified by subsection (b) and (c), together with an application and fee. Except where, under section 405(a), registration is made to preserve a copyright that would otherwise be invalidated because of omission of the notice, registration is not a condition of copyright protection.

Deposit for purpose of copyright registration

In general, and subject to various exceptions, the material to be deposited for copyright registration consists of one complete copy or phonorecord of an unpublished work, and two complete copies or phonorecords of the best edition in the case of a published work. Section 408(b) provides special deposit requirements in the case of a work first published abroad ("one complete copy or phonorecord as so published") and in the case of a contribution to a collective work ("one complete copy or phonorecord of the best edition of the collective work"). As a general rule the deposit of more than a tear sheet or similar fraction of a collective work is needed to identify the contribution properly and to show the form in which it was published. Where appropriate as in the case of collective works such as multivolume encyclopedias, multipart newspaper editions, and works that are rare or out of print, the regulations issued by the Register under section 408(c) can be expected to make exceptions or special provisions.

With respect to works published in the United States, a single deposit could be used to satisfy the deposit requirements of section 407 and the registration requirements of section 408, if the application and fee for registration are submitted at the same time and are accompanied by "any additional identifying material" required by regulations. To serve this dual purpose the deposit and registration would have to be made simultaneously; if a deposit under section 407 had already been made, an additional deposit would be required under section 408. In addition, since deposit for the Library of Congress and registration of a claim to copyright serve essentially different functions, section 408(b) authorizes the Register of Copyrights to issue regulations under which deposit of additional material, needed for identification of the work in which copyright is claimed, could be required in certain cases.

Administrative classification

It is important that the statutory provisions setting forth the subject matter of copyright be kept entirely separate from any classification of copyrightable works for practical administrative purposes. Section 408(c)(1) thus leaves it to the Register of copyrights to specify "the administrative classes into which works are to be placed for purposes of deposit and registration," and makes clear that this administrative classification "has no significance with respect to the subject matter of copyright or the exclusive rights provided by this title."

Optional deposit

Consistent with the principle of administrative flexibility underlying all of the deposit and registration provisions, subsection (c) of section 408 also gives the Register latitude in adjusting the type of material deposited to the needs of the registration system. The Register is authorized to issue regulations specifying "the nature of the copies or phonorecords to be deposited in the various classes" and, for particular classes, to require or permit deposit of identifying material rather than copies or phonorecords, deposit of one copy or phonorecord rather than two, or, in the case of a group of related works, a single rather than a number of separate registrations. Under this provision the Register could, where appropriate, permit deposit of phonorecords rather than notated copies of musical compositions, allow or require deposit of print-outs of computer programs under certain circumstances, or permit deposit of one volume of an encyclopedia for purposes of registration of a single contribution.

Where the copies or phonorecords are bulky, unwieldly, easily broken, or otherwise impractical to file and retain as records identifying the work registered, the Register would be able to require or permit the substitute deposit of material that would better serve the purpose of identification. Cases of this sort might include, for example, billboard posters, toys and dolls, ceramics and glassware, costume jewerly, and a wide range of three-dimensional objects embodying copyrighted material. The Register's authority would also extend to rare or extremely valuable copies which would be burdensome or impossible to deposit. Deposit of one copy or phonorecord rather than two would probably be justifiable in the case of most motion pictures, and in any case where the Library of Congress has no need for the deposit and its only purpose is identification.

The provision empowering the Register to allow a number of related works to be registered together as a group represents a needed and important liberalization of the law now in effect. At present the requirement for separate registrations where related works or parts of a work are published separately has created administrative problems and has resulted in unnecessary burdens and expenses on authors and other copyright owners. In a number of cases the technical necessity for separate applications and fees has caused copyright owners to forego copyright altogether. Examples of cases where these undesirable and unnecessary results could be avoided by allowing a single registration include the various editions or issues of a daily newspaper, a work published in serial installments, a group of related jewerly designs, a group of photographs by one photographer, a series of greeting cards related to each other in some way, or a group of poems by a single author.

Single registration

Section 408(c)(2) directs the Register of Copyrights to establish regulations permitting under certain conditions a single registration for a group of works by the same individual author, all first published as contributions to periodicals, including newspapers, within a twelve-month period, on the basis of a single deposit, application, and registration fee. It is required that each of the works as first published have a separate copyright notice, and that the name of the owner of copyright in the work, (or an abbreviation by which the name can be recognized, or a generally known alternative designation of the owner) is the same in each notice. It is further required that the deposit consist of one copy of the entire issue of the periodical, or of the entire section in the case of a newspaper, in which each contribution is first published. Finally, the application shall identify each work separately, including the periodical containing it and its date of first publication.

Section 408(c)(3) provides under certain conditions an alternative to the separate renewal registrations of subsection (a). If the specified conditions are met, a single renewal registration may be made for a group of works by the same individual author, all first published as contributions to perioricals, including newspapers, upon the filing of a single application and fee. It is required that the renewal claimant or claimants, and the basic of claim or claims under section 304(a), is the same for each of the works; that the works were all copyrighted upon their first publication, either through separate copyright notice and registration or by virtue of a general copyright notice in the periodical issue as a whole; that the renewal application and fees are received not more than twenty-eight or less than twenty-seven years after December 31 of the calendar year in which all of the works were first published; and that the renewal application identifies each work separately, including the periodical containing it and its date of first publication.

SENATE REPORT

The last sentence in the above paragraph reads:

It is required that the renewal claimant or claimants, and the basis of claim or claims under section 304(a), is the same for each of the works; that the works were all copyrighted upon their first publication, either through separate copyright notice and registration or by virtue of a general copyright notice in the periodical issue as a whole; that all of the works were first published not more than twenty-eight or less than twenty-seven years before the date of receipt of the renewal application and fee; and that the renewal application identifies each work separately, including the periodical containing it and its date of first publication.

HOUSE REPORT (Continued)

Corrections and amplifications

Another unsatisfactory aspect of the present law is the lack of any provision for correcting or amplifying the information given in a completed registration. Subsection (d) of section 408 would remedy this by authorizing the Register to establish "formal procedures for the filing of an application for supplementary registration," in order to correct an error or amplify the information in a copyright registration. The "error" to be corrected under subsection (d) is an error by the applicant that the Copyright Office could not have been expected to note during its examination of the claim; where the error in a registration is the result of the Copyright Office's own mistake or oversight, the Office can make the correction on its own initiative and without recourse to the "supplementary registration" procedure.

Under subsection (d), a supplementary registration is subject to payment of a separate fee and would be maintained as an independent record, separate and apart from the record of the earlier registration it is intended to supplement. However, it would be required to identify clearly "the registration to be corrected or amplified" so that the two registrations could be tied together by appropriate means in the Copyright Office records. The original registration would not be expunged or cancelled; as stated in the subsection: "The information contained in a supplementary registration augments but does not supersede that contained in the earlier registration."

Published edition of previously registered work

The present statute requires that, where a work is registered in unpublished form, it must be registered again when it is published, whether or not the published edition contains any new copyrightable material. Under the bill there would be no need to make a second registration for the published edition unless it contains sufficient added material to be considered a "derivative work" or "compilation" under section 103.

On the other hand, there will be a number of cases where the copyright owner, although not required to do so, would like to have registration made for the published edition of the work, especially since the owner will still be obliged to deposit copies or phonorecords of it in the Copyright Office under section 407. From the point of view of the public there are advantages in allowing the owner to do so, since registration for the published edition will put on record the facts about the work in the form in which it is actually distributed to the public. Accordingly, section 408(e), which is intended to accomplish this result, makes an exception to the general rule against allowing more than one registration for the same work.

COPYRIGHT OFFICE

Section 408(c)(1) permits the Register of Copyrights to exempt certain categories of works from the deposit requirements. Information about this dispensation appears on p. 49.

LAW

§ 409. Application for copyright registration

The application for copyright registration shall be made on a form prescribed by the Register of Copyrights and shall include—

(1) the name and address of the copyright claimant;

(2) in the case of a work other than an anonymous or pseudonymous work, the name and nationality or domicile of the author or authors, and, if one or more of the authors is dead, the dates of their deaths;

(3) if the work is anonymous or pseudonymous, the nationality or domicile of the author or authors;

(4) in the case of a work made for hire, a statement to this effect;

(5) if the copyright claimant is not the author, a brief statement of how the claimant obtained ownership of the copyright;

(6) the title of the work, together with any previous or alternative titles under which the work can be identified;

(7) the year in which creation of the work was completed;

(8) if the work has been published, the date and nation of its first publication;

(9) in the case of a compilation or derivative work, an identification of any preexisting work or works that it is based on or

incorporates, and a brief, general statement of the additional material covered by the copyright claim being registered;

(10) in the case of a published work containing material of which copies are required by section 601 to be manufactured in the United States, the names of the persons or organizations who performed the processes specified by subsection (c) of section 601 with respect to that material, and the places where those processes were performed; and

(11) any other information regarded by the Register of Copyrights as bearing upon the preparation or identification of the work or the existence, ownership, or duration of the copyright.

HOUSE REPORT

Section 409. Application for Registration

The various clauses of section 409, which specify the information to be included in an application for copyright registration, are intended to give the Register of Copyrights authority to elicit all of the information needed to examine the application and to make a meaningful record of registration. The list of enumerated items was not exhaustive; under the last clause of the section the application may also include "any other information regarded by the Register of Copyrights as bearing upon the preparation or identification of the work or the existence, ownership, or duration of the copyright."

The text between the asterisks in the following paragraph did not appear in the SENATE REPORT.

Among the enumerated items there are several that are not now included in the Copyright Office's application forms, but will become significant under the life-plus-50 term and other provisions of the bill. Clause (5), reflecting the increased importance of the interrelationship between registration of copyright claims and recordation of transfers of ownership, requires a statement of how a claimant who is not the author acquired ownership of the copyright.* Clause (9) requires that, "in the case of a compilation or derivative work" the application include "an identification of any preexisting work or works that it is based on or incorporates, and a brief, general statement of the additional material covered by the copyright claim being registered." It is intended that, under this requirement, the application covering a collection such as a song-book or hymnal would clearly reveal any works in the collection that are in the public domain, and the copyright status of all other previously-published compositions. This information will be readily available in the Copyright Office.*

The catch-all clause at the end of the section will enable the Register to obtain more specialized information, such as that bearing on whether the work contains material that is a "work of the United States Government." In the case of works subject to the manufacturing requirement, the application must also include information about the manufacture of the copies.

LAW

§ 410. Registration of claim and issuance of certificate

(a) When, after examination, the Register of Copyrights determines that, in accordance with the provisions of this title, the material deposited constitutes copyrightable subject matter and that the other legal and formal requirements of this title have been met, the Register shall register the claim and issue to the applicant a certificate of registration under the seal of the Copyright Office. The certificate shall contain the information given in the application, together with the number and effective date of the registration.

(b) In any case in which the Register of Copyrights determines that, in accordance with the provisions of this title, the material deposited does not constitute copyrightable subject matter or that the claim is invalid for any other reason, the Register shall refuse registration and shall notify the applicant in writing of the reasons for such refusal.

(c) In any judicial proceedings the certificate of a registration made before or within five years after first publication of the work shall constitute prima facie evidence of the validity of the copyright and of the facts stated in the certificate. The evidentiary weight to be accorded the certificate of a registration made thereafter shall be within the discretion of the court.

(d) The effective date of a copyright registration is the day on which an application, deposit, and fee, which are later determined by the Register of Copyrights or by a court of competent jurisdiction to be acceptable for registration, have all been received in the Copyright Office.

HOUSE REPORT

SECTION 410. REGISTRATION OF CLAIM AND ISSUANCE OF CERTIFICATE

The first two subsections of section 410 set forth the two basic duties of the Register of Copyrights with respect to copyright registration: (1) to register the claim and issue a certificate if the Register determines that "the material deposited constitutes copyrightable subject matter and that the other legal and formal requirements of this title have been met," and (2) to refuse registration and notify the applicant if the Register determines that "the material deposited does not constitute copyrightable subject matter or that the claim is invalid for any other reason."

Subsection (c) deals with the probative effect of a certificate of registration issued by the Register under subsection (a). Under its provisions, a certificate is required to be given prima facie weight in any judicial proceedings if the registration it covers was made "before or within five years after first publication of the work"; thereafter the court is given discretion to decide what evidentiary weight the certificate should be accorded. This five-year period is based on a recognition that the longer the lapse of time between publication and registration the less likely to be reliable are the facts stated in the certificate.

Under section 410(c), a certificate is to "constitute prima facie evidence of the validity of the copyright and of the facts stated in the certificate." The principle that a certificate represents prima facie evidence of copyright validity has been established in a long line of court decisions, and it is a sound one. It is true that, unlike a patent claim, a claim to copyright is not examined for basic validity before a certificate is issued. On the other hand, endowing a copyright claimant who has obtained a certificate with a rebuttable presumption of the validity of the copyright does not deprive the defendant in an infringement suit of any rights; it merely orders the burdens of proof. The plaintiff should not ordinarily be forced in the first instance to prove all of the multitude of facts that underline the validity of the copyright unless the defendant, by effectively challenging them, shifts the burden of doing so to the plaintiff.

Section 410(d), which is in accord with the present practice of the Coyright Office, makes the effective date of registration the day when an application, deposit, and fee "which are later determined by the Register of Copyrights or by a court of competent jurisdiction to be acceptable for registration" have all been received. Where the three necessary elements are received at different times the date of receipt of the last of them is controlling, regardless of when the Copyright Office acts on the claim. The provision not only takes account of the inevitable timelag between receipt of the application and other material and the issuance of the certificate, but it also recognizes the possibility that a court might later find the Register wrong in refusing registration.

See also the Transitional and Supplementary Provisions, Section 109, on p. 274.

LAW

§ 411. Registration as prerequisite to infringement suit

(a) Subject to the provisions of subsection (b), no action for infringement of the copyright in any work shall be instituted until registration of the copyright claim has been made in accordance with this title. In any case, however, where the deposit, application, and fee required for registration have been delivered to the Copyright Office in proper form and registration has been refused, the applicant is entitled to institute an action for infringement if notice thereof, with a copy of the complaint, is served on the Register of Copyrights. The Register may, at his or her option, become a party to the action with respect to the issue of registrability of the copyright claim by entering an appearance within sixty days after such service, but the Register's failure to become a party shall not deprive the court of jurisdiction to determine that issue.

(b) In the case of a work consisting of sounds, images, or both, the first fixation of which is made simultaneously with its transmission, the copyright owner may, either before or after such fixation takes place, institute an action for infringement under section 501, fully subject to the remedies provided by sections 502 through 506 and sections 509 and 510, if, in accordance with requirements that the Register of Copyrights shall prescribe by regulation, the copyright owner—

(1) serves notice upon the infringer, not less than ten or more than thirty days before such fixation, identifying the work and the specific time and source of its first transmission, and declaring an intention to secure copyright in the work; and

(2) makes registration for the work within three months after its first transmission.

HOUSE REPORT

Section 411. Registration as Prerequisite to Infringement Suit

The first sentence of section 411(a) restates the present statutory requirement that registration must be made before a suit for copyright infringement is instituted. Under the bill, as under the law now in effect, a copyright owner who has not registered his claim can have a valid cause of action against someone who has infringed his copyright, but he cannot enforce his rights in the courts until he has made registration.

The second and third sentences of section 411(a) would alter the present law as interpreted in *Vacheron & Constantin-Le Coultre Watches, Inc.* v. *Benrus Watch Co.*, 260 F. 2d 637 (2d Cir. 1958). That case requires an applicant, who has sought registration and has been refused, to bring an action against the Register of Copyrights to compel the issuance of a certificate, before suit can be brought against an infringer. Under section 411, a rejected claimant who has properly applied for registration may maintain an infringement suit if notice of it is served on the Register of Copyrights. The Register is authorized, though not required, to enter the suit within 60 days; the Register would be a party on the issue of registrability only, and a failure by the Register to join the action would "not deprive the court of jurisdiction to determine that issue."

Section 411(b) is intended to deal with the special situation presented by works that are being transmitted "live" at the same time they are being fixed in tangible form for the first time. Under certain circumstances, where the infringer has been given advance notice, an injunction could be obtained to prevent the unauthorized use of the* material included in the* "live" transmission.

SENATE REPORT

The words between asterisks in the above sentence did not appear in the SENATE REPORT.

LAW

§ 412. Registration as prerequisite to certain remedies for infringement

In any action under this title, other than an action instituted under section 411(b), no award of statutory damages or of attorney's fees, as provided by sections 504 and 505, shall be made for—

(1) any infringement of copyright in an unpublished work commenced before the effective date of its registration; or

(2) any infringement of copyright commenced after first publication of the work and before the effective date of its registration, unless such registration is made within three months after the first publication of the work.

HOUSE REPORT

SECTION 412. REGISTRATION AS PREREQUISITE TO CERTAIN REMEDIES

The need for section 412 arises from two basic changes the bill will make in the present law.

(1) Copyright registration for published works, which is useful and important to users and the public at large, would no longer be compulsory, and should therefore be induced in some practical way.

(2) The great body of unpublished works now protected at common law would automatically be brought under copyright and given statutory protection. The remedies for infringement presently available at common law should continue to apply to these works under the statute, but they should not be given special statutory remedies unless the owner has, by registration, made a public record of his copyright claim.

Under the general scheme of the bill, a copyright owner whose work has been infringed before registration would be entitled to the remedies ordinarily available in infringement cases: an injunction on terms the court considers fair, and his actual damages plus any applicable profits not used as a measure of damages. However, section 412 would deny any award of the special or "extraordinary" remedies of statutory damages or attorney's fees where infringement of copyright in an unpublished work began before registration or where, in the case of a published work, infringement commenced after publication and before registration (unless registration has been made within a grace period of three months after publication). These provisions would be applicable to works of foreign and domestic origin alike.

In providing that statutory damages and attorney's fees are not recoverable for infringement of unpublished, unregistered works, clause (1) of section 412 in no way narrows the remedies available under the present law. With respect to published works, clause (2) would generally deny an award of those two special remedies where infringement takes place before registration. As an exception, however, the clause provides a grace period of three months after publication during which registration can be made without loss of remedies; full remedies could be recovered for any infringement begun during the three months after publication if registration is made before that period has ended. This exception is needed to take care of newsworthy or suddenly popular works which may be infringed almost as soon as they are published, before the copyright owner has had a reasonable opportunity to register his claim.

LAW

Chapter 5.—COPYRIGHT INFRINGEMENT AND REMEDIES

§ 501. Infringement of copyright

(a) Anyone who violates any of the exclusive rights of the copyright owner as provided by sections 106 through 118, or who imports copies or phonorecords into the United States in violation of section 602, is an infringer of the copyright.

(b) The legal or beneficial owner of an exclusive right under a copyright is entitled, subject to the requirements of sections 205(d) and 411, to institute an action for any infringement of that particular right committed while he or she is the owner of it. The court may require such owner to serve written notice of the action with a copy of the complaint upon any person shown, by the records of the Copyright Office or otherwise, to have or claim an interest in the copyright, and shall require that such notice be served upon any person whose interest is likely to be affected by a decision in the case. The court may require the joinder, and shall permit the intervention, of any person having or claiming an interest in the copyright.

(c) For any secondary transmission by a cable system that embodies a performance or a display of a work which is actionable as an act of infringement under subsection (c) of section 111, a television broadcast station holding a copyright or other license to transmit or perform the same version of that work shall, for purposes of subsection (b) of this section, be treated as a legal or beneficial owner if such secondary transmission occurs within the local service area of that television station.

(d) For any secondary transmission by a cable system that is actionable as an act of infringement pursuant to section 111(c)(3), the following shall also have standing to sue: (i) the primary transmitter whose transmission has been altered by the cable system; and (ii) any broadcast station within whose local service area the secondary transmission occurs.

HOUSE REPORT

Section 501. Infringement of Copyright

The bill, unlike the present law, contains a general statement of what constitutes infringement of copyright. Section 501(a) identifies a copyright infringer as someone who "violates any of the exclusive rights of the copyright owner as provided by sections 106 through 118" of the bill, or who imports copies or phonorecords in violation of section 602. Under the latter section an unauthorized importation of copies or phonorecords acquired abroad is an infringement of the exclusive right of distribution under certain circumstances.

The principle of the divisibility of copyright ownership, established by section 201(d), carries with it the need in infringement actions to safeguard the rights of all copyright owners and to avoid a multiplicity of suits. Subsection (b) of section 501 enables the owner of a particular right to bring an infringement action in that owner's name alone, while at the same time insuring to the extent possible that the other owners whose rights may be affected are notified and given a chance to join the action.

The first sentence of subsection (b) empowers the "legal or beneficial owner of an exclusive right" to bring suit for "any infringement of that particular right committed while he or she is the owner of it." A "beneficial owner" for this purpose would include, for example, an author who had parted with legal title to the copyright in exchange for percentage royalties based on sales or license fees.

The second and third sentences of section 501(b), which supplement the provisions of the Federal Rules of Civil Procedure, give the courts discretion to require the plaintiff to serve notice of the plaintiff's suit on "any person shown, by the records of the Copyright Office or otherwise, to have or claim an interest in the copyright"; where a person's interest "is likely to be affected by a decision in the case" a court order requiring service of notice is mandatory. As under the Federal rules, the court has discretion to require joinder of "any person having or claiming an interest in the copyright"; but, if any such person wishes to become a party, the court must permit that person's intervention.

In addition to cases involving divisibility of ownership in the same version of a work, section 501(b) is intended to allow a court to permit or compel joinder of the owners of rights in works upon which a derivative work is based.

Section 501 contains two provisions conferring standing to sue under the statute upon broadcast stations in specific situations involving secondary transmissions by cable systems. Under subsection (c), a local television broadcaster licensed to transmit a work can sue a cable system importing the same version of the work into the broadcaster's local service area in violation of section 111(c). Subsection (d) deals with cases arising under section 111(c)(3), the provision dealing with substitution or alteration by a cable system of commercials or other programming; in such cases standing to sue is also conferred on: (1) the primary transmitter whose transmission has been altered by the cable system, and (2) any broadcast stations within whose local service area the secondary transmission occurs. These provisions are linked to section 509, a new provision on remedies for alteration of programming by cable systems, discussed below.

SENATE REPORT

The above paragraph did not appear in the SENATE REPORT. The following paragraph appeared in its place:

For purposes of subsection (b), subsection (c) of Section 501 provides that a television broadcast station holding a copyright or other license to transmit or perform the same version of a work shall be regarded as a legal or beneficial owner if a cable television system makes a secondary transmission which is actionable as an act of infringement under Section 111 if the transmission occurs within the local service area of the television broadcast station.

HOUSE REPORT (Continued)

Vicarious liability for infringing performances

The committee has considered and rejected an amendment to this section intended to exempt the proprietors of an establishment, such as a ballroom or night club, from liability for copyright infringement committed by an independent contractor, such as an orchestra laeder. A well-established principle of copyright law is that a person who violates any of the exclusive rights of the copyright owner is an infringer, including persons who can be considered related or vicarious infringers. To be held a related or vicarious infringer in the case of performing rights, a defendant must either actively operate or supervise the operation of the place wherein the performances occur, or control the content of the infringing program, and expect commercial gain from the operation and either direct or indirect benefit from the infringing performance. The committee has decided that no justification exists for changing existing law, and causing a significant erosion of the public performance right.

See also the Transitional and Supplementary Provisions, Section 112, on p. 275.

LAW

§ 502. Remedies for infringement: Injunctions

(a) Any court having jurisdiction of a civil action arising under this title may, subject to the provisions of section 1498 of title 28, grant temporary and final injunctions on such terms as it may deem reasonable to prevent or restrain infringement of a copyright.

(b) Any such injunction may be served anywhere in the United States on the person enjoined; it shall be operative throughout the United States and shall be enforceable, by proceedings in contempt or otherwise, by any United States court having jurisdiction of that person. The clerk of the court granting the injunction shall, when requested by any other court in which enforcement of the injunction is sought, transmit promptly to the other court a certified copy of all the papers in the case on file in such clerk's office.

HOUSE AND SENATE REPORTS

[Omitted to save space.]

LAW

§ 503. Remedies for infringement: Impounding and disposition of infringing articles

(a) At any time while an action under this title is pending, the court may order the impounding, on such terms as it may deem reasonable, of all copies or phonorecords claimed to have been made or used in violation of the copyright owner's exclusive rights, and of all plates, molds, matrices, masters, tapes, film negatives, or other articles by means of which such copies or phonorecords may be reproduced.

(b) As part of a final judgment or decree, the court may order the destruction or other reasonable disposition of all copies or phonorecords found to have been made or used in violation of the copyright owner's exclusive rights, and of all plates, molds, matrices, masters, tapes, film negatives, or other articles by means of which such copies or phonorecords may be reproduced.

HOUSE AND SENATE REPORTS

[Omitted to save space.]

LAW

§ 504. Remedies for infringement: Damages and profits

(a) In General.—Except as otherwise provided by this title, an infringer of copyright is liable for either—

(1) the copyright owner's actual damages and any additional profits of the infringer, as provided by subsection (b); or

(2) statutory damages, as provided by subsection (c).

(b) Actual Damages and Profits.—The copyright owner is entitled to recover the actual damages suffered by him or her as a result of the infringement, and any profits of the infringer that are attributable to the infringement and are not taken into account in computing the actual damages. In establishing the infringer's profits, the copyright owner is required to present proof only of the infringer's gross revenue, and the infringer is required to prove his or her deductible expenses and the elements of profit attributable to factors other than the copyrighted work.

(c) Statutory Damages.—

(1) Except as provided by clause (2) of this subsection, the copyright owner may elect, at any time before final judgment is rendered, to recover, instead of actual damages and profits, an award of statutory damages for all infringements involved in the action, with respect to any one work, for which any one infringer is liable individually, or for which any two or more infringers are liable jointly and severally, in a sum of not less than $250 or more than $10,000 as the court considers just. For the purposes of this subsection, all the parts of a compilation or derivative work constitute one work.

(2) In a case where the copyright owner sustains the burden of proving, and the court finds, that infringement was committed willfully, the court in its discretion may increase the award of statutory damages to a sum of not more than $50,000. In a case where the infringer sustains the burden of proving, and the court finds, that such infringer was not aware and had no reason to believe that his or her acts constituted an infringement of copyright, the court it its discretion may reduce the award of statutory

damages to a sum of not less than $100. The court shall remit statutory damages in any case where an infringer believed and had reasonable grounds for believing that his or her use of the copyrighted work was a fair use under section 107, if the infringer was: (i) an employee or agent of a nonprofit educational institution, library, or archives acting within the scope of his or her employment who, or such institution, library, or archives itself, which infringed by reproducing the work in copies or phonorecords; or (ii) a public broadcasting entity which or a person who, as a regular part of the nonprofit activities of a public broadcasting entity (as defined in subsection (g) of section 118) infringed by performing a published nondramatic literary work or by reproducing a transmission program embodying a performance of such a work.

HOUSE REPORT

SECTION 504. DAMAGES AND PROFITS

In general

A cornerstone of the remedies sections and of the bill as a whole is section 504, the provision dealing with recovery of actual damages, profits, and statutory damages. The two basic aims of this section are reciprocal and correlative: (1) to give the courts specific unambiguous directions concerning monetary awards, thus avoiding the confusion and uncertainty that have marked the present law on the subject, and, at the same time, (2) to provide the courts with reasonable latitude to adjust recovery to the circumstances of the case, thus avoiding some of the artificial or overly technical awards resulting from the language of the existing statute.

Subsection (a) lays the groundwork for the more detailed provisions of the section by establishing the liability of a copyright infringer for either "the copyright owner's actual damages and any additional profits of the infringer," or statutory damages. Recovery of actual damages and profits under section 504(b) or of statutory damages under section 504(c) is alternative and for the copyright owner to elect; as under the present law, the plaintiff in an infringement suit is not obliged to submit proof of damages and profits and may choose to rely on the provision for minimum statutory damages. However, there is nothing in section 504 to prevent a court from taking account of evidence concerning actual damages and profits in making an award of statutory damages within the range set out in subsection (c).

Actual damages and profits

[Omitted to save space.]

Statutory damages

Subsection (c) of section 504 makes clear that the plaintiff's election to recover statutory damages may take place at any time during the trial before the court has rendered its final judgment. The remainder of clause (1) of the subsection represents a statement of the general rates applicable to awards of statutory damages. Its principal provisions may be summarized as follows:

1. As a general rule, where the plaintiff elects to recover statutory damages, the court is obliged to award between $250 and $10,000. It can exercise discretion in awarding an amount within that range but, unless one of the exceptions provided by clause (2) is applicable, it cannot make an award of less than $250 or of more than $10,000 if the copyright owner has chosen recovery

under section 504(c).

2. Although, as explained below, an award of minimum statutory damages may be multiplied if separate works and separately liable infringers are involved in the suit, a single award in the $250 to $10,000 range is to be made "for all infringements involved in the action." A single infringer of a single work is liable for a single amount between $250 and $10,000, no matter how many acts of infringement are involved in the action and regardless of whether the acts were separate, isolated, or occurred in a related series.

3. Where the suit involves infringement of more than one separate and independent work, minimum statutory damages for each work must be awarded. For example, if one defendant has infringed three copyrighted works, the copyright owner is entitled to statutory damages of at least $750 and may be awarded up to $30,000. Subsection (c)(1) makes clear, however, that, although they are regarded as independent works for other purposes, "all the parts of a compilation or derivative work constitute one work" for this purpose. Moreover, although the minimum and maximum amounts are to be multiplied where multiple "works" are involved in the suit, the same is not true with respect to multiple copyrights, multiple owners, multiple exclusive rights, or multiple registrations. This point is especially important since, under a scheme of divisible copyright, it is possible to have the rights of a number of owners of separate "copyrights" in a single "work" infringed by one act of a defendant.

4. Where the infringements of one work were committed by a single infringer acting individually, a single award of statutory damages would be made. Similarly, where the work was infringed by two or more joint tortfeasors, the bill would make them jointly and severally liable for an amount in the $250 to $10,000 range. However, where separate infringements for which two or more defendants are not jointly liable are joined in the same action, separate awards of statutory damages would be appropriate.

Clause (2) of section 504(c) provides for exceptional cases in which the maximum award of statutory damages could be raised from $10,000 to $50,000, and in which the minimum recovery could be reduced from $250 to $100. The basic principle underlying this provision is that the courts should be given discretion to increase statutory damages in cases of willful infringement and to lower the minimum where the infringer is innocent. The language of the clause makes clear that in these situations the burden of proving willfulness rests on the copyright owner and that of proving innocence rests on the infringer, and that the court must make a finding of either willfulness or innocence in order to award the exceptional amounts.

The "innocent infringer" provision of section 504(c)(2) has been the subject of extensive discussion. The exception, which would allow reduction of minimum statutory damages to $100 where the infringer "was not aware and had no reason to believe that his or her acts constituted an infringement of copyright," is sufficient to protect against unwarranted liability in cases of occasional or isolated innocent infringement, and it offers adequate insulation to users, such as broadcasters and newspaper publishers, who are particularly vulnerable to this type of infringement suit. On the other hand, by establishing a realistic floor for liability, the provision preserves its intended deterrent effect; and it would not allow an infringer to escape simply because the plaintiff failed to disprove the defendant's claim of innocence.

In addition to the general "innocent infringer" provision clause (2) deals with the special situation of teachers, librarians, archivists, and public broadcasters, and the nonprofit institutions of which they are a part. Section 504(c)(2) provides that, where such a person or institution infringed copyrighted material in the honest belief that what they were doing constituted fair use, the court is precluded from awarding any statutory damages. It is intended that, in cases involving this provision, the burden of proof with respect to the defendant's good faith should rest on the plaintiff.

SENATE REPORT

In the SENATE REPORT, the preceding paragraph reads:

In addition to the general "innocent infringer" provision clause (2) deals with the special situation of teachers, libraries, and archivists in nonprofit institutions who reproduce copyrighted material in the honest belief that what they are doing constitutes fair use. In cases of this sort it would be possible for the court to find that there had been infringement and still reduce the statutory minimum or waive it altogether. This exception applies only where the defendant proves "that he believed and had reasonable grounds for believing that the reproduction was a fair use under section 107." It reflects the special problems of educational and scholarly uses of copyrighted material discussed in connection with that section.

CONFERENCE REPORT

[Omitted to save space.]

LAW

§ 505. Remedies for infringement: Costs and attorney's fees

In any civil action under this title, the court in its discretion may allow the recovery of full costs by or against any party other than the United States or an officer thereof. Except as otherwise provided by this title, the court may also award a reasonable attorney's fee to the prevailing party as part of the costs.

HOUSE REPORT

[Omitted to save space.]

LAW

§ 506. Criminal offenses

(a) CRIMINAL INFRINGEMENT.—Any person who infringes a copyright willfully and for purposes of commercial advantage or private financial gain shall be fined not more than $10,000 or imprisoned for not more than one year, or both: *Provided*, *however*, That any person who infringes willfully and for purposes of commercial advantage or private financial gain the copyright in a sound recording afforded by subsections (1), (2), or (3) of section 106 or the copyright in a motion picture afforded by subsections (1), (3), or (4) of section 106 shall be fined not more than $25,000 or imprisoned for not more than one year, or both, for the first such offense and shall be fined not more than $50,000 or imprisoned for not more than two years, or both, for any subsequent offense.

(b) FORFEITURE AND DESTRUCTION.—When any person is convicted of any violation of subsection (a), the court in its judgment of conviction shall, in addition to the penalty therein prescribed, order the forfeiture and destruction or other disposition of all infringing copies or phonorecords and all implements, devices, or equipment used in the manufacture of such infringing copies or phonorecords.

(c) FRAUDULENT COPYRIGHT NOTICE.—Any person who, with fraudulent intent, places on any article a notice of copyright or words of the same purport that such person knows to be false, or who, with fraudulent intent, publicly distributes or imports for public distribution any article bearing such notice or words that such person knows to be false, shall be fined not more than $2,500.

(d) FRAUDULENT REMOVAL OF COPYRIGHT NOTICE.—Any person who, with fraudulent intent, removes or alters any notice of copyright appearing on a copy of a copyrighted work shall be fined not more than $2,500.

(e) FALSE REPRESENTATION.—Any person who knowingly makes a false representation of a material fact in the application for copyright registration provided for by section 409, or in any written statement filed in connection with the application, shall be fined not more than $2,500.

HOUSE REPORT AND CONFERENCE REPORT

[Omitted to save space.]

LAW

§ 507. Limitations on actions

(a) CRIMINAL PROCEEDINGS.—No criminal proceeding shall be maintained under the provisions of this title unless it is commenced within three years after the cause of action arose.

(b) CIVIL ACTIONS.—No civil action shall be maintained under the provisions of this title unless it is commenced within three years after the claim accrued.

LAW

§ 508. Notification of filing and determination of actions

(a) Within one month after the filing of any action under this title, the clerks of the courts of the United States shall send written notification to the Register of Copyrights setting forth, as far as is shown by the papers filed in the court, the names and addresses of the parties and the title, author, and registration number of each work involved in the action. If any other copyrighted work is later included in the action by amendment, answer, or other pleading, the clerk shall also send a notification concerning it to the Register within one month after the pleading is filed.

(b) Within one month after any final order or judgment is issued in the case, the clerk of the court shall notify the Register of it, sending with the notification a copy of the order or judgment together with the written opinion, if any, of the court.

(c) Upon receiving the notifications specified in this section, the Register shall make them a part of the public records of the Copyright Office.

HOUSE REPORT

[Omitted to save space.]

LAW

§ 509. Seizure and forfeiture

(a) All copies or phonorecords manufactured, reproduced, distributed, sold, or otherwise used, intended for use, or possessed with intent to use in violation of section 506(a), and all plates, molds, matrices, masters, tapes, film negatives, or other articles by means of which such copies or phonorecords may be reproduced, and all electronic, mechanical, or other devices for manufacturing, reproducing, or assembling such copies or phonorecords may be seized and forfeited to the United States.

(b) The applicable procedures relating to (i) the seizure, summary and judicial forfeiture, and condemnation of vessels, vehicles, merchandise, and baggage for violations of the customs laws contained in title 19, (ii) the disposition of such vessels, vehicles, merchandise, and baggage or the proceeds from the sale thereof, (iii) the remission or mitigation of such forfeiture, (iv) the compromise of claims, and (v) the award of compensation to informers in respect of such forfeitures, shall apply to seizures and forfeitures incurred, or alleged to have been incurred, under the provisions of this section, insofar as applicable and not inconsistent with the provisions of this section; except that such duties as are imposed upon any officer or employee of the Treasury Department or any other person with respect to the seizure and forfeiture of vessels, vehicles, merchandise; and baggage under the provisions of the customs laws contained in title 19 shall be performed with respect to seizure and forfeiture of all articles described in subsection (a) by such officers, agents, or other persons as may be authorized or designated for that purpose by the Attorney General.

HOUSE REPORT AND CONFERENCE REPORT

[Omitted to save space.]

LAW

§ 510. Remedies for alteration of programing by cable systems

(a) In any action filed pursuant to section 111(c)(3), the following remedies shall be available:

(1) Where an action is brought by a party identified in subsections (b) or (c) of section 501, the remedies provided by sections 502 through 505, and the remedy provided by subsection (b) of this section; and

(2) When an action is brought by a party identified in subsection (d) of section 501, the remedies provided by sections 502 and 505, together with any actual damages suffered by such party as a result of the infringement, and the remedy provided by subsection (b) of this section.

(b) In any action filed pursuant to section 111(c)(3), the court may decree that, for a period not to exceed thirty days, the cable system shall be deprived of the benefit of a compulsory license for one or more distant signals carried by such cable system.

HOUSE REPORT

[Omitted to save space.]

LAW

Chapter 6.—MANUFACTURING REQUIREMENTS AND IMPORTATION

§ 601. Manufacture, importation, and public distribution of certain copies

(a) Prior to July 1, 1982, and except as provided by subsection (b), the importation into or public distribution in the United States of copies of a work consisting preponderantly of nondramtic literary material that is in the English language and is protected under this title is prohibited unless the portions consisting of such material have been manufactured in the United States or Canada.

(b) The provisions of subsection (a) do not apply—

(1) where, on the date when importation is sought or public distribution in the United States is made, the author of any substantial part of such material is neither a national nor a domiciliary of the United States or, if such author is a national of the United States, he or she has been domiciled outside the United States for a continuous period of at least one year immediately preceding that date; in the case of a work made for hire, the exemption provided by this clause does not apply unless a subsustantial part of the work was prepared for an employer or other person who is not a national or domiciliary of the United States or a domestic corporation or enterprise;

(2) where the United States Customs Service is presented with an import statement issued under the seal of the Copyright Office, in which case a total of no more than two thousand copies of any one such work shall be allowed entry; the import statement shall be issued upon request to the copyright owner or to a person designated by such owner at the time of registration for the work under section 408 or at any time thereafter;

(3) where importation is sought under the authority or for the use, other than in schools, of the Government of the United States or of any State or political subdivision of a State;

(4) where importation, for use and not for sale, is sought—

(A) by any person with respect to no more than one copy of any work at any one time;

(B) by any person arriving from outside the United States, with respect to copies forming part of such person's personal baggage; or

(C) by an organization operated for scholarly, educational, or religious purposes and not for private gain, with respect to copies intended to form a part of its library;

(5) where the copies are reproduced in raised characters for the use of the blind; or

(6) where, in addition to copies imported under clauses (3) and (4) of this subsection, no more than two thousand copies of any one such work, which have not been manufactured in the United States or Canada, are publicly distributed in the United States; or

(7) where, on the date when importation is sought or public distribution in the United States is made—

(A) the author of any substantial part of such material is an individual and receives compensation for the transfer or license of the right to distribute the work in the United States; and

(B) the first publication of the work has previously taken place outside the United States under a transfer or license granted by such author to a transferee or licensee who was not a national or domiciliary of the United States or a domestic corporation or enterprise; and

(C) there has been no publication of an authorized edition of the work of which the copies were manufactured in the United States; and

(D) the copies were reproduced under a transfer or license granted by such author or by the transferee or licensee of the right of first publication as mentioned in subclause (B), and the transferee or the licensee of the right of reproduction was not a national or domiciliary of the United States or a domestic corporation or enterprise.

(c) The requirement of this section that copies be manufactured in the United States or Canada is satisfied if—

(1) in the case where the copies are printed directly from type that has been set, or directly from plates made from such type, the setting of the type and the making of the plates have been performed in the United States or Canada; or

(2) in the case where the making of plates by a lithographic or photoengraving process is a final or intermediate step preceding the printing of the copies, the making of the plates has been performed in the United States or Canada; and

(3) in any case, the printing or other final process of producing multiple copies and any binding of the copies have been performed in the United States or Canada.

(d) Importation or public distribution of copies in violation of this section does not invalidate protection for a work under this title. However, in any civil action or criminal proceeding for infringement of the exclusive rights to reproduce and distribute copies of the work, the infringer has a complete defense with respect to all of the nondramatic literary material comprised in the work and any other parts of the work in which the exclusive rights to reproduce and distribute copies are owned by the same person who owns such exclusive rights in the nondramatic literary material, if the infringer proves—

(1) that copies of the work have been imported into or publicly distributed in the United States in violation of this section by or with the authority of the owner of such exclusive rights; and

(2) that the infringing copies were manufactured in the United States or Canada in accordance with the provisions of subsection (c); and

(3) that the infringement was commenced before the effective date of registration for an authorized edition of the work, the copies of which have been manufactured in the United States or

Canada in accordance with the provisions of subsection (c).

(e) In any action for infringement of the exclusive rights to reproduce and distribute copies of a work containing material required by this section to be manufactured in the United States or Canada, the copyright owner shall set forth in the complaint the names of the persons or organizations who performed the processes specified by subsection (c) with respect to that material, and the places where those processes were performed.

HOUSE REPORT

[This lengthy section has been omitted to save space, except for one subsection on the importation of educational and library materials.]

Limitations on importation and distribution of copies manufactured abroad

The basic purpose of the temporary manufacturing requirements of section 601, like that of the present manufacturing clause, is to induce the manufacture of an edition in the United States if more than a certain limited number of copies are to be distributed in this country. Subsection (a) therefore provides in general that "the importation into or public distribution in the United States" of copies not complying with the manufacturing clause is prohibited. Subsection (b) then sets out the exceptions to this prohibition, and clause (2) of that subsection fixes the importation limit at 2,000 copies.

Additional exceptions to the copies affected by the manufacturing requirements are set out in clauses (3) through (7) of subsection (b). Clause (3) permits importation of copies for governmental use, other than in schools, by the United States or by "any State or political subdivision of a State." Clause (4) allows importation for personal use of "no more than one copy of any work at any one time," and also exempts copies in the baggage of persons arriving from abroad and copies intended for the library collection of nonprofit scholarly, educational, or religious organizations. Braille copies are completely exempted under clause (5), and clause (6) permits the public distribution in the United States of copies allowed entry by the other clauses of that subsection. Clause (7) is a new exception, covering cases in which an individual American author has, through choice or necessity, arranged for publication of his work by a foreign rather than a domestic publisher.

The last sentence in the above paragraph did not appear in the SENATE REPORT.

CONFERENCE REPORT

[Omitted to save space.]

LAW

§ 602. Infringing importation of copies or phonorecords

(a) Importation into the United States, without the authority of the owner of copyright under this title, of copies or phonorecords of a work that have been acquired outside the United States is an infringement of the exclusive right to distribute copies or phonorecords under

section 106, actionable under section 501. This subsection does not apply to—

(1) importation of copies or phonorecords under the authority or for the use of the Government of the United States or of any State or political subdivision of a State, but not including copies or phonorecords for use in schools, or copies of any audiovisual work imported for purposes other than archival use;

(2) importation, for the private use of the importer and not for distribution, by any person with respect to no more than one copy or phonorecord of any one work at any one time, or by any person arriving from outside the United States with respect to copies or phonorecords forming part of such person's personal baggage; or

(3) importation by or for an organization operated for scholarly, educational, or religious purposes and not for private gain, with respect to no more than one copy of an audiovisual work solely for its archival purposes, and no more than five copies or phonorecords of any other work for its library lending or archival purposes, unless the importation of such copies or phonorecords is part of an activity consisting of systematic reproduction or distribution, engaged in by such organization in violation of the provisions of section 108(g)(2).

(b) In a case where the making of the copies or phonorecords would have constituted an infringement of copyright if this title had been applicable, their importation is prohibited. In a case where the copies or phonorecords were lawfully made, the United States Customs Service has no authority to prevent their importation unless the provisions of section 601 are applicable. In either case, the Secretary of the Treasury is authorized to prescribe, by regulation, a procedure under which any person claiming an interest in the copyright in a particular work may, upon payment of a specified fee, be entitled to notification by the Customs Service of the importation of articles that appear to be copies or phonorecords of the work.

HOUSE REPORT

SECTION 602. INFRINGING IMPORTATION

Scope of the section

Section 602, which has nothing to do with the manufacturing requirements of section 601, deals with two separate situations: importation of "piratical" article (that is, copies or phonorecords made without any authorization of the copyright owner), and unauthorized importation of copies or phonorecords that wree lawfully made. The general approach of section 602 is to make unauthorized importation an act of infringement in both cases, but to permit the United States Customs Service to prohibit importation only of "piratical" articles.

Section 602(a) first states the general rule that unauthorized importation is an infringement merely if the copies or phonorecords "have been acquired outside the United States", but then enumerates three specific exceptions: (1) importation under the authority or for the use of a governmental body, but not including material for use in schools or copies of an audiovisual work imported for any purpose other than archival use; (2) importation for the private use of the importer of no more than one copy or phonorecord of a work at a time, or of articles in the personal baggage of travelers from abroad;

or (3) importation by nonprofit organizations "operated for scholarly, educational, or religious purposes" of "no more than one copy of an audiovisual work solely for archival purposes, and no more than five copies or phonorecords of any other work for its library lending or archival purposes."

SENATE REPORT

The SENATE REPORT adds at this point:

Under the definition in section 101, "audiovisual works" include motion pictures.

HOUSE REPORT (Continued)

The first sentence in this section did not appear in the SENATE REPORT:

The bill specifies that the third exception does not apply if the importation "is part of an activity consisting of systematic reproduction or distribution, engaged in by such organization in violation of the provisions of section 108(g)(2)."

If none of the three exemptions applies, any unauthorized importer of copies or phonorecords acquired abroad could be sued for damages and enjoined from making any use of them, even before any public distribution in this country has taken place.

Importation of "piratical" copies

Section 602(b) retains the present statute's prohibition against importation of "piratical" copies or phonorecords—those whose making "would have constituted an infringement of copyright if this title had been applicable." Thus, the Customs Service could exclude copies or phonorecords that were unlawful in the country where they were made; it could also exclude copies or phonorecords which, although made lawfully under the domestic law of that country, would have been unlawful if the U.S. copyright law could have been applied. A typical example would be a work by an American author which is in the public domain in a foreign country because that country does not have copyright relations with the United States; the making and publication of an authorized edition would be lawful in that country, but the Customs Service could prevent the importation of any copies of that edition.

Importation for infringing distribution

The second situation covered by section 602 is that where the copies or phonorecords were lawfully made but their distribution in the United States would infringe the U.S. copyright owner's exclusive rights. As already said, the mere act of importation in this situation would constitute an act of infringement and could be enjoined. However, in cases of this sort it would be impracticable for the United States Customs Service to attempt to enforce the importation prohibition, and section 602(b) provides that, unless a violation of the manufacturing requirements is also involved, the Service has no authority to prevent importation, "where the copies or phonorecords were lawfully made." The subsection would authorize the establishment of a procedure under which copyright owners could arrange for the Customs Service to notify them whenever articles appearing to infringe their works are imported.

LAW

§ 603. Importation prohibitions: Enforcement and disposition of excluded articles

(a) The Secretary of the Treasury and the United States Postal Service shall separately or jointly make regulations for the enforcement of the provisions of this title prohibiting importation.

(b) These regulations may require, as a condition for the exclusion of articles under section 602—

(1) that the person seeking exclusion obtain a court order enjoining importation of the articles; or

(2) that the person seeking exclusion furnish proof, of a specified nature and in accordance with prescribed procedures, that the copyright in which such person claims an interest is valid and that the importation would violate the prohibition in section 602; the person seeking exclusion may also be required to post a surety bond for any injury that may result if the detention or exclusion of the articles proves to be unjustified.

(c) Articles imported in violation of the importation prohibitions of this title are subject to seizure and forfeiture in the same manner as property imported in violation of the customs revenue laws. Forfeited articles shall be destroyed as directed by the Secretary of the Treasury or the court, as the case may be; however, the articles may be returned to the country of export whenever it is shown to the satisfaction of the Secretary of the Treasury that the importer had no reasonable grounds for believing that his or her acts constituted a violation of law.

HOUSE REPORT

[Omitted to save space.]

LAW

Chapter 7.—COPYRIGHT OFFICE

§ 701. The Copyright Office: General responsibilities and organization

(a) All administrative functions and duties under this title, except as otherwise specified, are the responsibility of the Register of Copyrights as director of the Copyright Office of the Library of Congress. The Register of Copyrights, together with the subordinate officers and employees of the Copyright Office, shall be appointed by the Librarian of Congress, and shall act under the Librarian's general direction and supervision.

(b) The Register of Copyrights shall adopt a seal to be used on and after January 1, 1978, to authenticate all certified documents issued by the Copyright Office.

(c) The Register of Copyrights shall make an annual report to the Librarian of Congress of the work and accomplishments of the Copyright Office during the previous fiscal year. The annual report of the Register of Copyrights shall be published separately and as a part of the annual report of the Librarian of Congress.

(d) Except as provided by section 706(b) and the regulations issued thereunder, all actions taken by the Register of Copyrights under this title are subject to the provisions of the Administrative Procedure Act of June 11, 1946, as amended (c. 324, 60 Stat. 237, title 5, United States Code, Chapter 5, Subchapter II and Chapter 7).

HOUSE REPORT

[Omitted to save space.]

LAW

§ 702. Copyright Office regulations

The Register of Copyrights is authorized to establish regulations not inconsistent with law for the administration of the functions and duties made the responsibility of the Register under this title. All regulations established by the Register under this title are subject to the approval of the Librarian of Congress.

HOUSE REPORT

[The report did not comment on this section.]

LAW

§ 703. Effective date of actions in Copyright Office

In any case in which time limits are prescribed under this title for the performance of an action in the Copyright Office, and in which the last day of the prescribed period falls on a Saturday, Sunday, holiday, or other nonbusiness day within the District of Columbia or the Federal Government, the action may be taken on the next succeeding business day, and is effective as of the date when the period expired.

HOUSE REPORT

[The report did not comment on this section.]

LAW

§ 704. Retention and disposition of articles deposited in Copyright Office

(a) Upon their deposit in the Copyright Office under sections 407 and 408, all copies, phonorecords, and identifying material, including those deposited in connection with claims that have been refused registration, are the property of the United States Government.

(b) In the case of published works, all copies, phonorecords, and identifying material deposited are available to the Library of Congress for its collections, or for exchange or transfer to any other library. In the case of unpublished works, the Library is entitled, under regulations that the Register of Copyrights shall prescribe, to select any deposits for its collections or for transfer to the National Archives of the United States or to a Federal records center, as defined in section 2901 of title 44.

(c) The Register of Copyrights is authorized, for specific or general categories of works, to make a facsimile reproduction of all or any part of the material deposited under section 408, and to make such reproduction a part of the Copyright Office records of the registration, before transferring such material to the Library of Congress as provided by subsection (b), or before destroying or otherwise disposing of such material as provided by subsection (d).

(d) Deposits not selected by the Library under subsection (b), or identifying portions or reproductions of them, shall be retained under the control of the Copyright Office, including retention in Government storage facilities, for the longest period considered practicable and desirable by the Register of Copyrights and the Librarian of Congress. After that period it is within the joint discretion of the Register and the Librarian to order their destruction or other disposition; but, in the case of unpublished works, no deposit shall be knowingly or intentionally destroyed or otherwise disposed of during its term of copyright unless a facsimile reproduction of the entire deposit has been made a part of the Copyright Office records as provided by subsection (c).

(e) The depositor of copies, phonorecords, or identifying material under section 408, or the copyright owner of record, may request retention, under the control of the Copyright Office, of one or more of such articles for the full term of copyright in the work. The Register of Copyrights shall prescribe, by regulation, the conditions under which such requests are to be made and granted, and shall fix the fee to be charged under section 708(a)(11) if the request is granted.

HOUSE REPORT

Retention and disposition of deposited articles

A recurring problem in the administration of the copyright law has been the need to reconcile the storage limitations of the Copyright Office with the continued value of deposits in identifying copyrighted works. Aside from its indisputable utility to future historians and scholars, a susbtantially complete collection of both published and unpublished deposits, other than those selected by the Library of Congress, would avoid the many difficulties encountered when copies needed for identification in connection with litigation or other purposes have been destroyed. The basic policy behind section 704 is that cpyright deposits should be retained as long as possible, but that the Register of Copyrights and the Librarian of Congress should be empowered to dispose of them under appropriate safeguards when they decide that it has become necessary to do so.

Under subsection (a) of section 704, any copy, phonorecord, or identifying material deposited for registration, whether registered or not, becomes "the property of the United States Government." This means that the copyright owner or person who made the depodsit cannot demand its return as a matter of right, even in rejection cases, although the provisions of section 407 and 408 are flexible enough to allow for special arrangements in exceptional cases. On the other hand, Government ownership of deposited articles under section 704(a) carries with it no privileges under the copyright itself; use of a deposited article in violation of the copyright owner's exclusive rights would be infringement.

With respect to published works, section 704(b) makes all deposits available to the Library of Congress "for its collections, or for exchanges or transfer to any other library"; where the work is unpublished, the Library is authorized to select any deposit for its own collections* or for transfer to the National Archives of the United States or to a Federal records center.

SENATE REPORT

The text following the asterisk in the above sentence did not appear in the SENATE REPORT; the following text appeared in its place:

or for exchange or transfer to any other library.

HOUSE REPORT (Continued)

Motion picture producers have expressed some concern lest the right to transfer copies of works, such as motion pictures, that have been published under rental, lease, or loan arrangements, might lead to abuse. However, the Library of Congress has not knowingly transferred works of this sort to other libraries in the past, and there is no reason to expect it to do so in the future.

The Committee added a new subsection (c) to section 704, under which the Register is authorized to make microfilm or other record copies of copyright deposits before transferring or otherwise disposing of them.

The preceding paragraph did not appear in the SENATE REPORT.

For deposits not selected by the Library, subsection (d) provides that they, or "identifying portions or reproductions of them," are to be retained under Copyright Office control "for the longest period considered practicable and desirable" by the Register and the Librarian. When and if they ultimately decide that retention of certain deposited articles is no longer "practicable and desirable," the Register and Librarian have joint discretion to order their "destruction or other disposition." Because of the unique value and irreplaceable nature of unpublished deposits, the subsection prohibits their intentional destruction during their copyright term, unless a facsimile reproduction has been made.

SENATE REPORT

The last sentence in the above paragraph reads:

Because of the unique value and irreplaceable nature of unpublished deposits, the subsection requires their preservation throughout their own term of copyright.

HOUSE REPORT (Continued)

Subsection (e) of section 704 establishes a new procedure under which a copyright owner can request retention of deposited material for the full term of copyright. The Register of Copyrights is authorized to issue regulations prescribing the fees for this service and the "conditions under which such requests are to be made and granted."

LAW

§ 705. Copyright Office records: Preparation, maintenance, public inspection, and searching

(a) The Register of Copyrights shall provide and keep in the Copyright Office records of all deposits, registrations, recordations, and other actions taken under this title, and shall prepare indexes of all such records.

(b) Such records and indexes, as well as the articles deposited in connection with completed copyright registrations and retained under the control of the Copyright Office, shall be open to public inspection.

(c) Upon request and payment of the fee specified by section 708, the Copyright Office shall make a search of its public records, indexes, and deposits, and shall furnish a report of the information they disclose with respect to any particular deposits, registrations, or recorded documents.

HOUSE REPORT

[The report did not comment on this section.]

LAW

§ 706. Copies of Copyright Office records

(a) Copies may be made of any public records or indexes of the Copyright Office; additional certificates of copyright registration and copies of any public records or indexes may be furnished upon request and payment of the fees specified by section 708.

(b) Copies or reproductions of deposited articles retained under the control of the Copyright Office shall be authorized or furnished only under the conditions specified by the Copyright Office regulations.

HOUSE REPORT

[The report did not comment on this section.]

LAW

§ 707. Copyright Office forms and publications

(a) CATALOG OF COPYRIGHT ENTRIES.—The Register of Copyrights shall compile and publish at periodic intervals catalogs of all copyright registrations. These catalogs shall be divided into parts in accordance with the various classes of works, and the Register has discretion to determine, on the basis of practicability and usefulness, the form and frequency of publication of each particular part.

(b) OTHER PUBLICATIONS.—The Register shall furnish, free of charge upon request, application forms for copyright registration and general informational material in connection with the functions of the Copyright Office. The Register also has the authority to publish compilations of information, bibliographies, and other material he or she considers to be of value to the public.

(c) DISTRIBUTION OF PUBLICATIONS.—All publications of the Copyright Office shall be furnished to depository libraries as specified under section 1905 of title 44, and, aside from those furnished free of charge, shall be offered for sale to the public at prices based on the cost of reproduction and distribution.

HOUSE REPORT

Catalog of copyright entries

Section 707(a) of the bill retains the present statute's basic requirement that the Register compile and publish catalogs of all copyright registrations at periodic intervals, but provides for "discretion to determine, on the basis of practicability and usefulness the form and frequency of publication of each particular part". This provision will in no way diminish the utility or value of the present catalogs, and the flexibility of approach, coupled with use of the new mechanical and electronic devices now becoming available, will avoid waste and result in a better product.

LAW

§ 708. Copyright Office fees

(a) The following fees shall be paid to the Register of Copyrights:

(1) for the registration of a copyright claim or a supplementary registration under section 408, including the issuance of a certificate of registration, $10;

(2) for the registration of a claim to renewal of a subsisting copyright in its first term under section 304(a), including the issuance of a certificate of registration, $6;

(3) for the issuance of a receipt for a deposit under section 407, $2;

(4) for the recordation, as provided by section 205, of a transfer of copyright ownership or other document of six pages or less, covering no more than one title, $10; for each page over six and each title over one, 50 cents additional;

(5) for the filing, under section 115(b), of a notice of intention to make phonorecords, $6;

(6) for the recordation, under section 302(c), of a statement revealing the identity of an author of an anonymous or pseudonymous work, or for the recordation, under section 302(d), of a statement relating to the death of an author, $10 for a document of six pages or less, covering no more than one title; for each page over six and for each title over one, $1 additional;

(7) for the issuance, under section 601, of an import statement, $3;

(8) for the issuance, under section 706, of an additional certificate of registration, $4;

(9) for the issuance of any other certification, $4; the Register of Copyrights has discretion, on the basis of their cost, to fix the fees for preparing copies of Copyright Office records, whether they are to be certified or not;

(10) for the making and reporting of a search as provided by section 705, and for any related services, $10 for each hour or fraction of an hour consumed;

(11) for any other special services requiring a substantial amount of time or expense, such fees as the Register of Copyrights may fix on the basis of the cost of providing the service.

(b) The fees prescribed by or under this section are applicable to the United States Government and any of its agencies, employees, or officers, but the Register of Copyrights has discretion to waive the requirement of this subsection in occasional or isolated cases involving relatively small amounts.

(c) All fees received under this section shall be deposited by the Register of Copyrights in the Treasury of the United States and shall be credited to the appropriation for necessary expenses of the Copyright Office. The Register may, in accordance with regulations that he or she shall prescribe, refund any sum paid by mistake or in excess of the fee required by this section; however, before making a refund in any case involving a refusal to register a claim under section 410(b), the Register may deduct all or any part of the prescribed registration fee to cover the reasonable administrative costs of processing the claim.

The first sentence of 708(c) was amended by the Legislative Branch Appropriation Act of 1978 (P.L. 95-94; 91 Stat. 653, 676, 682), which was signed by President

Carter on August 5, 1977. The amendment went into effect on January 1, 1978, the effective date for the Copyright Revision Act of 1976.

HOUSE REPORT

[Omitted to save space.]

LAW

§ 709. Delay in delivery caused by disruption of postal or other services

In any case in which the Register of Copyrights determines, on the basis of such evidence as the Register may by regulation require, that a deposit, application, fee, or any other material to be delivered to the Copyright Office by a particular date, would have been received in the Copyright Office in due time except for a general disruption or suspension of postal or other transportation or communications services, the actual receipt of such material in the Copyright Office within one month after the date on which the Register determines that the disruption or suspension of such services has terminated, shall be considered timely.

HOUSE REPORT

[Omitted to save space.]

LAW

§ 710. Reproduction for use of the blind and physically handicapped: Voluntary licensing forms and procedures

The Register of Copyrights shall, after consultation with the Chief of the Division for the Blind and Physically Handicapped and other appropriate officials of the Library of Congress, establish by regulation standardized forms and procedures by which, at the time applications covering certain specified categories of nondramatic literary works are submitted for registration under section 408 of this title, the copyright owner may voluntarily grant to the Library of Congress a license to reproduce the copyrighted work by means of Braille or similar tactile symbols, or by fixation of a reading of the work in a phonorecord, or both, and to distribute the resulting copies or phonorecords solely for the use of the blind and physically handicapped and under limited conditions to be specified in the standardized forms.

HOUSE REPORT

Reproductions for the blind and handicapped

Section 710 directs the Register of Copyrights to establish by regulation forms and procedures by which the copyright owners of certain categories of works may voluntarily grant to the Library of Congress a license to reproduce and distribute copies or phonorecords of the work solely for the use of the blind and physically handicapped.

LAW

Chapter 8.—COPYRIGHT ROYALTY TRIBUNAL

§ 801. Copyright Royalty Tribunal: Establishment and purpose

(a) There is hereby created an independent Copyright Royalty Tribunal in the legislative branch.

(b) Subject to the provisions of this chapter, the purposes of the Tribunal shall be—

(1) to make determinations concerning the adjustment of reasonable copyright royalty rates as provided in sections 115 and 116, and to make determinations as to reasonable terms and rates of royalty payments as provided in section 118. The rates applicable under sections 115 and 116 shall be calculated to achieve the following objectives:

(A) To maximize the availability of creative works to the public;

(B) To afford the copyright owner a fair return for his creative work and the copyright user a fair income under existing economic conditions;

(C) To reflect the relative roles of the copyright owner and the copyright user in the product made available to the public with respect to relative creative contribution, technological contribution, capital investment, cost, risk, and contribution to the opening of new markets for creative expression and media for their communication;

(D) To minimize any disruptive impact on the structure of the industries involved and on generally prevailing industry practices.

(2) to make determinations concerning the adjustment of the copyright royalty rates in section 111 solely in accordance with the following provisions:

(A) The rates established by section 111(d)(2)(B) may be adjusted to reflect (i) national monetary inflation or deflation or (ii) changes in the average rates charged cable subscribers for the basic service of providing secondary transmissions to maintain the real constant dollar level of the royalty fee per subscriber which existed as of the date of enactment of this Act: *Provided*, That if the average rates charged cable system subscribers for the basic service of providing secondary transmissions are changed so that the average rates exceed national monetary inflation, no change in the rates established by section 111(d)(2)(B) shall be permitted: *And provided further*, That no increase in the royalty fee shall be permitted based on any reduction in the average number of distant signal equivalents per subscriber. The Commission may consider all factors relating to the maintenance of such level of payments including, as an extenuating factor, whether the cable industry has been restrained by subscriber rate regulating authorities from increasing the rates for the basic service of providing secondary transmissions.

(B) In the event that the rules and regulations of the Federal Communications Commission are amended at any time after April 15, 1976, to permit the carriage by cable systems of additional television broadcast signals beyond the local service area of the primary transmitters of such signals, the royalty rates established by section 111(d)(2)(B) may be adjusted to insure that the rates for the additional distant signal equivalents resulting from such carriage are reasonable in the light of the changes effected by the amendment to such rules and regulations. In determining the reasonableness of rates proposed following an amendment of Federal Communications Commission rules and regulations, the Copyright Royalty Tribunal shall consider, among other factors, the economic impact on copyright owners and users: *Provided*, That no adjustment in royalty rates shall be made under this subclause with respect to any distant signal equivalent or fraction thereof represented by (i) carriage of any signal permitted under the rules and regulations of the Federal Communications Commission in effect on April 15, 1976, or the carriage of a signal of the same type (that is, independent, network, or noncommercial educational) substituted for such permitted signal, or (ii) a television broadcast signal first carried after April 15, 1976, pursuant to an individual waiver of the rules and regulations of the Federal Communications Commission, as such rules and regulations were in effect on April 15, 1976.

(C) In the event of any change in the rules and regulations of the Federal Communications Commission with respect to syndicated and sports program exclusivity after April 15, 1976, the rates established by section 111(d)(2)(B) may be adjusted to assure that such rates are reasonable in light of the changes to such rules and regulations, but any such adjustment shall apply only to the affected television broadcast signals carried on those systems affected by the change.

(D) The gross receipts limitations established by section 111(d)(2)(C) and (D) shall be adjusted to reflect national monetary inflation or deflation or changes in the average rates charged cable system subscribers for the basic service of providing secondary transmissions to maintain the real constant dollar value of the exemption provided by such section; and the royalty rate specified therein shall not be subject to adjustment; and

(3) to distribute royalty fees deposited with the Register of Copyrights under sections 111 and 116, and to determine, in cases where controversy exists, the distribution of such fees.

(c) As soon as possible after the date of enactment of this Act, and no later than six months following such date, the President shall publish a notice announcing the initial appointments provided in section 802, and shall designate an order of seniority among the initially-appointed commissioners for purposes of section 802(b).

SENATE REPORT

[The SENATE REPORT for Chapter 8 differs greatly from Chapter 8 in the HOUSE REPORT. Because of its length and its limited value to this book's intended audience, it has been omitted to save space.]

HOUSE REPORT

CHAPTER 8. COPYRIGHT ROYALTY COMMISSION

Chapter 8 establishes a Copyright Royalty Commission for the purpose of periodically reviewing and adjusting statutory royalty rates for use of copyrighted materials pursuant to compulsory licenses provided in sections 111 (secondary transmissions by cable systems), 115 (mechanical royalties) and 116 (jukebox) of the bill. In addition, the Commission will make determinations as to reasonable terms and rates of royalty payments as provided in section 118 (public broadcasting), and to resolve disputes over the distribution of royalties paid pursuant to the statutory licenses in sections 111 and 116.

The Committee recognizes that the industries affected by the royalty rates over which the Commission has jurisdiction are very different, and it is therefore expected that any adjustment of a rate by the Commission shall be based on the economic conditions peculiar to the industries affected by that rate. Likewise, the Committee recognizes the fact that the cable television industry is a developing industry in transition, whereas the recording and jukebox industries are long-established. Therefore, the Committee has chosen periods of different lengths in which the Commission is to review the rates affecting those industries. Rates for retransmission of copyrighted works by cable television systems will be reviewed in 1980 and each subsequent fifth year. Rates established for mechanical reproduction will be reviewed in 1980, 1987, and in each subsequent 10th year. Rates for performance by jukebox will be reviewed in 1980, and in each subsequent 10th year. Rates and terms under section 118 will be reviewed in 1982 and in each subsequent fifth year. The Committee does not intend that rate changes, whether up or down, should necessarily be made as the result of such periodic reviews.

The Committee has chosen to stagger the times for review of the various rates established under the bill so as to balance the workload of the Commission. Cable and copyright owners agreed to a set of standards for the adjustment of rates which the Committee in large measure has accepted. No specific standards governing the establishment or adjustment of rates by the Commission, other than rates for cable transmissions, have been detailed in the legislation, because the Committee did not wish to limit the factors that the Commission might consider in a world of constantly changing economics and technology. However, it is anticipated that the Commission will consider the following objectives in determining a reasonable rate under sections 115 and 116:

The report then repeats Sections 180(b)(1) and (2) of the LAW. This part has been omitted to save space.

Similar considerations are noted in connection with Commission review of rates and terms for public broadcasting in the discussion of section 118, above.

CONFERENCE REPORT

[The text of this report appears at the end of Section 802.]

LAW

§ 802. Membership of the Tribunal

(a) The Tribunal shall be composed of five commissioners appointed by the President with the advice and consent of the Senate for a term of seven years each; of the first five members appointed, three shall be designated to serve for seven years from the date of the notice specified in section 801(c), and two shall be designated to serve for five years from such date, respectively. Commissioners shall be compensated at the highest rate now or hereafter prescribe for grade 18 of the General Schedule pay rates (5 U.S.C. 5332).

(b) Upon convening the commissioners shall elect a chairman from among the commissioners appointed for a full seven-year term. Such chairman shall serve for a term of one year. Thereafter, the most senior commissioner who has not previously served as chairman shall serve as chairman for a period of one year, except that, if all commissioners have served a full term as chairman, the most senior commissioner who has served the least number of terms as chairman shall be designated as chairman.

(c) Any vacancy in the Tribunal shall not affect its powers and shall be filled, for the unexpired term of the appointment, in the same manner as the original appointment was made.

HOUSE REPORT

Structure of the Copyright Royalty Commission

The Senate bill provides that, upon certifying the existence of a controversy concerning distribution of statutory royalty fees or upon periodic petition for review of statutory royalty rates by an interested party, the Register of Copyrights, is to convene a three member panel to constitute a Copyright Royalty Tribunal for the purpose of resolving the controversy or reviewing the rates.

The Senate bill provides that the Tribunal be appointed by the Register from among the membership of the American Arbitration Assocation or similar organization. The Tribunal is to exist within the Library of Congress.

Due to constitutional concern over the provision of the Senate bill that the Register of Copyrights, an employee of the Legislative Branch, appoint the members of the Tribunal, the Committee adopted an amendment providing for direct appointment of three individuals by the President. The name of the Tribunal was changed to the Copyright Royalty Commission.

Although under the Committee Amendment, the Commission is to be an independent authority, it is to receive administrative support from the Library of Congress.

The Commission is authorized to appoint a staff to assist it in carrying out its responsibilities. However, it is expected that the staff will consist only of sufficient clerical personnel to provide one full time secretary for each member and one or two additional employees to meet the clerical needs of the entire Commission. Members of the Commission are expected to perform all professional responsibilities themselves, except where it is necessary to employ outside experts on a consulting basis. Assistance in matters of administration, such as payroll and budgeting, will be available from the Library of Congress.

The Committee expects that the President shall appoint members of the Commission from among persons who have demonstrated professional competence in the field of copyright policy.

CONFERENCE REPORT

COPYRIGHT ROYALTY TRIBUNAL

Senate bill

Chapter 8 of the Senate bill established a Copyright Royalty Tribunal in the Library of Congress, for the purpose of periodically reviewing and adjusting statutory royalty rates with respect to the four compulsory licenses provided by the bill, and of resolving disputes over the distribution of royalties from cable transmissions and jukebox performances. Upon certifying the existence of a controversy concerning distribution of statutory royalty fees, or upon periodic petition for review of statutory royalty rates by an interested party, the Register of Copyrights was to convene a three-member panel to constitute a Copyright Royalty Tribunal to resolve the controversy or review the rates. Determinations by the Tribunal were to be submitted to the two Houses of Congress, and were to be final unless voted upon and rejected by one of the two Houses within a specified period. Rate adjustments were not subject to judicial review, and the grounds for judicial review of royalty distributions were limited to misconduct or corruption of a Tribunal member.

House bill

The House bill amended chapter 8 to provide for a permanent three-member Copyright Royalty Commission, which was to be an independent body but would receive administrative support from the Library of Congress. The commissioners were to be appointed by the President for staggered five-year terms, and the Commission's proceedings were made generally subject to the Administrative Procedure Act. Any final determinations of the Commission would be reviewable by the U.S. Court of Appeals on the basis of the record before the Commission. Under sections 111, 116, and chapter 8 of the House bill, the Register of Copyrights was to perform the recording functions and do the paperwork and initial accounting connected with the compulsory licensing procedures established for cable transmissions and jukebox performances. However, after the Register had deducted the costs involved in these procedures and deposited the royalties in the U.S. Treasury, the Commission would assume all duties involved in distributing the royalties, regardless of whether or not there were a dispute.

Conference substitute

The conference substitute conforms in general to the House bill, but with several changes. The body established by chapter 8 is to be named the Copyright Royalty Tribunal, and is to consist of five commissioners appointed for staggered seven-year terms by the President with the advice and consent of the Senate. The Tribunal is to be an independent agency in the legislative branch; a new section defines the responsibilities of the Library of Congress to provide administrative support to the Tribunal, and establishes specific regulatory authority governing the procedures and responsibilities for disbursement of funds. The House receded on its language appearing in the last sentence of section 801(b)(1), and the conference agreed to a substitute for that language.

LAW

§ 803. Procedures of the Tribunal

(a) The Tribunal shall adopt regulations, not inconsistent with law, governing its procedure and methods of operation. Except as otherwise provided in this chapter, the Tribunal shall be subject to the provisions of the Administrative Procedure Act of June 11, 1946, as amended (c. 324, 60 Stat. 237, title 5, United States Code, chapter 5, subchapter II and chapter 7).

(b) Every final determination of the Tribunal shall be published in the Federal Register. It shall state in detail the criteria that the Tribunal determined to be applicable to the particular proceeding, the various facts that it found relevant to its determination in that proceeding, and the specific reasons for its determination.

HOUSE REPORT

Adjustment of Cable Television Royalty Rates

[Omitted to save space.]

Increase in the Number of Distant Signals

[Omitted to save space.]

Change in the Syndicated and Sports Program Exclusivity Rules

[Omitted to save space.]

Adjustment of the Small System Royalty Fees

[Omitted to save space.]

Distribution of Royalty Fees

[Omitted to save space.]

LAW

§ 804. Institution and conclusion of proceedings

(a) With respect to proceedings under section 801(b)(1) concerning the adjustment of royalty rates as provided in sections 115 and 116, and with respect to proceedings under section 801(b)(2)(A) and (D)—

(1) on January 1, 1980, the Chairman of the Tribunal shall cause to be published in the Federal Register notice of commencement of proceedings under this chapter; and

(2) during the calendar years specified in the following schedule, any owner or user of a copyrighted work whose royalty rates are specified by this title, or by a rate established by the Tribunal, may file a petition with the Tribunal declaring that the petitioner requests an adjustment of the rate. The Tribunal shall make a determination as to whether the applicant has a significant interest in the royalty rate in which an adjustment is requested. If the Tribunal determines that the petitioner has a significant interest, the Chairman shall cause notice of this determination, with the reasons therefor, to be published in the Federal Register, together with notice of commencement of proceedings under this chapter.

(A) In proceedings under section 801(b)(2) (A) and (D), such petition may be filed during 1985 and in each subsequent fifth calendar year.

(B) In proceedings under section 801(b)(1) concerning the adjustment of royalty rates as provided in section 115, such petition may be filed in 1987 and in each subsequent tenth calendar year.

(C) In proceedings under section 801(b)(1) concerning the adjustment of royalty rates under section 116, such petition may be filed in 1990 and in each subsequent tenth calendar year.

(b) With respect to proceedings under subclause (B) or (C) of section 801(b)(2), following an event described in either of those subsections, any owner or user of a copyrighted work whose royalty rates are specified by section 111, or by a rate established by the Tribunal, may, within twelve months, file a petition with the Tribunal declaring that the petitioner requests an adjustment of the rate. In this event the Tribunal shall proceed as in subsection (a)(2), above. Any change in royalty rates made by the Tribunal pursuant to this subsection may be reconsidered in 1980, 1985, and each fifth calendar year thereafter, in accordance with the provisions in section 801(b)(2) (B) or (C), as the case may be.

(c) With respect to proceedings under section 801(b)(1), concerning the determination of reasonable terms and rates of royalty payments as provided in section 118, the Tribunal shall proceed when and as provided by that section.

(d) With respect to proceedings under section 801(b)(3), concerning the distribution of royalty fees in certain circumstances under sections 111 or 116, the Chairman of the Tribunal shall, upon determination by the Tribunal that a controversy exists concerning such distribution, cause to be published in the Federal Register notice of commencement of proceedings under this chapter.

(e) All proceedings under this chapter shall be initiated without delay following publication of the notice specified in this section, and the Tribunal shall render its final decision in any such proceeding within one year from the date of such publication.

HOUSE REPORT

Institution and Conclusion of Proceedings

[Omitted to save space.]

Periodic Adjustment of Certain Rates

[Omitted to save space.]

Immediate Review of Cable Television Rates for Certain Purposes

[Omitted to save space.]

Institution of Proceedings to Adjust Public Broadcasting Royalty Rates

Section 804(c) provides that the institution of proceedings under Section 801(b)(1) concerning the determination of reasonable terms and rates of royalty payments as provided in Section 118 shall proceed when and as provided in that section.

Institution of Proceedings to Distribute Royalty Fees

[Omitted to save space.]

Prompt Resolution of Proceedings

[Omitted to save space.]

LAW

§ 805. Staff of the Tribunal

(a) The Tribunal is authorized to appoint and fix the compensation of such employees as may be necessary to carry out the provisions of this chapter, and to prescribe their functions and duties.

(b) The Tribunal may procure temporary and intermittent services to the same extent as is authorized by section 3109 of title 5.

HOUSE REPORT

The comments on this section appear in Section 802 of the HOUSE REPORT.

LAW

§ 806. Administrative support of the Tribunal

(a) The Library of Congress shall provide the Tribunal with necessary administrative services, including those related to budgeting, accounting, financial reporting, travel, personnel, and procurement. The Tribunal shall pay the Library for such services, either in advance or by reimbursement from the funds of the Tribunal, at amounts to be agreed upon between the Librarian and the Tribunal.

(b) The Library of Congress is authorized to disburse funds for the Tribunal, under regulations prescribed jointly by the Librarian of Congress and the Tribunal and approved by the Comptroller General. Such regulations shall establish requirements and procedures under which every voucher certified for payment by the Library of Congress under this chapter shall be supported with a certification by a duly authorized officer or employee of the Tribunal, and shall prescribe the responsibilities and accountability of said officers and employees of the Tribunal with respect to such certifications.

HOUSE REPORT

[The report does not comment on this section.]

LAW

§ 807. Deduction of costs of proceedings

Before any funds are distributed pursuant to a final decision in a proceeding involving distribution of royalty fees, the Tribunal shall assess the reasonable costs of such proceeding.

HOUSE REPORT

[The report does not comment on this section.]

LAW

§ 808. Reports

In addition to its publication of the reports of all final determinations as provided in section 803(b), the Tribunal shall make an annual report to the President and the Congress concerning the Tribunal's work during the preceding fiscal year, including a detailed fiscal statement of account.

HOUSE REPORT

[The report does not comment on this section.]

LAW

§ 809. Effective date of final determinations

Any final determination by the Tribunal under this chapter shall become effective thirty days following its publication in the Federal Register as provided in section 803(b), unless prior to that time an appeal has been filed pursuant to section 810, to vacate, modify, or correct such determination, and notice of such appeal has been served on all parties who appeared before the Tribunal in the proceeding in question. Where the proceeding involves the distribution of royalty fees under sections 111 or 116, the Tribunal shall, upon the expiration of such thirty-day period, distribute any royalty fees not subject to an appeal filed pursuant to section 810.

HOUSE REPORT

[The report does not comment on this section.]

LAW

§ 810. Judicial review

Any final decision of the Tribunal in a proceeding under section 801(b) may be appealed to the United States Court of Appeals, within thirty days after its publication in the Federal Register by an aggrieved party. The judicial review of the decision shall be had, in accordance with chapter 7 of title 5, on the basis of the record before the Tribunal. No court shall have jurisdiction to review a final decision of the Tribunal except as provided in this section.

HOUSE REPORT

[The report does not comment on this section.]

TRANSITIONAL AND SUPPLEMENTARY PROVISIONS

HOUSE REPORT

Sec. 101 of S. 22 consists of the completely revised text of title 17 of the United States Code, containing eight chapters and 71 sections running from section 101 through section 809. Sections 102 through 115 of the bill are "transitional and supplementary" provisions which would not be a part of the new title 17.

LAW

SEC. 102. This Act becomes effective on January 1, 1978, except as otherwise expressly provided by this Act, including provisions of the first section of this Act. The provisions of sections 118, 304(b), and chapter 8 of title 17, as amended by the first section of this Act, take effect upon enactment of this Act.

HOUSE REPORT

Effective date

Under Sec. 102 of the transitional and supplementary provisions, the revised title 17 would come into effect on January 1, 1978, "except as otherwise expressly provided by this Act." Specific exceptions are made for the provisions of sections 118, 304(b), and Chapter 8, which take effect immediately upon enactment. The reference to section 304 (b) is necessary to take account of the specified cases of subsisting renewal copyrights that have already been extended under Public Laws 87–668, 89–142, 90–141, 90–416, 91–147, 91–555, 92–170, 92–566, and 93-573 of renewal copyrights scheduled to expire during 1977 and of copyrights for which renewal registration is made between December 31, 1976, and December 31, 1977. In these cases the new statute would operate, before its effective date, to extend the total duration of copyright to 75 years from the date it was secured.

LAW

SEC. 103. This Act does not provide copyright protection for any work that goes into the public domain before January 1, 1978. The exclusive rights, as provided by section 106 of title 17 as amended by the first section of this Act, to reproduce a work in phonorecords and to distribute phonorecords of the work, do not extend to any nondramatic musical work copyrighted before July 1, 1909.

HOUSE REPORT

Works in the public domain

Since there can be no protection for any work that has fallen into the public domain before January 1, 1978, Sec. 103 makes clear that lost or expired copyrights cannot be revived under the bill. The second sentence of the section, which prohibits recording rights in nondramatic musical works copyrighted before July 1, 1909, relates to the provision in the 1909 act limiting recording rights to musical works copyrighted after its effective date.

LAW

Sec. 104. All proclamations issued by the President under section 1(e) or 9(b) of title 17 as it existed on December 31, 1977, or under previous copyright statutes of the United States, shall continue in force until terminated, suspended, or revised by the President.

Sec. 105.

This section identifies seven amendments to existing federal statutes and regulations resulting from the passage of the Copyright Revision Act. Most of them consist of minor changes in terminology or changes in references to sections of the act. This section has been omitted to save space.

HOUSE AND SENATE REPORTS

[Omitted to save space.]

LAW

Sec. 106. In any case where, before January 1, 1978, a person has lawfully made parts of instruments serving to reproduce mechanically a copyrighted work under the compulsory license provisions of section 1(e) of title 17 as it existed on December 31, 1977, such person may continue to make and distribute such parts embodying the same mechanical reproduction without obtaining a new compulsory license under the terms of section 115 of title 17 as amended by the first section of this Act. However, such parts made on or after January 1, 1978, constitute phonorecords and are otherwise subject to the provisions of said section 115.

HOUSE AND SENATE REPORTS

[Omitted to save space.]

LAW

Sec. 107. In the case of any work in which an ad interim copyright is subsisting or is capable of being secured on December 31, 1977, under section 22 of title 17 as it existed on that date, copyright protection is hereby extended to endure for the term or terms provided by section 304 of title 17 as amended by the first section of this Act.

HOUSE AND SENATE REPORTS

[Omitted to save space.]

LAW

SEC. 108. The notice provisions of sections 401 through 403 of title 17 as amended by the first section of this Act apply to all copies or phonorecords publicly distributed on or after January 1, 1978. However, in the case of a work published before January 1, 1978, compliance with the notice provisions of title 17 either as it existed on December 31, 1977, or as amended by the first section of this Act, is adequate with respect to copies publicly distributed after December 31, 1977.

HOUSE REPORT

Notice in copies of previously published works

Since the notice requirements of the new statute are different and, with respect to the year date, more inclusive that those of the present law, a transitional provision is needed to cover works first published before the effective date of the revised law. Sec. 108 makes clear that, as a general rule, the notice provisions of the new law apply to "all copies or phonorecords publicly distributed after January 1, 1978," but adds that, in the case of a work published before that date, "compliance with the notice provisions of title 17 either as it existed on December 31, 1977, or as amended by the first section of this Act, is adequate with respect to copies publicly distributed after December 31, 1977."

This is particularly significant in terms of evaluating the validity of copyright notices in maps, art works, and the like, since the year of creation or publication was lawfully omitted from the copyright notices on these works.

LAW

SEC. 109. The registration of claims to copyright for which the required deposit, application, and fee were received in the Copyright Office before January 1, 1978, and the recordation of assignments of copyright or other instruments received in the Copyright Office before January 1, 1978, shall be made in accordance with title 17 as it existed on December 31, 1977.

HOUSE AND SENATE REPORTS

[Omitted to save space.]

LAW

SEC. 110. The demand and penalty provisions of section 14 of title 17 as it existed on December 31, 1977, apply to any work in which copyright has been secured by publication with notice of copyright on or before that date, but any deposit and registration made after that date in response to a demand under that section shall be made in accordance with the provisions of title 17 as amended by the first section of this Act.

HOUSE AND SENATE REPORTS

[Omitted to save space.]

LAW

SEC. 111. Section 2318 of title 18 of the United States Code is amended to read as follows:

"§ 2318. Transportation, sale or receipt of phonograph records bearing forged or counterfeit labels

"(a) Whoever knowingly and with fraudulent intent transports, causes to be transported, receives, sells, or offers for sale in interstate or foreign commerce any phonograph record, disk, wire, tape, film, or other article on which sounds are recorded, to which or upon which is stamped, pasted, or affixed any forged or counterfeited label, knowing the label to have been falsely made, forged, or counterfeited shall be fined not more than $10,000 or imprisoned for not more than one year, or both, for the first such offense and shall be fined not more than $25,000 or imprisoned for not more than two years, or both, for any subsequent offense.

"(b) When any person is convicted of any violation of subsection (a), the court in its judgment of conviction shall, in addition to the penalty therein prescribed, order the forfeiture and destruction or other disposition of all counterfeit labels and all articles to which counterfeit labels have been affixed or which were intended to have had such labels affixed.".

"(c) Except to the extent they are inconsistent with the provisions of this title, all provisions of section 509, title 17, United States Code, are applicable to violations of subsection (a).".

HOUSE AND SENATE REPORTS

[Omitted to save space.]

LAW

SEC. 112. All causes of action that arose under title 17 before January 1, 1978, shall be governed by title 17 as it existed when the cause of action arose.

HOUSE AND SENATE REPORTS

[Omitted to save space.]

LAW

SEC. 113. (a) The Librarian of Congress (hereinafter referred to as the "Librarian") shall establish and maintain in the Library of Congress a library to be known as the American Television and Radio Archives (hereinafter referred to as the "Archives"). The purpose of the Archives shall be to preserve a permanent record of the television and radio programs which are the heritage of the people of the United States and to provide access to such programs to historians and scholars without encouraging or causing copyright infringement.

(1) The Librarian, after consultation with interested organizations and individuals, shall determine and place in the Archives such copies and phonorecords of television and radio programs transmitted to the public in the United States and in other countries which are of present or potential public or cultural interest, historical significance, cognitive value, or otherwise worthy of preservation, including copies and phonorecords of published and unpublished transmission programs—

(A) acquired in accordance with sections 407 and 408 of title 17 as amended by the first section of this Act; and

(B) transferred from the existing collections of the Library of Congress; and

(C) given to or exchanged with the Archives by other libraries, archives, organizations, and individuals; and

(D) purchased from the owner thereof.

(2) The Librarian shall maintain and publish appropriate catalogs and indexes of the collections of the Archives, and shall make such collections available for study and research under the conditions prescribed under this section.

(b) Notwithstanding the provisions of section 106 of title 17 as amended by the first section of this Act, the Librarian is authorized with respect to a transmission program which consists of a regularly scheduled newscast or on-the-spot coverage of news events and, under standards and conditions that the Librarian shall prescribe by regulation—

(1) to reproduce a fixation of such a program, in the same or another tangible form, for the purposes of preservation or security or for distribution under the conditions of clause (3) of this subsection; and

(2) to compile, without abridgment or any other editing, portions of such fixations according to subject matter, and to reproduce such compilations for the purpose of clause (1) of this subsection; and

(3) to distribute a reproduction made under clause (1) or (2) of this subsection—

(A) by loan to a person engaged in research; and

(B) for deposit in a library or archives which meets the requirements of section 108(a) of title 17 as amended by the first section of this Act,

in either case for use only in research and not for further reproduction or performance.

(c) The Librarian or any employee of the Library who is acting under the authority of this section shall not be liable in any action for copyright infringement committed by any other person unless the Librarian or such employee knowingly participated in the act of infringement committed by such person. Nothing in this section shall be construed to excuse or limit liability under title 17 as amended by the first section of this Act for any act not authorized by that title or this section, or for any act performed by a person not authorized to act under that title or this section.

(d) This section may be cited as the "American Television and Radio Archives Act".

HOUSE REPORT

The following section did not appear in the SENATE REPORT.

American Television and Radio Archives

The American Television and Radio Archive established by this bill will provide a repository for the preservation of our nation's television and radio heritage. The need for such a repository has become more pressing as the importance of television's role in American society has increased, and particularly as television news has become more heavily relied upon by Americans as an important source of news. The provisions of the bill establishing an American Television and Radio Archive attempt to ensure preservation and limited distribution (for research purposes) of this material while at the same time not causing or encouraging copyright infringement.

Under this section, the Librarian of Congress shall estblish the Archive in the Library of Congress. After consulting with interested organizations and individuals, the Librarian shall place in the Archives fixations of those television and radio programs which are of present or potential public or cultural interest, historical significance, cognitive value, or otherwise worthy of preservation. These may include copies and phonorecords of transmission programs, both published and unpublished, acquired in accordance with the provisions of sections 407 and 408 of Title 17, transferred from the existing collections of the Library of Congress; given to or exchanged with the Archive by other libraries, archives, organizations or individuals; or purchased from the owner.

The Librarian shall also maintain and publish appropriate catalogs and indexes of the collections or the Archives, and make the collections available for study and research under the conditions prescribed in this section. It is expected that in compiling its index of collected materials, and particularly in establishing an indexing system for retrieval of those news broadcasts eligible for distribution under this section, the Librarian will make use of existing indexes which may have been prepared by the owners of copyrighted news product and shall attempt to make this indexing process as complete and accurate as possible. In any event, however, it is expected that any such index compiled by the Librarian shall be a list of items in the collections of the Library (without summaries or other commentary), and shall not be regarded as an official determination of the appropriateness or completeness of the categories contained therein or the items contained within those categories.

The functions of the Archive in serving as a central distribution point for research uses of broadcast news products are also provided for in this section. The Librarian is authorized to reproduce transmission programs consisting of regularly scheduled newscasts or on-the-spot coverage of news events; to compile by subject matter, without abridgement or any other editing, portions of these reproductions; and to reproduce these compilations and distribute any such reproductions by loan to a person engaged in research, and for deposit in a library or archive meeting the requirements of section 108(a) of Title 17. The distribution of such reproductions shall be for use only in research and not for further reproduction or performance. By regularly scheduled newscasts and on-the-spot coverage of news events, the committee intends to conform to the substantial precedents of the Federal Communications Commission in developing these terms.

The committee recognizes the difficulty of properly responding to requests for research materials under this section. The Librarian is authorized to establish standards and conditions for this process through regulation. The committee believes that these standards should indicate that no compilation undertaken by the Librarian shall be deemed for any purposes or proceeding to be an official determination of the subject matter covered by such a compilation. Further, the committee urges the Librarian to make compilations available to individual researchers under section 113(b)(3)(A) only if the researcher indicates the particular segments of news broadcasts he or she wishes to receive in compiled form, on the basis of the index prepared by the Librarian, which index would be supplied to the researcher requesting material from the Archive. Finally, the committee believes such regulations should indicate that any compilations should be in chronological order and should include enough material broadcast directly before and after the segment requested to ensure the researcher that the entire segment was included.

The proper functioning of the Archive will also depend on its ability to ensure the copyright integrity of materials it distributes for research purposes. The committee believes the Librarian, through regulation, should establish procedures which will facilitate proper use of any materials loaned for research or deposited for archival purposes in other libraries. These conditions should include provisions to implement the section's prohibition on performance or reproduction.

LAW

SEC. 114. There are hereby authorized to be appropriated such funds as may be necessary to carry out the purposes of this Act.

HOUSE REPORT

See the comment following Section 115, below.

LAW

SEC. 115. If any provision of title 17, as amended by the first section of this Act, is declared unconstitutional, the validity of the remainder of this title is not affected.

HOUSE REPORT

Authorization and severability clause

Sec. 114 is a general authorization provision, except that "no more than $500,000 shall be appropriated annually for the operations of the Copyright Royalty Commission." Sec. 115 is the familiar clause preserving the constitutionality of the remainder of the statute if any part of it is held unconstitutional.

This statement did not appear in the SENATE REPORT.

LAW

Approved October 19, 1976.

HOUSE REPORT

OVERSIGHT

Oversight of the Copyright Office and the Copyright Royalty Commission is the responsibility of the Committee on the Judiciary of the U.S. House of Representatives. The legislation requires that the Copyright Office and the Copyright Royalty Commission shall submit reports on their activities each year to each House of Congress.

SENATE REPORT

The "Oversight" section does not appear in the SENATE REPORT.

HOUSE REPORT

[The remaining routine announcements, which did not appear in the SENATE REPORT, were omitted to save space.]

SENATE REPORT

The Senate Bill and the SENATE REPORT contain a lengthy section identified as "Title II–Protection of Ornamental Designs of Useful Articles." As noted below in the CONFERENCE REPORT, the section was deleted by the House of Representatives. This section of the bill and the report have been omitted to save space. The design protection section omitted from the Copyright Act was reintroduced, with minor changes by Representative Tom Railsback in the first session of the Ninety-sixth Congress as H.R. 2706, where it died in the House Judiciary Committee.

CONFERENCE REPORT

ORNAMENTAL DESIGNS OF USEFUL ARTICLES AND WORKS OF APPLIED ART

Senate bill

Title II of the Senate bill proposed to establish a new form of protection for "original ornamental designs of useful articles." The title, which consisted of 35 sections, offered a limited short-term form of protection for designs. This protection was based on copyright principles but was provided separately from the copyright law itself.

House amendment

The House amendment deleted title II of the bill entirely, together with two subsections of section 113 dealing with the interrelationship between titles I and II. It revised the definition of "pictorial, graphic, and sculptural works" in section 101 to clarify the distinction between works of applied art subject to protection under the bill and industrial designs not subject to copyright protection.

Conference substitute

The conference substitute adopts the House amendments.

For further information about this section, see the note above under SENATE REPORT.

LEGISLATIVE HISTORY

Both the HOUSE and SENATE REPORTS include a "Statement" detailing the legislative history of the Copyright Act. The two accounts are quite different, and when read together, they provide a wealth of information about the 20 years of legislative activity leading to the Copyright Revision Act of 1976. The two accounts have been omitted because of their length; they appear on pp. 47-50 of the HOUSE REPORT and pp. 47-50 of the SENATE REPORT.

SELECTED BIBLIOGRAPHY

GOVERNMENT DOCUMENTS

The present volume reproduces the Copyright Act as it existed in April, 1980, and relevant parts of the three key congressional committee reports explaining the law, plus certain other documents. It is updated and expanded by:

Nicholas, Henry. *Copyright, Congress and Technology: The Public Record.* Phoenix: Oryx Press, 1979-80. 5 vols. About $112.00.

An extensive collection of copyright documents issued between 1958 and 1977 by the Copyright Office, congressional committees, the National Commission on the New Technological Uses of Copyrighted Works (CONTU), and the like.

U.S. Code of Federal Regulations: Title 37, Patents, Trademarks, and Copyrights. Washington, DC: Office of the Federal Register. Issued annually in the fall. About $6.00.

Includes a comprehensive collection of Copyright Office regulations. It is updated by Copyright Office announcements in the *Federal Register.*

U.S. Copyright Office. *Announcement.* Irregular. Free.

Includes Copyright Office publicity releases and reprints of Copyright Office announcements in the *Federal Register.* It is distributed to persons on the Copyright Office mailing list.

U.S. Copyright Office. *Annual Report of the Register of Copyrights.* Annual. Free.

Reports the activities of the Copyright Office and significant activities in the national and international copyright field. It is especially useful for its analysis of important copyright court decisions of the past year. The report also appears as a part of the *Annual Report of the Librarian of Congress.* Copies are distributed to persons on the Copyright Office mailing list.

U.S. Copyright Office. *Circular.* Irregular. Free.

Pamphlets summarizing key points in the copyright law. Copies are distributed to persons on the Copyright Office mailing list. A collection of recent issues may be obtained by requesting a complimentary copy of the Copyright Office "Information Kit."

Recent publications in this series include:

R 1 "The Nuts and Bolts of Copyright," 1980, 11p.

R 15 "Renewal of Copyright," 1978, 5p.

R 21 "Reproduction of Copyrighted Works by Educators and Librarians," 1978, 26p.

R 38a "International Copyright Relations of the United States," 1979, 7p. (This circular is revised frequently.)

R 38c "International Copyright Conventions," 1977, 35p. (Contains the texts of the four international copyright conventions to which the United States is a party.)

R 63 "Reproductions of Copyrighted Works for the Blind and and Physically Handicapped," 1977, 4p.

R 99 "Highlights of the New Copyright Law," 1978, 4p.

U.S. Copyright Office. *Concordance: Title 17, Copyright Law Keyword-in-Context Index.* Washington, DC: Government Printing Office, 1979. $7.00.

Prepared under contract by Aspen Systems Corp. Although it does not index the important congressional reports, it helps to identify the desired passages in the reports by locating the related words or statements in the act.

U.S. Copyright Office. *Decisions of the United States Courts Involving Copyright.* Washington, DC: Government Printing Office, 1909- . Frequency varies, now issued biennially. About $14.00 for recent volumes. The 1909-1970 set, with a cumulative index, is available for $195.05.

Contains substantially all federal and state copyright cases as well as cases involving related subjects in the field of intellectual property. A supplemental list of related cases is included.

MONOGRAPHS

The monographs issued before the passage of the Copyright Revision Act in 1976 are largely out of date, although a few of them retain their value for serious students of copyright. Although there have been a number of books published since the law passed, only a few appear to be useful to the intended audience of this book. Some of the older works that have retained their value are:

Kaplan, Benjamin. *Cases on Copyright, Unfair Competition, and Other Topics Bearing on the Protection of Literary, Musical, and Artistic Works.* 2nd ed. by Ralph S. Brown, Jr. Mineola, NY: Foundation Press, 1974.

A textbook for law school copyright courses.

Kaplan, Benjamin. *An Unhurried View of Copyright.* New York: Columbia University Press, 1967.

A reprint of Professor (now Judge) Kaplan's James S. Carpentier lectures delivered at the Columbia University School of Law in March 1966. It remains a classic work on the philosophy of copyright protection.

More recent works are:

Miller, Jerome K. *Applying the New Copyright Law: A Guide for Educators and Librarians*. Chicago: American Library Association, 1979. $10.00.

Attempts to explain the application of the copyright law to schools, colleges, and libraries. It includes chapters on securing copyright protection and obtaining permission to duplicate copyrighted works.

Nimmer, Melville B. *Nimmer on Copyright: A Treatise on the Law of Literary, Musical and Artistic Property, and the Protection of Ideas*. Rev. ed. New York: Matthew Bender, 1978. 4 vols., looseleaf, with annual supplements. $275.00, plus an annual service fee of about $50.00.

The preeminent, scholarly work in the field. It supersedes the two-volume first edition issued in 1963.

CONTINUATIONS

Educators and librarians who attempt to remain current in the copyright literature are soon frustrated by the lack of a journal devoted to their interests. The significant scholarly articles are scattered throughout the law reviews and other journals. The better articles written for educators and librarians are spread throughout the professional journals. *American Libraries* has published a number of useful articles on Section 107, and *Instructional Innovator* (formerly *Audiovisual Instruction*) regularly includes articles on fair use and educational transmissions. The few journals that concentrate on copyright are oriented to members of the patent, trademark, and copyright bar and tend to be very expensive in relation to their value to educators and librarians. Some of the better titles are:

BNA's Patent, Trademark & Copyright Journal. Weekly. $252.00.

A newsletter devoted chiefly to patent and trademark issues, useful for identifying recent congressional and court activities.

Bulletin of the Copyright Society of the U.S.A. Six times a year. $35.00.

Most issues contain a single scholarly article. The great value of the journal is its comprehensive, annotated, international, multi-lingual bibliography of recently published monographs, law review articles, legislative and administrative documents, court decisions, treaties, and conventions throughout the world. Monographs and journal articles published in the United States for the communication and entertainment industries are selectively indexed. Many issues are late.

Copyright Law Symposium: Nathan Burkan Memorial Competition Sponsored by the American Society of Composers, Authors and Publishers. New York: Columbia University Press. Annual. Price varies, about $15.00 per volume.

Contains three to six award-winning papers from the Nathan Burkan Memorial Competition for law school students. Although this is a very convenient reference series, most of the articles appeared earlier in the law reviews. Some volumes include a cumulative table of contents for the series. A three to five-year publication delay is not uncommon.

Copyright Management. Monthly. $60.00.

Billed as "an information/educational journal–for individuals and companies concerned with intellectual property." It is devoted to late-breaking news and to lengthy reviews of recent books.

U.S. Patents Quarterly. Weekly. $317.00.

Reprints court decisions in the patent, trademark, and copyright field.

INDEX TO DOCUMENTS CONTAINED IN THE WORK

INDEX

Prepared by Jackie Kahn